DREAM CARS

DREAM
CARS

NEW
BURLINGTON
BOOKS

A QUINTET BOOK

Published by New Burlington Books.
6 Blundell Street
London N7

ISBN: 1-85348-132-7

This book was designed and produced by
Quintet Publishing Limited
6 Blundell Street
London N7 9BH

Art Director: Peter Bridgewater
Editors: Mark Chivers, Sarah Goodwin,
Nicholas Law, John Varnom
Photography: John McGovren

Typeset in Great Britain by
Central Southern Typesetters, Eastbourne
Manufactured in Hong Kong by
Regent Publishing Services Limited

The authors and publishers would like to
thank the following for supplying pictures:

Aston Martin Lagonda Ltd, pp.97-102;
J. Baker Collection, pp.73; Chris Harvey,
pp.20-21, 22-23, 29, 34-59, 67;
James O. Barron, pp.110;
Long Island Automotive Museum, pp.8-9, 12-13, 36,37, 45, 48,49;
Midland Motor Museum; pp.10-11, 14-15; Mirco Decet, pp.64-65, 80-81,
82-83, 88, 89, 90, 94; Andrew Moreland, pp.24-25, 26-27, 30, 31, 34-35, 36-37,
42, 43, 44-45, 46-47, 49, 54-55, 60, 61, 62-63, 64, 65, 67, 68, 74-75, 76-77,
78, 79, 84, 85, 86, 87; *Performance Car Magazine*, pp.13, 16, 17, 18, 19, 32-33,
38-39, 40, 41, 55, 65, 74-75, 78-79, 92-93, 94-95, 98-99, 100-101,
102-103, 105, 107, 109; Jasper Spencer Smith, pp.228.

Every effort has been made by the
publishers to trace the owners of the
photographs used in this book, and we apologize for any inadvertent ommissions.

The material in this book previously
appeared in *Classic Sportscars, The World's Fastest
Cars* and *Glamorous Cars.*

DREAM CARS

Contents

Classic
Sportscars

1911 MERCER 35R RACEABOUT

Before the Mercer Automobile Co in Mercer County, N.J., introduced the Mercer Type 35 Raceabout in 1911, there were racing cars and there were sporting versions of touring cars. The racing cars typically comprised very big engines shoehorned into massive chassis, stripped to the bare bones and with minimal bodywork – all in an effort to save weight. In their rudimentary way, they were as specialised as any racing car of today and definitely not for everyday use. The sporting cars were generally little more than touring cars divested of the heavier creature comforts to improve performance.

The new Mercer though was something else. It was perhaps the first car that could genuinely be called a 'sportscar'; it was neither a single-purpose racing car nor a compromised tourer, but a car designed specifically for everyday motoring excitement, with more than just a dash of style.

That may not be a complete definition of a sportscar, but any car which fulfils it is well on its way to qualifying for the name.

The Raceabout was designed by Mercer's new chief engineer, Finley Robertson Porter, as a road car which could also be used as a racer by the amateur sportsman – and there was no shortage of those in pre-World War I America. It had a four-cylinder 55 h.p. T-head engine, two bucket seats, a handbrake, gearshift – four wheels and not much else. Even the throttle pedal was outboard of the driver's seat.

As an option, the Mercer driver could order a distinctive monocle windshield that fitted onto the long, exposed steering column – the sum total of weather protection for the Raceabout driver and his passenger!

The bodywork involved no more than a low bonnet, long rakish wings (with small running boards), and a massive bolster fuel tank on the tail, surmounted by two spare tyres on detachable rims. Mercer tended to go the whole hog and paint the already rather conspicuous Raceabout in garish colours with flamboyant pinstriping. One of the most popular schemes was a bright sunshine yellow with black.

It was definitely a car to be seen in, but it was more than just a pretty face; it also backed up its looks with performance. Mercer guaranteed the standard Raceabout to have a top speed of at least 70mph/113kph which was certainly enough to leave most other cars of the day trailing by a handsome margin, and with

its very light weight it would reach such speeds in spirited fashion.

The penalty of the light weight, shortish wheelbase and hard, semi-elliptic springing was a spectacularly lively ride on the often appalling roads of the day. However, the steering was light and precise, the gearshift incredibly slick by prevailing standards, and the roadholding was a tail-sliding delight. The brakes were terrible, but that never seemed to stop

the Mercer driver from using his car's performance to the full.

The Raceabout was not just an expensive toy either; at a very reasonable $2,250 in 1911 it created a large market for itself and the imitators which inevitably followed. Best known among these was the Stutz Bearcat, which had most of the Raceabout's looks but far from all its performance.

The racing versions of the Raceabout were used to great effect by such all-American heroes as Barney Oldfield and Ralph de Palma. In 1913 Spencer Wishart took a racing type 35F, the smallest car in the race, to second place at Indianapolis and in 1914 Eddie Pullen won the American Grand Prize for Mercer, who now advertised the Raceabout as 'The Champion Light Car'.

Unfortunately, as well as being perhaps the first real sportscar, the Raceabout was also one of the first to demonstrate that manufacturers can easily ignore the potential of their models. When Porter left in 1914, Mercer went on to replace the classic 35R with a stodgy, L-head engined model, the 22/70 Raceabout, which, tellingly, was also available as a touring model.

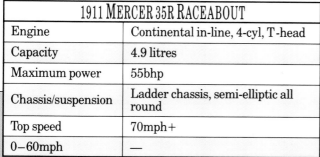

1911 MERCER 35R RACEABOUT	
Engine	Continental in-line, 4-cyl, T-head
Capacity	4.9 litres
Maximum power	55bhp
Chassis/suspension	Ladder chassis, semi-elliptic all round
Top speed	70mph +
0–60mph	—

BELOW *Lightweight (and almost non-existent!) bodywork coupled with a 4.9 litre engine, gave the Mercer Raceabout sparkling acceleration and a 70 mph/112 kph+ top-speed. Creature comforts are few and far between, and stopping the car is a bit of a problem, but who cares? Available in only the most garish colours, the Raceabout is definitely the car to be seen in!*

1912 HISPANO-SUIZA ALFONSO

If the American Mercer Raceabout could stake a claim to being the first sportscar in the world, the Hispano-Suiza Alfonso, introduced shortly after the Mercer in 1911, had an equally strong claim as the first production sportscar in Europe.

It was designed by the great Swiss engineer Marc Birkigt, Hispano-Suiza's young technical director, and based on his successful voiturette racing design of 1909. A long-stroke 2.6-litre development of that car won the Coupe de l'Auto GP des Voiturettes in 1910 and this first of several Hispanos to bear the Alfonso name emerged the following year, as a production version of the voiturette, with a side-valve four-cylinder engine, further enlarged to 3.6 litres.

It became available in a number of two- and four-seater versions; all of them with the same sporting character, and they took their name from Hispano's enthusiastic royal patron, King Alfonso XIII – of Spain, where the Hispano-Suiza company had been founded in 1904.

It was one of the few Spanish-built Hispanos to achieve any special distinction. All the great Hispanos of later years, mostly much larger and more complex cars than the Alfonso, came from the French branch of the company, set up in 1911, initially as an assembly plant for the Spanish cars, but later as a manufacturer in its own right. Although the Spanish factory in Barcelona made far more cars than the French operation, they were mostly just cheaper versions of the French models.

French built versions of the extremely popular Alfonso soon went into production and for a while there were even plans to build the model in Russia, a possibility which was eventually frustrated by the outbreak of World War I.

By the heavyweight standards of the day, the Alfonso looked almost frail, with a high chassis (available in either short- or long-wheelbase versions), delicate looking wings and narrow, wire-spoked wheels. Its looks, however, belied a rugged design typical of Birkigt's original thinking.

The 3.6-litre engine was notable mainly for its very long stroke – more than twice the bore size and a feature originally prompted by racing rules. It gave about 65bhp at something less than 2,500rpm, which was enough to give the compact little car a top speed in the region of 75mph/121kph – plus exceptional

1912 HISPANO-SUIZA 'ALFONSO'	
Engine	In-line, 4-cyl, SV
Capacity	3.6 litres
Maximum power	65bhp
Chassis/suspension	Ladder chassis, semi-elliptic all round
Top speed	75mph
0–60mph	—

ABOVE AND RIGHT *Delicate-looking bodywork disguises a rugged chassis design. Its lightness gives the car good handling, and underneath lies* *a powerful racing-derived, 3.6-litre engine.*

flexibility thanks to the torque typical of the long stroke layout. This engine was installed in unit with the gearbox, unlike most of its contemporaries which still tended to treat the latter as a separate component, often accommodated somewhere quite remote from the engine.

Even in 1911, there were faster cars than the Alfonso, but only either out-and-out racing cars or a very few large tourers. Where the Alfonso really differed was in its nimbleness and, like the Mercer Raceabout, in its style. The Mercer had been able to run rings round the generally much more powerful opposition in its racing days and those similar handling characteristics were successfully transferred to the Alfonso – but without demanding the skills of a racing driver to make use of them.

For once, it was not the manufacturer who was responsible for the demise of a classic model but in this case the onset of World War I. Although the Spanish factory continued to build cars more or less throughout the war, it obviously considered the Alfonso to be somewhat inappropriate for the climate of the period and concentrated instead on larger touring cars.

The French factories built large numbers of Birkigt-designed aero-engines and after hostilities had ceased put their wartime profits and engineering lessons to good use with some magnificent luxury cars – but never again anything quite so sporty as the Alfonso.

1928 BUGATTI TYPE 43

When people talk of genius in the same breath as the motor car, they will usually talk of one man: Ettore Bugatti. Genius may be the right sentiment but the wrong word; Bugatti was really an artist whose medium happened to be motor cars – and like most artists he combined eccentricity with his brilliance.

Bugatti, born in Milan in 1881, came from a family of artists. His father was an architect and furniture-maker whose work is now highly regarded. His younger brother was a distinguished sculptor, but although Ettore dabbled in the fine arts he was always more drawn to mechanical designs.

He had no formal engineering training; he designed essentially by eye, with a seemingly intuitive appreciation of material strength which he steadfastly declined to back with conventional calculations.

His other great passion was for thoroughbred horses and he obviously saw parallels in designing thoroughbred cars; he even referred to his line of cars as 'le pur-sang' – literally, thoroughbred.

He designed his first car in 1901, before working on designs for several manufacturers, one of which subsequently re-emerged in 1909 as the prototype Bugatti, in production from 1910.

Almost from the beginning he entered his cars in races and adapted the lessons of the racetrack to his sporting road cars. His greatest racing success was as much commercial as sporting; the legendary Type 35 Grand Prix car and its derivatives were designed not just as cars for the works team but also as 'over the counter' racers. Not only did they become probably the most successful racing cars of all time, they also contributed greatly to one of Bugatti's finest road cars – the Type 43.

The Type 43, introduced in 1927, used a very slightly detuned version of the Type 35B Grand Prix car's supercharged 2.3-litre straight-eight engine in a chassis derived from the underpowered Type 38 tourer, the main difference being a slightly shorter wheelbase. What this created was the world's first 100mph production car, not just in the fanciful realms of a catalogue or on a closed race track, but for real, on almost any decent road. In fact the 43 was good for at least 110mph, or supposedly as much as 125mph with the optional higher final drive ratio – at

RIGHT A true supercar in its day, and no slouch even by today's standards, the Bugatti Type 43 is quite literally a racing car for the road. The first production car to be capable of more than 100 mph/160 kph, its supercharged eight-cylinder engine would whisk it to a 110 mph/176 kph maximum in fourth gear alone!

BELOW *Classic lines of the Type 43 conceal the secret of Bugatti's success. The chassis, suspension and brakes are all superbly engineered to give the car handling and stopping power to match its performance.*

1928 BUGATTI TYPE 43	
Engine	In-line, 8-cyl, sohc
Capacity	2.3 litres
Maximum power	120bhp
Chassis/suspension	Ladder chassis, semi-elliptic front, quarter-elliptic rear
Top speed	110mph
0–60mph	11.7 seconds

a time when 70mph was considered quick for a production car.

It was sold, very expensively, as a 3½-seater sports tourer, the odd half being an occasional seat alongside a full-sized rear seat. The engineering was typically Bugatti; the engine, externally square-cut and plain looking, concealed its artistry inside. It also concealed one of Bugatti's weaknesses, a built-up crankshaft with roller bearings and no forced lubrication, which he stubbornly ignored even though it was plainly necessary. This crank was lovely to look at but like much of Bugatti's work needed constant attention to his own standards to keep it serviceable.

When all was well its 120bhp and massive torque gave the 43 quite remarkable performance. It was flexible enough to take the car from a standstill to maximum speed in top gear. More conventionally, through the slick, four-speed gearbox, with the supercharger taking effect above about 1500rpm, it would reach 60mph in less than 12 seconds and cover a standing quarter-mile in only 17 seconds.

This performance was matched by a superb chassis – the secret of much of Bugatti's success, but again dependant on the car being maintained to Bugatti standards. Very firm suspension, semi-elliptic at the front and quarter-elliptic at the back, with friction shock absorbers, was hung on an elegant, rigid chassis and gave precise, grippy handling with feedback worthy of any racing car. Its brakes were probably the best of its day, cable operated but brilliantly laid out to give positive servo action through their own torque reaction – the brighter side of Bugatti's genius.

The Bugatti remains the archetype of the supremely elegant sports car, the epitome of an Art Deco car. It is also notorious as the car that caused the death of the American dancer Isadora Duncan, who was strangled when her fashionably long scarf became entangled in the wire wheels as she speeded along.

The 43 was made until 1931, latterly as an overbodied American-inspired version, the 43A. In a way it contributed to its own demise. Bugatti gave three 43s to American racing star Leon Duray in exchange for two track racing Miller cars in which Duray had campaigned in Europe. Bugatti based his own first twin-cam engine design, the Type 51 racer, on the fabulous Millers – and its roadgoing derivative, the 55, ultimately replaced the 43.

1930 4½-LITRE 'BLOWER' BENTLEY

If there is any single universal image of the vintage sportscar, the 'Blower' Bentley is undoubtedly it. The massive British Racing Green cars which Bentley's arch-rival Ettore Bugatti is alleged to have described as 'les plus vites camions du monde' – the fastest trucks in the world – are the cars that most people think of as the Bentleys that won Le Mans; in that at least they are mistaken.

The racing 'Blower' cars, strictly speaking, were not even built by Bentley themselves; W. O. Bentley personally hated them and all they stood for. What the company did build was the run of 50 or so supercharged 4½-litre production cars which regulations demanded be offered for sale in order to qualify the model for international racing. W.O. did so under protest, grudgingly allocating a corner of his Cricklewood factory to producing touring and sportscars with the blown engine.

Specifically, his objection was to supercharging, which he held to be a vastly inferior and less reliable route to more power than increasing capacity. He was more or less forced into accepting the blower idea by the financial state of his company, which at the time was existing largely through the backing of the enormously wealthy Woolf Barnato.

Both Barnato and Bentley saw racing as important to the company. Barnato as a driver (as well as the company chairman) and Bentley as a salesman; they simply didn't agree on methods.

While the production cars were built in the works, however reluctantly, the racing cars were built by the ostensibly private Birkin-Paget racing team in Welwyn Garden City (now a London suburb). Birkin was the racing driver Sir Henry 'Tim' Birkin, and Paget was the Hon. Dorothy Paget, the team's benefactress.

There were only four of the real, racing 'Blower' Bentleys, each of them different and none of them, in spite of popular misconceptions, particularly successful. The first became a single seater, the second a short-wheelbase four-seater, the third a longer four-seater and the last, completed in 1930 (and the most successful of the four), a short-chassis car which, stripped to the bare necessities, finished second in the 1930 Pau Grand Prix, driven by Birkin himself.

The unsupercharged 'works' 4½-litre Bentley (whose development from the earlier 3-litre four-cylinder model had been paid for by Barnato) had won Le Mans in 1928 (Barnato himself sharing the driving with Bernard Rubin), but the blown cars were not even ready to put up a fight in the 1929 running of the 24-Hour classic. Instead, W.O. was able to gloat over yet another works victory gained by an unsupercharged car – in this case the 6½-litre Speed Six, which had been his answer to the 'Blower'

as a way to increasing performance.

Whatever W.O.'s personal misgivings, the big supercharged car is indisputably a classic. The production cars, of which the 26 open Vanden Plas-bodied cars at least looked like the racers, could boast about 175bhp, but the Birkin cars could muster over 250bhp at a very low 3750rpm. That, combined with staggering torque at almost any engine speed, was enough to give even this two-ton-plus car exceptional performance.

On the long Mulsanne straight at Le Mans (after which the turbocharged 1980s Bentley is named) the big Blower 4½ might have touched around 130mph. It took maybe 8½ seconds to get to 50mph but after that its massive power gave it enormous high speed flexibility, which was just as well, as the gearbox, though extremely strong, was extraordinarily awkward to use.

The roadholding was surprisingly good, and the handling was certainly very forgiving, but there was no disguising how much kinetic energy the huge drum brakes had to destroy from very high speeds.

It all matters very little, of course; no-one is particularly interested in the shortcomings of a car like the big Bentley; to the man in the street it is still one of the greatest of all classic sportscars.

1930 BENTLEY 4½-LITRE S/C	
Engine	In-line, 4-cyl, sohc, s/c, 16v
Capacity	4.5 litres
Maximum power	250bhp
Chassis/suspension	Ladder chassis, semi-elliptic all round
Top speed	130mph
0–60mph	8.5 seconds

LEFT AND OVERLEAF *The classic supercharged 4½-litre Bentley.*

ABOVE *British engineering at its best – the cockpit of the 'Blower' Bentley.*

1932 ALFA ROMEO 8C MONZA

The Alfa Romeo 8C is a car for all reasons. In various guises, it was a Le Mans winner (four times in a row), a Grand Prix winner (on circuits as diverse as the super-fast Monza autodrome and the tight, round-the-houses Monte Carlo street circuit), and it was also a superb roadgoing sportscar.

Even by today's standards it is exceptionally quick, particularly in its classic Monza 2,600 guise, but it is also a car which can quite easily serve for everyday use – a sportscar by any definition.

The 8C series was Alfa's sporting mainstay from its introduction in sports racing form in 1931 right through to the enforced end of production in 1939 with the onset of World War II. It was designed by the greatest of all Alfa Romeo's engineers, Vittorio Jano, who had joined the company in September, 1923. He was enticed over to Alfa from Fiat's racing department by Enzo Ferrari – who became famous as a racing driver and team organiser with Alfa Romeo long before he began to build cars under his own name. Fiat were not very pleased with Jano's defection, but Alfa Romeo were delighted . . .

The 8C first appeared in long wheelbase 2,300 sportscar format, early in 1931. On its radiator cowl was the distinctive Alfa Romeo badge, combining the red-on-white St George's Cross of Alfa's native Milan and the bizarre emblem of the ancient Milanese rulers, the Viscontis – a writhing, crowned serpent swallowing a small child. The laurel wreath which surrounds the badge commemorates Alfa Romeo's victory in the first official world championship, achieved in 1924 with Jano's very first Alfa design, the all-conquering P2 Grand Prix car.

In May, 1931, only weeks after its introduction, the sports version of the 8C won the gruelling Targa Florio road race in Sicily. Two weeks later two short-

LEFT AND ABOVE RIGHT *Like many cars of the period, the Alfa Romeo Monza is super-charged to give it truly remarkable acceleration and a top speed of 135 mph/216 kph. The comfortable, well-laid-out cockpit is relatively roomy, and has surprisingly comprehensive instrumentation.*

chassis models, stripped of lights, wings and other non-essential running gear, were entered in the Italian Grand Prix at Monza. They finished first and second and the rare short-chassis racing model has been known as the Monza ever since.

The heart of the 8C is Jano's magnificent, super-charged, twin-overhead-cam, straight-eight engine. It started life as a 2.3-litre unit but later grew to 2.6-litres, originally in the racing team cars run by Ferrari and, later, through modification, in many customer cars. It is a beautiful looking-engine, with its long twin cam-covers and its heavily finned inlet manifolding leading from the Roots-type super-charger, which, like the camshafts, is driven from a central vertical gear-train between the individual halves of the all-alloy engine.

It is a very strong unit, superbly balanced and quite capable of much higher revs than most of its contemporaries. Even in its sports versions it was good for somewhere near 150bhp and the works racing Monzas gave as much as 180bhp, while remaining perfectly tractable and trouble-free.

Although the Monza was quite definitely a racing model, it also makes a very impressive roadgoing sportscar. Its cockpit is roomier and more comfort-able than might be expected from its vintage, and its controls are surprisingly modern in layout – the only exception being the placing of the throttle pedal

between clutch and brakes, a layout common to many cars of its period.

From behind the big steering wheel it actually feels quite small and its performance is truly remark-able. A Monza geared for short sprints will reach 60mph/96.5kph in less than seven seconds and at the other end of the scale might approach 140mph/225kph.

On rock-hard suspension and damping its ride is bumpy but its smooth surface grip is astonishing. Its quick, accurate steering and powerful, mechanically operated brakes make it a delightful car to drive even in the 1980s, especially as today's improved road surfaces give a smoother ride than would have been possible in the 1930s.

What it must have felt like in its day is surely the true measure of Jano's genius.

1932 ALFA ROMEO 8C MONZA	
Engine	In-line, 8-cyl, 2ohc, s/c
Capacity	2.6 litres
Maximum power	150bhp (180bhp for racing)
Chassis/suspension	Ladder chassis, semi-elliptic all round
Top speed	135mph
0–60mph	7.0 seconds

1935 AUBURN 851 SPEEDSTER

ABOVE *Flamboyant styling makes the Auburn Speedster really stand out from the crowd, while the supercharged, straight-eight engine makes sure it goes as well as it looks. Every car guaranteed to top 100 mph/160 kph!*

If imitation is the sincerest form of flattery, there can be little doubt that Auburn's various Speedsters have been flattered from the day they were made. The spectacularly sporty-looking cars became style leaders in the age of style, and right up to the present day they have inspired numerous replica builders both in America and Europe.

Anyone who dismisses replicas as nothing more than a mish-mash of other people's bits and pieces would do well to look at the original Speedsters. Like most Auburns, they were assembled around unsophisticated 'proprietary' engines, and running gear from the company parts bin. What made the Speedsters memorable where the vast majority of Auburns were eminently forgettable was their combination of brash styling and promise of near racing car performance, at least in Auburn's skilful sales pitches. They owed more, in fact, to one man's incredible talent as a salesman than to any particular engineering excellence.

The man was Errett Lobban Cord, who eventually linked the name of Auburn with those of Cord and Duesenberg in a classic trilogy of American sporting marques, but who arrived at Auburn, in 1924, at a time when the company was close to bankruptcy on the strength of an image of extreme mediocrity. Cord, who by his mid-20s had already made and lost several fortunes, revamped Auburn's dowdy range, treated them to a major sales splash and turned the name into a respectable seller.

As ever, competition exposure played its part, as Auburn began to take part in stock car racing and record breaking – and the sporting image was cleverly exploited in pulling customers who had no real intention of buying a sportscar into the corporate showrooms.

The first Speedster, sensationally styled by Count Alexis de Sakhnoffsky, appeared in 1928 on the eight-cylinder, Lycoming-engined 8-115 chassis, establishing its performance credentials with a 108mph run at Daytona Beach. Even more surprising than the Speedster's performance though was its price, which was less than half that of its most obvious rival, the Stutz Black Hawk. Not surprisingly, it helped Auburn to its best sales year to date.

Cord made one of his occasional mistakes in 1929, with the spectacular Cabin Speedster sedan; long,

low, racily streamlined and with every possible weight-saving trick, including wicker seats, it was just a bit too much of a good thing and though most people marvelled, very few bought. Cord quickly reverted to slightly more conservative models and gave Auburn its best ever sales year in the middle of the 1930s depression, topping off his audacious marketing style in 1932 by offering the first and last twelve-cylinder car ever to be sold for less than $1000 – with the inevitable Speedster option at only $1600.

Whether it was the depression or the thought that a V12, even a Lycoming-engined V12, was too good to be true at the price, the car didn't sell and it was dropped in 1934, to make way in 1935 for the greatest of all the Speedsters, the classic Type 851.

The 851, styled almost as a parody of the earlier models by Gordon Buehrig, had the archetypal pointed tail, a huge bonnet (hood) (which in this case housed a centrifugally supercharged straight-eight Lycoming engine of about 150bhp), vast, flexible outside exhaust pipes and a short two-seater cabin behind a tiny, steeply-raked windscreen. On the dashboard of every 851 was a small plaque which guaranteed that the car had exceeded 100mph on test

in the hands of Auburn racer and and record breaker Ab Jenkins.

It was indeed a staggering performer, with an easily selected option of high or low axle ratios for top speed or acceleration, but every 851 was sold at a loss. A very slightly revised model, the 852, replaced the 851 in 1936 but time was running out for Auburn and the 500 or so 851/852 Speedsters sold became Auburn's monument rather than its saviour as the company went out of business in 1937. Here is another example of a superb car that is no longer in production due to management problems, despite the excellence of the product.

1935 AUBURN SPEEDSTER	
Engine	Lycoming in-line, 8-cyl, sv, s/c
Capacity	4.6 litres
Maximum power	150bhp
Chassis/suspension	Ladder chassis, semi-elliptic all round
Top speed	100mph+
0–60mph	—

1935 SS100 JAGUAR

Although Jaguar did not appear as a make in its own right until 1945, its history goes back well beyond that. It began in the British seaside resort of Blackpool with the Swallow Sidecar Co, which built motorcycle sidecars in the early 1920s, then grew as the Swallow Sidecar and Coachbuilding Co, which built special, usually very sporty bodies on various makes of saloon car during the late 1920s.

From 1931 the company (which became known as SS Cars Ltd in 1933) built complete cars, though still initially using bought-in engines and chassis. The first of these were known as the SSI and SSII saloons, sporty cars, but not yet sportscars.

The company's first *real* sportscar appeared in March 1935: a rakish two-seater with a 2.7-litre, 86bhp, six-cylinder Standard side-valve engine in a shortened SSI underslung chassis. It was dubbed the SS90, alluding, slightly optimistically, to its top speed.

The company never actually admitted to what SS meant in their own minds: Super Sports, Super Swallow, Swallow Sports – take your pick.

Only 23 SS90s were built, up to September 1935 – when SS announced two new cars with overhead-valve engines. They were the SS Jaguar saloon and the SS Jaguar 100 – the logical development of the SS90.

What started as a model name quickly gained prominence, and in 1945, when SS wasn't exactly an ideal title, the company became Jaguar Cars Ltd.

The SS100, with its sweeping wings, wire wheels and huge, mesh-covered headlamps, looked very like the two-seater SS90 but was much better developed.

It used a purpose-built chassis rather than a cut-down saloon type, with an alloy body over an ash frame. It had a four-speed gearbox and non-indepen-

RIGHT *Performance and style at a budget price? The classic SS100 Jaguar sports car is a far cry from the company's original products – motorcycle sidecars. Faultless handling, superb brakes, and a willing, flexible engine make the SS100 a real driver's car.*

1935 SS100 3½-LITRE	
Engine	In-line, 6-cyl, ohv
Capacity	3.5 litres
Maximum power	125bhp
Chassis/suspension	Ladder chassis, semi-elliptic all round
Top speed	101mph
0–60mph	11.5 seconds

dent suspension all round, on long, semi-elliptic springs with a mixture of hydraulic and friction damping – basically like the SS90 but with improved mouldings. The big, finned drum brakes changed from cable to rod operation, but the biggest improvement of all was the new engine.

The overhead valve conversion and twin carbs put the quoted power output up to 100bhp and the 100 again represented the claimed top speed. As with the SS90, it was a bit optimistic to start with, by 4 or 5mph according to most tests, but the SS100, like Jaguars ever since, offered quite exceptional value for money – at only around one third of the price of a contemporary 'thoroughbred' of similar performance.

The 2.7-litre SS100 stayed in production until 1939 and a total of 198 were eventually built, but towards the end of 1937 the car was finally able to live up to its name when a 3.5-litre version was introduced alongside the 2.7.

The bigger engine, with slightly higher compression, offered 125bhp, great flexibility and a genuine roadgoing top speed of 101mph. Sparkling acceleration took it to 60mph in about 11½ seconds and to a standing quarter-mile in just 17 seconds.

Its roadholding and handling, with very quick steering, were impeccable – even if the ride was a bit hard – and its brakes were superb.

Just 116 3.5-litre SS100s were built before they too ceased production, in 1939. Of the total of 314 SS100s of both types which were built, probably 200 survive, most of them in the USA, where the Jaguar reputation for performance with style and value is now perhaps stronger than ever, one of the few British cars to enjoy such a reputation.

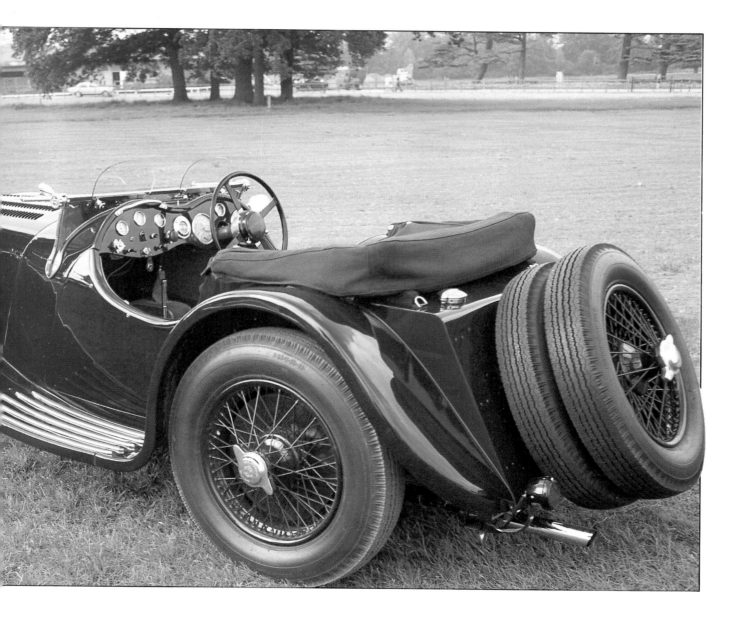

1937 BMW 328

Considering the strength of BMW's high-tech sporting image today, it is difficult to believe that the company's first venture as a car manufacturer was in building a version of the humble Austin Seven. BMW was already well known for its motorcycles and aeroengines (the famous quartered blue and white badge is the stylised blur of a spinning propellor) before it acquired the German manufacturing rights for the Seven, by taking over Dixi in 1928 and relaunching Dixi's interpretation of the Seven as the BMW 3/15, on New Year's Day 1929.

A close look at the way the 3/15 evolved showed that later developments were hardly surprising. It took BMW very little time to discover, as many had before them, that motor sporting success was a surefire way of selling motor cars and the German Seven soon became a very sporty car indeed. BMW offered the little car as either a roadster or open tourer and it started its four-wheel racing career by winning a

team prize in the 1929 Alpine Trial, followed by a class win in the 1930 Monte Carlo Rally.

The company's real sporting fame, however, sprang from the arrival in 1933 of its first six-cylinder model, the 303 saloon – a tiny car for a six, with just 1175cc and about 30bhp to its name! Predictably, this soon grew a little bit bigger and quicker as it evolved into the 1.5-litre 315, with twin

1937 BMW 328	
Engine	In-line, 6-cyl, sohc
Capacity	1.9 litres
Maximum power	80bhp
Chassis/suspension	Tubular, transverse leaf/wishbone ifs, semi-elliptic rear
Top speed	95mph
0–60mph	—

BELOW *Elegance and superb engineering rolled into one, sum up the BMW 328. Its advanced, wind-cheating bodywork looks good, while independent front suspension gives the 328 the comfort of a saloon car ride with racing car levels of roadholding.*

carburettors and a four-speed gearbox for 1934, but still only 34bhp.

Alongside the basic 315 however, BMW gave another hint of its true colours with the sporty 315/1 roadster, which had triple carbs, 40bhp and a top speed of over 75mph/121kph. This model was good enough to win the Alpine Trial outright among its many sporting successes, before it gave way to the next of the series, a little bit larger again, at 1.9-litres, the excellent 319.

The 319 was the final forerunner of the classic 328, which had none of the reticence of the previous models about its true character; it was a real sports-car through and through. It was unveiled in the summer of 1936 when it won the prestigious Eiffel-rennen sportscar race and it went on sale early in 1937. It was based on the 319's well-proven tubular chassis, now with an engine of close to 2 litres and using a clever hemispherical head design with in-clined valves operated by a single camshaft and a crossover pushrod arrangement. This gave the new engine most of the advantages of a real twin-cam design but without the complexity and manufactur-ing expense.

The engine quickly earned a reputation for being both reliable and delightfully crisp. It also had a much increased power output; with three down-draught carbs (and the ability to use an unusually high compression ratio thanks to the advanced head design) it produced 80bhp and gave the roadgoing 328 a very respectable top speed of almost 95mph/153kph.

Additionally, it set new standards of roadholding and handling – with much of the refinement of a saloon car ride combined with racing car standards of grip. Much of that was due to the 328's brave insist-ence on using independent front suspension at a time when beam axles were generally the order of the day on sportscars, but it said even more about the overall integrity of the chassis design.

To complete this magnificent mechanical package, the BMW engineers came up with a beautiful and aerodynamically efficient body which made most other sportscars of the day look positively primitive. It even had a smooth full-length undertray to drama-tically cut drag below the car.

Not only BMW themselves reaped the benefits of the 328; it was imported into Britain as the Frazer-Nash BMW and through that connection, as war reparations after World War II, it was adopted by Bristol as the basis of their new luxury sporting saloons. It was also widely used in racing for many years, even after the war.

BMW themselves may have lost out in the short term, but the engineering skills which created the 328 would not lay dormant for long.

1946 MG TC

Few cars come closer to the popular concept of a sportscar than the splendid MG TC Midget, introduced in November 1945 and in production until the end of 1949.

No car could have been a better celebration of the recent end of World War II. For not much more than the cost of a small saloon car, it brought cheap and cheerful wind-in-the-hair sporting motoring to thousands who could never have afforded it before – and might anyway never have had the freedom of spirit to drive such a car.

The TC was the archetypal British sportscar of the period, but more than that, it became known everywhere as the MG that took the British sportscar to America – although only just over 2000 were actually sold there, mostly around the sunny and always sportscar conscious west coast, from a total production run of exactly 10,000.

With lean, rakish lines derived from the small pre-war MG sportscars, a simple steel ladder chassis and a long-stroke, overhead-valve 1250cc four-cylinder engine with twin carburettors, this third in the series of T-type Midgets was low on technology but very high on entertainment.

It was strictly a two-seater, in the pre-war style, with very little by way of luggage space but a surprisingly roomy and comfortable cockpit considering its compact exterior dimensions. Its lovely body had deeply cutaway doors, an impressively long, louvred bonnet (hood), a huge slab fuel tank, knock-on wire wheels and beautiful sweeping wings (fenders). It looked every inch the breath of freedom that the new postwar motoring market wanted, and it was.

It wasn't particularly fast, even by the generally mediocre standards of the time, and its mere 54bhp gave it a top speed of about 75mph – with 0–60mph taking a leisurely 22 seconds, or about twice as long as a very ordinary family saloon of today. But what it lacked in outright performance it more than made up for with its outstanding character and drivability.

It was so small and nimble that on the relatively uncluttered roads of the day it was possible to maintain near 60mph averages without ever needing to go over 70mph! The steering, with a massive sprung-spoke steering wheel on a telescopically adjustable column, was very quick (with less than two turns from lock-to-lock) and precise and the four gear ratios

1946 MG TC	
Engine	In-line, 4-cyl, ohv
Capacity	1.2 litres
Maximum power	54bhp
Chassis/suspension	Ladder chassis, semi-elliptic all round
Top speed	75mph
0–60mph	22.5 seconds

were perfectly matched to the engine performance – with a lovely slick change through a stubby little lever. The big instruments under the sweeping lines of the scuttle (with the rev counter set ahead of the driver and the speedometer set in front of the passenger!) told the TC driver everything he needed to know that he wasn't already feeling through the seat of his pants.

On such tall, narrow tyres it was quite exciting to throw a TC around on narrow lanes, the car compensating for its lack of outright grip by very forgiving manners and even a fairly comfortable ride for such a lightweight. It didn't have enough power to get into real trouble accidentally, but it did have enough to offer a controllable amount of oversteering fun.

Of course, if the driver really did want more, it was a very easy car to endow with more power and few TCs stayed completely standard for very long. Even with a tuned engine, the hydraulic drum brakes were quite good enough to stop the light little car solidly and with no more drama than a little wheel locking on a wet road – and if it *did* rain there was always a reasonably waterproof and easy to erect soft top on the outside and a rudimentary heater inside!

With its small, reliable engine and relatively simple engineering it cost very little to run or to repair, and, of course, when the sun shone (and usually even when it didn't) the top came off and the world was the TC owner's oyster.

The TC and the other T-series Midgets typified the MG name in particular on both sides of the Atlantic for almost 20 years, from the first TA of 1936 to the last TF of 1955 – and it will typify the sportscar ethic in general forever.

LEFT *Post-war Britain was looking for an affordable, fun, wind-in-the-hair sports car, and the MG TC fits the bill. Generally regarded as the classic sports MG, the TC isn't fast even by 1946 standards, but it positively oozes panache!*

BELOW *Long, low and sleek, the MG TC is a true two-seater sports car – there's little room for more than driver and passenger. For those less hardy souls, the TC comes as a convertible with heater. Luxury indeed!*

1951 ALLARD J2

Had Sydney Herbert Allard been alive today he would probably still be looking for the biggest, most powerful V8 he could find, then building the smallest possible amount of car to put it in. Allard died in April 1966, but at least he missed most of the frustration of seeing ever-increasing legislation shoving out the only sort of car he loved – simple, big-engined specials that were much bigger on character than on sophistication. Sophistication certainly was not Allard's forté, but he has to be respected for his unswerving conviction that anything, however un-likely, that made an Allard go faster was good. What made most Allards go faster was muscle – V8 muscle.

'The Guvnor', as he was always known, was a big, broad man who had started a garage business in South London in 1930 and quickly discovered the joys of the very English sport of trialling, with a modified Ford V8. In 1937 he started selling V8-powered specials, mostly for the mud-plugging trials but including a couple of road cars. He even built a few Lincoln V12-engined cars before World War II and, after the war, soon started building Ford V8 models again in fairly large numbers – some two-seaters, some four-seaters, a few drophead coupés and some short-chassis competition cars. In 1952 Allard won the Monte Carlo Rally in one of his own saloons, the only person ever to win driving his own make of car.

The Allard that everyone remembers, though, is

RIGHT *Allard lives! On the road or the racetrack, big is beautiful as far as Allards are concerned. This J2 model is powered by a 4.4 litre Mercury V-8 engine – getting the power down on to the road is helped by slinging a large fuel tank over the rear wheels.*

1950 ALLARD J2	
Engine	Mercury V8 ohv conversion
Capacity	4.3 litres
Maximum power	150bhp
Chassis/suspension	Ladder chassis, coil spring/lower arm ifs, De Dion rear
Top speed	120mph
0–60mph	—

the spectacular J2, a car that was equally successful on both sides of the Atlantic (as it was always planned to be) as a road car or a racer.

Allard competed with the first J2 at the famous Prescott hillclimb in the summer of 1949, winning his class in this 4.4-litre flathead Mercury V8-powered car. Unfortunately, because of postwar import problems, the J2 was generally restricted to flathead engines in Britain (albeit highly modified), so the real performance was reserved for the USA, where the choice of engine was almost boundless – a real paradise for Allard!

With overhead-valve Ford, Chrysler and Cadillac V8s (and sometimes with supercharging too) the J2 was a major success in America from its arrival in April 1950. Allard shipped rolling chassis with their good-looking, cycle-winged (fendered) aluminium bodies and left the customer to drop in whatever engine would fit.

The chassis could certainly handle it, with deep, stiff side rails and ample cross bracing. The front axle was a traditional Allard split-beam, but with coil springs, and the rear, also on coils, used a De Dion layout. The brakes too were especially good for their day, with big, hydraulically-operated drums all round.

Allard's way of ensuring enough traction for the more potent J2s included hanging a 40-gallon fuel tank over the back axle, and with maybe 300bhp in some cars it was needed – helping the quickest J2s to as much as 140mph/225kph. The racing J2X derivative was quicker still, capable of 150mph/241kph at Le Mans with full aerodynamic bodywork. With massive V8 torque in a car weighing little more than a ton it goes without saying that acceleration was spectacular even by today's standards.

Sadly, a car like the J2 could not last – even in the 1950s – there was just too much civilized competition from the likes of Jaguar beginning to appear. Ford dropped the V8 in Britain and Allard started looking at other projects by 1952 – but in 1981 the J2 reappeared, built with 1950s character but 1980s running gear in Mississauga, Canada – by Allard's son!

29

1952 CUNNINGHAM C3 CONTINENTAL COUPÉ

Briggs Swift Cunningham was the epitome of the all-American millionaire sportsman. Born in 1907 into a substantial family fortune based on investments and stockholdings, he was a gifted track and field athlete in his college days who gave up his place in the 1929 US Olympic squad when he decided he was more interested in competitive sailing – and became a very capable yachtsman.

Eventually, his interests shifted again, this time to motor sports, which, like everything else, he pursued with a passion. Rich though he was, Cunningham would not go out and buy guaranteed success. A big part of the challenge would be in doing it himself, as a car constructor as well as just a driver – and in the big time, not the little league. He wanted to be a road racer European-style, rather than a track racer, and as well as building and racing his own cars he became actively involved in running the Automobile Racing

Club of America and its successor, the Sports Car Club of America.

He built his first car in 1940 and, at a time when it was fashionable to put American engines in European chassis, he did it the other way round, dropping a Mercedes engine into a stripped Buick to make the Bu-Merc.

The war put an end to that episode and Cunningham raced more conventional machinery, including MGs and Austin Healeys – plus the first Ferrari ever imported into the USA.

His interest in European racing and European cars was one thing, but his patriotism was another and he decided that he wanted to beat the Europeans at their own sportscar racing game, on home ground at Le Mans, with an all-American car.

His first entry (and the first American entry since 1935) was in 1950 with two Model 61 Cadillacs – one almost stock and the other with ugly 'streamlined' bodywork which earned it the nickname *le monstre*. They went well enough to make him pursue his Le Mans ambitions for many years, and from the later Le Mans project emerged a few roadgoing Cunningham sportscars, which might even have gone into serious production but for the pressures and expense of racing.

He started with the road car idea in 1951, planning to build Cunningham C2 production sportscars alongside the C1 racers in his new Palm Beach workshops. Four 1951 cars were built but only one was a road car, with a Cadillac V8, where the racers had Chrysler Hemis. One ran in second place at Le Mans before fuel problems pushed it back to 18th at the finish.

Cunningham even advertised his proposed roadgoing C2 derivatives late in 1951, as 'the ultimate in sportscars', but again he only built one, early in 1952, before Le Mans pressures took over again. More than ever though, he intended to build a road car and from February, 1952 he catalogued a 210bhp, 331cu in a Chrysler-powered, Vignale-bodied coupé, the C3 Continental.

It was fast, at almost 140mph/225kph but very, very expensive. A convertible, introduced in 1953, was even more expensive . . .

While the racing Cunninghams continued to give the Europeans an uncomfortably close run at Le Mans (with fourth place in 1952 and third in 1953), the Cunningham road cars sold just 18 coupés and nine convertibles before production petered out in 1955.

Briggs S, having for once failed to beat them, joined them – becoming Jaguar's US racing representative in 1956. He started his long association with Jaguar by using one of their engines in the 1957 C6RD Le Mans car – the last of the Cunninghams.

BELOW *American muscle versus the Europeans. Advertised as 'the ultimate in sportscars' the Cunningham C3 Continental Coupé was the road-going version of the racing cars built to challenge the likes of Jaguar at Le Mans.*

1952 CUNNINGHAM C3 CONTINENTAL COUPÉ	
Engine	Chrysler V8, ohv
Capacity	5.4 litres
Maximum power	210bhp
Chassis/suspension	Tubular chassis, coil spring/ wishbone ifs, De Dion rear
Top speed	138mph
0–60mph	—

1953 JAGUAR XK120

If ever one sportscar company truly lived up to the old adage of racing improving the breed, it is Jaguar. Through the 1950s Jaguar, with its C-Type and D-Type racing sportscars, took on the might of Ferrari and Mercedes-Benz at the highest levels of the sport, and frequently won – crowning its racing achievements with five Le Mans wins, including a hat-trick between 1955 and 1957.

The lessons of the racing Jaguars (most famously, disc brakes) were enthusiastically adopted for subsequent road cars and where Jaguar led, others followed. But the process really started in reverse, because the first great racing Jaguar, the C-Type, was actually developed from a Jaguar road car, the outstanding XK120 sports roadster.

The two-seater roadster version of the XK120 was introduced at the London Motor Show in 1948, rushed into what Jaguar envisaged as only limited production as a stop-gap model in which to introduce the company's new twin overhead camshaft XK-series engines – which were primarily intended for the forthcoming MkVII luxury saloon.

A four-cylinder XK100 was never put into production but the six-cylinder 3.4-litre XK120, with its beautifully sleek, modern lines, was the sensation of the show. Plans for a total run of 200 aluminium-bodied cars quickly gave way to full, steel-bodied production from 1949 and the XK line continued until the last XK150s of 1961 bowed out to the E-Type. The XK engine in various sizes was even longer lived, carrying over into the E-Type itself and into the saloon ranges; its basic layout is still instantly recognisable in six-cylinder Jaguars today.

As ever, the 120 part of the model designation represented Jaguar's top speed claim for the car – but in this case it was, if anything, a considerable understatement. A totally standard production model powered by the ultra-reliable 160bhp twin-carb engine was tested at the time at over 125mph/201kph. A works car, mildly tidied up aerodynamically, achieved almost 133mph/214kph and a later car, highly tuned and even more streamlined, recorded over 172mph/277kph in 1953.

The XK120 had roadholding to match its performance and looks, with a massive, cross-braced box-section chassis, independent torsion bar front suspension and semi-elliptic rear suspension. Ironi-

1953 JAGUAR XK120	
Engine	In-line, 6-cyl, 2ohv
Capacity	3.4 litres
Maximum power	160bhp
Chassis/suspension	Cross-braced, box-section, torsion bar ifs, semi-elliptic rear
Top speed	125mph
0–60mph	9.6 seconds

BELOW *Creating a motoring sensation with a stop-gap car. The Jaguar XK120 continued the theme of the SS100 with driveability and roadholding par excellence.*

RIGHT AND BELOW RIGHT *Modern sweeping lines of the XK120 were a revelation. The smooth six-cylinder engine used in the XK continued in production until 1986.*

cally, the only real weakness on the early XKs was the hydraulic drum brakes and after Jaguar had developed their disc system through the racing programme they were eventually transferred onto the later XK150s.

A fixed head coupe version of the XK120 was available from 1951 and a proper drophead coupé – as opposed to the original, rather spartan, roadster style – was introduced in 1953.

The XK120 was in production until 1954, when it was superseded by the more powerful but otherwise similar XK140. Over 12,000 120s were built and over 90 per cent were exported, around 60 per cent of them to the USA, where it firmly established Jaguar's reputation.

As well as amassing its own distinguished racing and rallying record, the XK120 also formed the basis in 1951 of the streamlined, tubular-framed C-Type, Jaguar's first out-and-out racing car. When Jaguar returned to Le Mans in the mid-1980s, they were looking to extend a record started when the C-Type won the 24-hour classic outright in 1951 and again in 1953. The C-Type might never have existed but for the popularity of the first XK120 show car.

1953 TRIUMPH TR2

The Triumph TR2 is a wonderful example of how to make something out of nothing – or at least out of not very much: a cut-price classic from the corporate parts bin.

The TR part stands for Triumph Roadster, the name given to the first open-topped post World War II Triumph, which appeared in 1946 – shortly after the company had been taken over by Standard.

The Roadster, on a shortened 1800 saloon chassis, followed the lines of a one-off convertible built for the company's new chairman, Sir John Black; it was more of a well-equipped open tourer with sporting looks than a sportscar, but it had a lot to do with why Triumph wanted to be in the sportscar market.

Its original four-cylinder engine was the one that Standard had supplied to Jaguar's prewar predecessor, SS Cars. After World War II, Sir John Black, himself a great motoring enthusiast, wanted nothing more than to show Jaguar that he could build sports-

BELOW *Hurried into production, the slab-sided TR2 was not the sleekest new sportscar around. However, what it lacked in looks it made up for in driveability on both road and track.*

ABOVE RIGHT *The most inexpensive 100 mph sportscar on the market, the chunky body style of the TR2 enclosed mechanics borrowed from the Triumph saloon range to help keep costs down.*

cars too. He wanted to beat Jaguar and he wanted to beat MG, not least because he was well aware of the giant US market potential for a particular type of cheap and cheerful British sportscar.

He even tried to buy the Morgan company but failed and so he asked his engineers to come up, in a hurry, with a low-priced sportscar, based on available production parts. In six months they had a prototype ready for the 1952 London Motor Show, based on components largely from the 2-litre Standard Vanguard saloon – many of which were also used on the Ferguson tractor!

The car was well received and with a few months' refinement it re-emerged in mid-1953 as the production TR2.

The TR2 now had its own chassis, underslung at the rear, an engine linered-down to just under 2-litres (a competition class limit), gearbox and semi-elliptic rear axle also from the Vanguard, and front wishbone and coil spring suspension from Triumph's small 'razor-edge' saloon, the Mayflower.

Its chunkily-attractive slab-sided body also reflected low tooling costs and hurried development, but somehow it all clicked and the little Triumph was a major success – as a racing and rally car as well as just in the showroom.

On 15-in wire wheels and quite narrow tyres, it handled well, if a little twitchily at the back, with a reasonable ride and a good level of comfort. It was well trimmed, acceptably roomy, and there was even a worthwhile boot (trunk) – even though the whole car had been built as small as possible to keep down material costs, weight and frontal area, the last two to help it to its target of 100mph/161kph performance.

It actually did its planned 100mph/161kph, in fact it could manage about 105mph/169kph, and at the time it was the cheapest 100mph/161kph car on the British market.

Most TR2s were not sold in their native Britain; of the 250 cars built in 1953, 200 were exported – almost all (no doubt to Sir John Black's delight) to the USA, where the TR quickly began to challenge the popularity of the suddenly dating T-series MGs as the 'in' sportscar.

From those small beginnings, production started properly in 1954 and over 8,600 TR2s were built up to 1955, which saw the arrival of the slightly more powerful and mildly restyled TR3, later to become the first British production car to use front-wheel disc brakes.

Through the TR3 and TR3A, the basic TR2 body shape survived for another six years; and so did its popularity, with more than 83,000 more examples being sold before the very different TR4 arrived in 1961 to start a new TR line.

1953 TRIUMPH TR2	
Engine	In-line, 4-cyl, ohv
Capacity	2.0 litres
Maximum power	90bhp
Chassis/suspension	Ladder chassis, coil spring/ wishbone ifs, semi-elliptic rear
Top speed	105mph
0–60mph	11.9 seconds

1954 PORSCHE 356 SPEEDSTER

Strictly speaking, the rear-engined layout, with the engine behind the gearbox, aft of the rear axle line, is a dubious configuration for any car, let alone a sportscar, which might reasonably be expected to be driven somewhere near its limits. So much weight concentrated so far back should inevitably make the tail want to wag the dog.

Yet Porsche, one of the most respected and successful of sportscar makers, has stuck doggedly to this contrary layout for almost 40 years, even persisting with it alongside more 'conventional' designs. Their current 911 types, even the enormously powerful Turbo, have the same basic configuration as the pro-

ABOVE *The mark of genius. Light and aerodynamic, the short-lived Porsche 356 Speedster uses the classic rear-engine configuration still used by Porsche to this day.*

duction 356 of 1948 – and there is no sign of Porsche abandoning it yet.

If, as has been said many times, the Porsche is a triumph of development over design, it is a triumph nonetheless.

The 356 was the first car to bear the Porsche name, though not the first to bear the stamp of Porsche's genius. Nominally, it was the 356th design of the Porsche design bureau, set up in Stuttgart in 1930. This was somewhat misleading, because Dr Porsche

1954 PORSCHE 356 'SPEEDSTER'	
Engine	A/c, flat 4-cyl
Capacity	1.3 litres
Maximum power	—
Chassis/suspension	Rear engined platform chassis, torsion bar independent
Top speed	120mph
0–60mph	10.0 seconds

started with Project 7, to avoid his first customers thinking he was inexperienced.

The first 356 prototype was based on Porsche's Berlin-Rome Axis Race streamliner of 1939, in turn based on the VW Beetle – which started life as Porsche Project 60 . . .

The 356 (designed by Dr Porsche's son Ferry to his father's brief, and completed in May 1948) had an open body and mid-engine (ahead of the gearbox and rear axle line), but all subsequent cars were rear-engined, to offer adequate cockpit space.

They used the platform chassis and all-torsion-bar trailing front/swing arm rear suspension of the Beetle, with a mildly tuned 40bhp version of the 1,131cc air-cooled flat-four Beetle engine.

Light weight and clean aerodynamics helped the car to a top speed of 85mph/137kph.

In August, 1948, Porsche completed the first 356 coupé and started small-scale production, launching the car officially early in 1949. Having built 50 cars in an interim workshop, Porsche got its Stuttgart works back from the US military in 1950 and started production in earnest.

The 356 developed rapidly, with the first capacity increase, to 1286cc, in 1951, followed by another, to 1582cc, in 1955 – this being the basic capacity until the last of the 356s in 1965. There was only one major body change, in 1959, with a larger windscreen and slight raising of the bumpers and headlamps, but there were many variations on the 356 theme, both open and closed.

One was the first Carrera; ultimately quickest of the 356s, in its 1965 130bhp 2-litre form, it took its name from the Carrera Panamericana, the Mexican road race in which Porsche won the small sportscar class at its first attempt in 1953. Porsche also won its class first time out at Le Mans, in 1951 with a racing coupé, quickly becoming a worldwide sales success too – especially on the west coast of the USA.

The most distinctive of all 356s was created for that market: the stunning but short-lived Speedster.

The Speedster, a sparsely equipped, lightweight, open 356 with a chopped down windscreen, clearly evoked the racing image. It had near racing perform-ance too, with a 120mph/193kph top speed, 10-second 0–60mph/96.5kph times and superb brakes and transmission. Whatever people said about Porsche handling, very few cars could pass one.

It was introduced in 1954 after American importer Max Hoffman had bought a racing Spyder and mooted the lookalike to Porsche. It was dropped fairly quickly when Porsche realised they could not pos-sibly make money on such a basic car however many they sold.

There are some miracles that even Porsche cannot work . . .

1955 MERCEDES-BENZ 300SL

The gull-winged Mercedes-Benz 300SL is one of the most distinctive of all sportscars. Outstandingly successful on both road and track, it was pioneering in many ways, though some of its most striking features were pure compromise. Yet it remains one of the greatest of all sporting classics.

It started life as a racing model, when three cars (including a little used open example) were built for the 1952 season. This was Mercedes' first racing effort after World War II and the budget by their standards was tiny.

Logically enough, the 300SL was designed around Mercedes' biggest production engine – a 3-litre straight-six, introduced in 1951 and then used in the big, 110mph/177kph 300S saloon.

300SL stood for 3-litre *Sport-Leicht*, or light sportscar, and light was the key word. The engine was big and heavy so the rest of the car had to be as light as possible, to which end the competition department designed a frighteningly complicated, stressed multi-tubular spaceframe, which weighed little more than 110lb. To this they bolted coil spring front suspension, swinging arm rear suspension and an aluminium coupé body with the famous gullwing doors. It was their only reasonable option, as the chassis had to be so deep in the sills to achieve the desired stiffness that conventional doors were out of the question.

To keep the bonnet (hood) line low the engine was canted through 40° *and* offset to one side.

Among its four major racing successes in its first year was a win at Le Mans – which every sportscar manufacturer still recognises as the one motor racing event with truly worldwide impact.

It was Mercedes' New York agent who suggested turning the 300SL into a road car and when the company expressed doubts he eased their uncertainty with a firm order for 1,000 cars!

The first production prototype was unveiled at the New York Auto Show in February, 1954 and production proper started in August. The road car looked very similar to the racing original, save for a few styling bulges and a different headlamp arrangement, but it had several major differences.

Most of the body (except the slightly larger doors, the boot (trunk) and bonnet (hood)) were steel, and the interior was fully trimmed – though it retained

LEFT *Probably the most famous Mercedes of all-time, the gull-wing 300SL is race-bred. 140 mph/224 kph and stunning acceleration are combined with somewhat treacherous handling – not a car for the faint-hearted.*

LEFT AND RIGHT *Wearing its three-pointed star with pride. Super-sleek styling and hand-built craftsmanship combine to make the 300SL look right from every angle.*

the tilting steering wheel which made entry merely difficult rather than totally impossible.

Where the Le Mans engine had used carburettors, production engines pioneered the use of Bosch direct fuel injection, and all road engines were also dry-sumped.

Although the road car was substantially heavier than the racer, and slower, it was still streets ahead of any opposition. With 195bhp (or an optional 215) it was good for maybe 140mph/225kph, and up to 228lb ft of torque gave instant pulling power from as little as 15mph/24kph in top gear. On the lowest of three optional axle ratios it would reach 60mph/96.5kph in under 7½ seconds and 100mph/161kph in less than 15 seconds.

The chassis was a mixture of good and bad; the huge aluminium-finned drum brakes, with servo-assistance, were exceptional, but the swinging arm rear suspension gave the sort of high speed oversteer that only a really gifted driver could cope with. On the newly fashionable radial tyres, it was especially

difficult . . .

In 1957, the gullwing was replaced (after 1,400 had been hand-built) by a roadster – largely on the strength of the Californian market. It had lower sills and conventional doors, plus many other refinements – notably to the rear suspension – which gave it better manners but not nearly so much character. Although it sold 1,858 copies by 1963, it will inevitably be remembered only as the mighty gullwing's lesser cousin.

1955 MERCEDES-BENZ 300 SL	
Engine	In-line, 6-cyl, sohc
Capacity	3.0 litres
Maximum power	195bhp
Chassis/suspension	Multi-tubular spaceframe, coil spring ifs, swinging arm irs
Top speed	140mph
0–60mph	7.5 seconds

1956 CHEVROLET CORVETTE

In America in the mid-1950s, auto industry engineers and stylists were a lot more interested in building sportscars than the public was in buying them. The few odd-balls who did want open-top two-seaters either bought European or went to the small but expensive specialist builders like Kurtis and Cunningham. To the Big Three they were a weird minority, not a potential profit area. Not, that is, until General Motors took the plunge with the Corvette – a nameplate which has survived ever since as the all-time biggest selling American sports-car.

Of all manufacturers, GM had perhaps the best idea of what people would buy in the future, gauged largely through what extravagances they could get away with in their annual Motorama showcars.

That was how the Corvette idea began. With the arrival of the new generation overhead-valve V8s in the early 1950s, America was quick to come to terms with horsepower, but GM was undoubtedly surprised by the enthusiastic reaction to the Corvette prototype which the Chevrolet Division showed at the 1953 Motorama.

It was a thoroughly European two-seater, far smaller than anything GM might reasonably have expected to gain public approval; and far from having all the trimmings of the typical showcar, it was basic in the extreme. It was so small because the engineers had ignored convention and designed it that way, placing all the major components as close together as they would go, and it looked so good because they had entrusted the fibreglass bodyshell to master-stylist Harley Earl.

So loud was the cheering for the Corvette that GM decided to plunge straight into production – intending to use fibreglass for the first 300 cars to give them time to tool into metal. They never had to – the public accepted the new material, production methods were refined and America's first mass-produced sportscar stayed plastic.

Given this open-armed enthusiasm, it is amazing how close GM came to getting the Corvette totally wrong. It was launched in 1953 with a 150bhp version of the elderly 235cu in the Chevy Six and the stodgy auto that went with it. GM had had a late attack of conservatism and aimed the Corvette mid-market. Its excellent chassis and sporty looks became

1956 CHEVROLET CORVETTE	
Engine	V8, ohv
Capacity	4.3 litres
Maximum power	225bhp
Chassis/suspension	Perimeter frame, coil spring/wishbone ifs, semi-elliptic rear
Top speed	120mph
0–60mph	7.5 seconds

an embarrassment when big, gin-palace-trimmed sedans with gutsy V8s could wallow by on any decent straight stretch.

What saved the Corvette was the 1955 option of the new and brilliant 265 Chevy V8 and a 1956 restyling. The result was equally spectacular looks *and* performance. With options up to 225bhp, the milestone 1956 Corvette became an outstanding car, well capable of over 120mph/193kph and 0–60mph/96.5kph in just 7½ seconds. Tuned for racing, a 1955 Corvette would touch 150mph/241kph and racing development further improved the already good production chassis. With the arrival of a three-speed, close ratio manual gearbox, superbly balanced handling and refined horsepower, the 1956 Corvette was a sportscar worthy of any company.

It was just a little too late for the boom sales year of 1955, and just a bit too expensive at over $3,100, but it had now become so good that Corvette sales soon far exceeded anything Chevrolet had ever envisaged back in 1953.

The Corvette became an American institution. It gained bigger and better V8s over the years and changed dramatically with the arrival of the Stingray in 1963. The 1956 Corvette probably remains America's closest approach to the universal sportscar, though Corvettes since have continued to be outstanding.

RIGHT *Corvette – the all-American sportscar. Compact by American standards, the Corvette sports a fibreglass bodyshell powered by a Chevy V-8 engine. A superbly-engineered chassis endows the car with razor-sharp handling. In road trim, a Corvette would reach 120 mph/192 kph – racing versions were good for another 30 mph/48 kph.*

1956 FORD THUNDERBIRD

In 1951, Ford's Vice President, Lewis Crusoe, and his assistant, George Walker, looked around the Paris Salon at the proliferation of Ferraris, Porsches and Jaguars and decided, there and then, that a sportscar was just what Ford needed to bolster its badly jaded image. Walker, a freelance designer, called his own studio and by the time the two of them arrived back in the USA his staff had already drawn up the outline of what would become the Thunderbird.

Although the Ford management quickly agreed to the idea, the company's dire financial problems committed them to building their sportscar on the cheap. It was planned as a fairly lightweight two-seater with soft-top and V8 power. The catch was that it had to use as many existing Ford parts as possible and it had to happen quickly – to give Ford a competitor for the newly launched Chevrolet Corvette.

The good news was that the Ford stylists, who were traditionally poor relations to the engineers, were given an unusually free hand – including a good deal of cooperation with the mechanical layout. Early tests were carried out using a shortened sedan chassis, with relatively soft suspension, but the T'bird's own chassis and running gear, with the engine set lower down and further back just as the stylists had asked, was developed in parallel.

The first prototype, early in 1954, already looked wonderful – low, sleek and largely free of the usual flashiness, but it was too heavy. Conveniently, Ford was able to take a quick look at the sales problems of the early Corvettes and chicken out of calling the Thunderbird a sportscar. Not only did they not have to go on an expensive and time consuming crash diet but they felt free to load on even more weight, in the form of an optional hardtop and power everything, thereby upgrading the Thunderbird to what Ford dubbed a 'personal car'.

As such, the Thunderbird went on sale, with the soft-top now optional, in October, 1954. At $2,695 it was even cheaper than the spartan six-cylinder Corvette and not surprisingly it outsold the early Chevy quite handsomely – by more than twenty to one in 1955, with over 16,000 sales.

The best of the T'birds was generally reckoned to be the 1956 model, which was still as near as made no odds to a sportscar, whatever Ford chose to call it. It

had put right the few problems of the earlier cars but actually changed very little. Even so, it was the most distinguishable of all Thunderbirds, with a one-year-only adoption of a 'continental' spare wheel location (vertically at the rear) and optional portholes in the rear quarters of the hardtop. It used a 202bhp version of Ford's 292cu in V8 and manual transmission as standard, with the 312cu in V8 as an option.

With softer rear springs and lower geared steering than the earlier examples its handling was less

1956 FORD THUNDERBIRD	
Engine	V8, ohv
Capacity	4.8 litres
Maximum power	202bhp
Chassis/suspension	Cross-braced ladder chassis, coil spring/wishbone ifs, semi-elliptic
Top speed	115mph
0–60mph	9.5 seconds

BELOW *Stylish competition for the Corvette, the Ford Thunderbird went upmarket with 'power-assisted*

everything'. A sports car in everything but name, the Thunderbird has become a legend.

twitchy and the good looking car would reach around 115mph/185kph, with 60mph/96.5kph coming up in under ten seconds. As such it lagged a little way behind the contemporary Corvette (now with the V8 it always needed) in everything but sales – but with the Chevy rapidly gaining ground to cut the margin to about three to one.

Ironically, that reflected a complete reversal of roles; the Corvette, which had started out as a mid-market car, had turned into a real sportscar, while the T'bird, which should have been a sportscar, had softened up into a 'personal' car.

The reversal continued, with the Thunderbird turning into an ordinary four-seater only a year or so later and the Corvette beating it in both sales and performance terms.

Maybe Americans really did want a sportscar in the 1950s, after all. It would not be the first time that the American market had been misjudged by a major American manufacturer.

1957 LOTUS 7 (CATERHAM 7)

The Caterham Super Seven has often been described as the nearest thing to a motor-cycle on four wheels, and that is probably still the best description there can be for this extraordinary car – which has been around with few fundamental changes since 1957!

It was launched as the Lotus Seven, a kit-built sportscar designed by Colin Chapman, the genius behind Lotus and a man well known for his absolute refusal to compromise.

There was certainly no compromise about the Seven. It was, and is, an out-and-out sportscar with absolutely no pretensions to being anything else. It has two seats and virtually no luggage space, rudimentary weather protection in the guise of an awkward-to-erect hood and side screens (which, when up, make getting in and out virtually impossible), and very few other creature comforts. However, it does have a race-bred tubular chassis and suspension which contribute to roadholding and

handling well beyond all normal realms – and with any of the vast choice of engines which have been available over the years, and barely half-ton of car has a blistering straightline performance. With any of the more potent engine options it will nudge six seconds for the dash to 60mph/96.5kph – even though its top speed is limited by the aerodynamics. Impressively, it achieves all this for no more than the cost of a sporty hatchback and combines its performance with a style as individual as anything on the road.

Everything about the Seven flatters the enthusiastic driver: beautifully precise controls; strictly functional instruments and trim; even the laid-back driving position which is so exhilaratingly close to the road. Barring a few aesthetic drawbacks, driving the Caterham Super Seven is a pure joy.

Over the years, engine options grew from small pushrod units, through Formula Ford type units, the famous Lotus Twincam in various stages of tune, to that engine's modern replacement, the big-valve,

LEFT BELOW *Four-wheeled motorbike? The thoroughly individual Caterham 7 pays no heed to modern comforts. The basic design of the car hasn't changed since 1957 – it's fast, it's fun and it's oh so impractical!*

1957 LOTUS 7 (CATERHAM 7)	
Engine	In-line, 4-cyl, ohv
Capacity	1690cc
Maximum power	135bhp
Chassis/suspension	Tubular space frame, aluminium-clad ifs, live axle rear
Top speed	112mph
0–60mph	5.6 seconds

BELOW *Light-weight body and powerful engine add up to true supercar performance. Limpet-like grip and phenomenal levels of handling complement the blistering acceleration.*

twin-cam built for Caterham by Lotus preparation specialists Vegantune.

In the early days, almost all Sevens were sold in kit form to take advantage of a British tax concession of the time, but in 1973 that exemption was withdrawn, putting prices up substantially and all but killing the Seven. Where many other specialist cars were prematurely buried because of this, the Seven survived.

It was saved by a long-time Lotus dealer, Caterham Cars, in Surrey, who acquired production rights (though not use of the Lotus name) from Lotus in May 1973 and have been producing the car, with constant improvements, ever since.

Although Caterham actually took over the angu-lar, fibreglass-bodied Series 4 car (which Lotus had only recently introduced) customer opinion soon persuaded them to revert to the classic, alloy-panelled, fibreglass-nosed and -winged Series 3 design which survives today.

In 1982 Caterham added a long-cockpit option to give bigger drivers a touch more leg-room but neither that nor the myriad engine and chassis variations have changed the essential character of the Super Seven in the slightest. On a warm summer's day and an open road the Seven still offers about as much fun as it is possible to have in any road car at any price, which is quite an achievement for a car that started out as a kit!

1961 JAGUAR E-TYPE

By 1961, Jaguar were used to having their new cars acclaimed as 'sensational'. In the 1920s, their Swallow-bodied forerunners were seen as the essence of style; in the 1930s the SS100 offered unbeatable performance for its price; in 1948 the XK120 combined speed, style and amazing value for money; and in the 1950s the racing D-Types beat the world. But none of them caused the same sensation as the exquisite E-Type, unveiled in March, 1961 at the Geneva Show. Its incredible looks, world-beating performance and almost unbelievably low price instantly rendered all its mass-produced contemporaries also-rans.

The E-Type's relationship with the D-Type showed quite clearly both above and below the surface. The sleek shape was very much like a longer, lower D-Type and had actually started to evolve as early as 1953 on an interim car between the C- and D-Types. A fastback coupé was offered alongside the roadster and, of course, all the E-Types were much better equipped than the spartan, racing Ds.

Under the skin, the new car had the familiar central monocoque with tubular subframes at front and rear, but, for the first time, Jaguar used an all-independent suspension. The front was based on wishbones and torsion bars; the clever new rear arrangement housed the final drive (with its inboard

disc brakes) in a frame attached to the rear of the monocoque, fixed length driveshafts acted as a top link, and there were wide-based lower wishbones and radius arms – all controlled by two big coil spring damper units at each side.

It worked brilliantly and the layout is still essentially unchanged on all Jaguars today, including the nearest thing to a sportscar, the V12 engined XJ-S Cabriolet.

Both open and closed E-Types, powered by the 265bhp 3.8-litre triple carb XK twin-cam engine, would do as near 150mph/241kph as made no difference – the coupé perhaps 1mph more, the less aerodynamic drophead (for which a detachable hardtop was available) perhaps 1mph under. Both could reach 60mph/96.5kph in seven seconds and return a respectable 20mpg/14lp100km – thanks to their exceptional aerodynamics and acceptably light weight.

Handling and roadholding were superb, letting even the ordinary driver enjoy much of the extraordinary performance; but the E-Type did have its faults. The earliest cars were quite cramped; they tended to overheat; the faired-in headlamps were hopeless (they were changed in 1967 for new US regulations); the all-disc brakes were marginal for such performance; and the early gearboxes were dreadfully slow and heavy.

Jaguar overcame most problems very quickly, ironically because they had again totally underestimated demand and had only planned a limited run! They cured many faults simply by going into proper tooling.

And, of course, the E-Type developed over the years anyway – though not always for the better.

The first cars were never surpassed for outright performance, with later power increases always offset by added weight. In 1964 the E-Type was given a 4.2-litre engine and an excellent new all-syncro gearbox. In 1966 the less attractive, high-roofed, long wheelbase 2+2 was introduced, with an automatic gearbox option. The car adapted to new US regulations in the late 1960s but the biggest change came in 1970 when Jaguar launched its magnificent 5.3-litre V12 engine in the E-Type, replacing the XK sixes.

This 272bhp engine, still considered one of the finest in the world, brought the E-Type a new refinement and a very different image – as a grand tourer rather than an outright sportscar.

E-Type production continued until early 1975, by which time more than 72,500 had been built, including some 15,000 V12s.

The XJ-S which replaced it was even less of a sportscar than the last E-Type. Even for Jaguar, the original E-Type was a very hard act to follow.

1961 JAGUAR E-TYPE	
Engine	In-line, 6-cyl, 2ohc
Capacity	3.8 litres
Maximum power	265bhp
Chassis/suspension	Central monocoque, tubular subframes, torsion bar ifs, coil spring irs
Top speed	150mph
0–60mph	7.0 seconds

BELOW *Cat that got the cream.*
The E-type Jaguar is the
sportscar of the 1960s.

1962 AC COBRA

The AC Cobra was an Anglo-american hybrid which actually worked, and the final fling of the no-holds-barred sportscar before the Ralph Nader era put a stop to such overt overkill. After Nader's book *Unsafe At Any Speed* (Grossman, New York, 1965) was published and the 'consumer protection' lobby grew, motoring in America and around the world changed dramatically. Gone was the hey-day of the musclecar, the horsepower race and the open top; in came downsizing, detoxing and crash testing; and out went cars like the Cobra with its big engine in a lightweight chassis, massive performance, open top and all. Happily, the Cobra had already guaranteed its own immortality as one of the fastest, most evocative sportscars of any era.

It evolved from 1961, when American racing driver Carroll Shelby took his version of the 'US engine/European chassis' idea to AC Cars in Britain. He had already been turned down by Aston Martin (even though he had won Le Mans for them in 1959), Jensen and Maserati, but he timed his arrival at AC perfectly – just as they were looking for more power for their excellent 2.6-litre Ford-powered Ace chassis.

By September, 1961 the project was under way. Ford, committed to its image-building 'total performance' programme, saw Shelby's idea as a way to pull buyers into Ford showrooms and responded to his approaches by giving him two of their latest 221cu in V8s to work with. The first example of what Shelby dubbed the Cobra ran in Britain in January, 1962, before several chassis, based on the Ace but much stronger, were shipped to the USA to be fitted with engines – which by then had grown to 260cu in.

Where others had failed, the Cobra triumphed, combining exceptional straightline performance with the handling and braking that AC always knew their chassis could provide. Shelby arranged to sell the cars through Ford dealers in the USA and the first 100 were commissioned late in 1962 in an effort to qualify the Cobra for international racing.

Late in 1962 the Cobra lost its inboard rear disc brakes but gained the classic 271bhp 289cu in Ford V8, to become the Mark II – sold in America as the Shelby Ford Cobra. This 289 Cobra was already in-decently quick, giving -second 0–60 times and a 000mph top speed, but there was much more to come.

1965 AC COBRA 427	
Engine	Ford V8, ohv
Capacity	7 litres
Maximum power	425bhp
Chassis/suspension	Tubular ladder, coil spring suspension all round
Top speed	160mph
0–60mph	4.5 seconds

BELOW AND RIGHT *The immortal AC Cobra (here in 7-litre form) is amazingly quick by any standards. The massive V8 in the lightweight body will propel the Cobra to 60 mph/96 kph in 4½ seconds and on to a maximum of 160 mph/256 kph!*

Racing was part of the Cobra's *raison d'etre* and it was obviously capable, with modification, of coping with considerably more horsepower. One product of Ford's NASCAR sedan racing programme was the famous 427 engine, which in 'standard' form gave some 425bhp. Shelby soon adopted it as a way to challenge the big Corvettes in American sportscar racing, allowing the Cobra to dominate for several years.

Derivatives, including the Daytona coupé which appeared in 1964, were very successful in international racing, just missing the world endurance championship in 1964 before becoming the first ever American winner of the World Manufacturers' Championship for GT cars in 1965.

In January, 1965 the staggeringly quick 427 (typically capable of 160mph/257kph and 12-second standing quarters) was launched as a road car. Ford had helped design new coil spring suspension and a stronger chassis but some of the 427's straightline muscle ws compromised by less agile handling than the 289.

The leaf-sprung chassis was dropped when the 427 arrived but AC put 289 engines into the later chassis as the AC 289 Mark III – and some cars were made with the cheaper 355bhp 'police special' 428 engine from the Ford Galaxie.

However, *every* Cobra was a classic, some just more than others. Only post-Nader legislation and consumer activists could beat the Cobra and production stopped in 1967. The Cobra lives on though – in 1982, with AC's approval, the British company Autocraft began to make genuine AC Mark IVs on the original 427 jigs. Perhaps the American enthusiasts will be able to enjoy the Cobra again, this time an imported version.

1964 AUSTIN HEALEY 3000 MkIII

They were affectionately called the 'Big Healeys', by almost everyone, and the Austin Healey 3000s really were larger-than-life in many respects – almost the end of the line for macho sportscars, before brute force, sadly, became less than socially acceptable.

The family line started in 1952 when specialist car builder Donald Healey exhibited his open, two-seater Healey 100 at the London Motor Show. Powered by a 2.6-litre four-cylinder engine derived from the big Austin A90 saloon and with a straghtforward ladder chassis and simply running gear, it attracted the approval of BMC management. They were looking for just such a sportscar, which they could build cheaply around existing Austin parts and fill what they saw as a yawning market gap between the small MGs and Triumphs and the bigger, more specialized Jaguars. They soon came to an agreement with Healey and his car went into production in 1953 as the Austin Healey 100, with a top speed of 102mph/164kph. The bodies were built by another specialist sportscar maker, Jensen, whose own 1952 Motor Show design had also impressed BMC, but not quite so much as the Healey.

The four-cylinder cars, including the tuned 100S, which started a distinguished competition career for the Healeys, were built until 1956, when a 102bhp six-cylinder 2.6-litre engine was introduced. In a slightly longer, slightly heavier but still very similar looking shell (mainly different in offering a token passenger space behind the front seats), this became known as the 100-6. It carried on the tradition of good performance with few frills and continued to sell in large numbers – almost all earning valuable export income.

In 1959 the car underwent a fairly major revision, with some chassis strengthening, front disc brakes and a capacity increase to 2.9 litres, to emerge as the Austin Healey 3000.

With power up to 124bhp from a triple-carburettor engine, the 3000 gave an even more vivid performance, with a top speed of about 116mph/187kph and predictably impressive low-speed flexibility.

In 1961 a MkII version was introduced with 132bhp and in 1964 the definitive MkIII appeared, now with only two carbs but with power up to 148bhp, for a top speed of 123mph/198kph and quite brutal

1964 AUSTIN HEALEY 3000 MK III	
Engine	In-line, 6-cyl, ohv
Capacity	2.9 litres
Maximum power	148bhp
Chassis/suspension	Cross-braced ladder coil spring/ wishbone ifs, semi-elliptic rear
Top speed	123mph
0–60mph	—

acceleration in the lower gears. Such refinements as wind-up windows and new walnut dash trim did nothing to change the uncompromising muscularity of the beast at all – which was a good thing.

Certainly the Big Healey had some shortcomings. Though capable of being docile, and with its overdrive gearing quite relaxed at speed, the brakes were heavy, it was a brute to drive hard, short on driver space (especially around the pedals), shorter still on luggage space, and the seats belied their comfortable looks. Regardless of any complaints, the 3000 built an exceptional reputation as a rally car. The famous red and white, alloy-bodied, 210bhp works cars scored literally dozens of major victories – including the 1964 Alpine Rally and two Liège–Sofia–Liège Rallies – and it was a successful circuit racer in its class for many years.

It lasted until the end of 1967, and of the 43,000 cars built, well over 90 per cent were exported.

1964 FORD MUSTANG

Ford has a longstanding habit of getting it right, and this was exemplified by the Mustang, the original pony-car. In its early days at least, the Mustang was much closer to being a sportscar than most Americans had ever thought they would buy. But buy it they did, in their millions.

For Ford, it was a calculated change of image from conservative to glamorous and a change of market from middle age to youth – aimed right at the millions who had grown up, with money in their pockets, from the postwar baby boom.

It emerged at the time of Ford's 'total performance' programme and America's growing awareness of the smaller, sportier European cars. The Mustang, like 'total performance', was dreamed up by the young, go-ahead new boss of the Ford Division, Lee Iacocca – now boss of Chrysler. The Mustang I was a 1962 mid-engined two-seater show car, but was never intended for production. The first *real* Mustang, thoroughly conventional but with the elusive spark of style, was seen in April 1964 at the New York World's Fair. Within hours of the car going on sale in the same month, Ford's $65 million development and $10 million advertising investments began to look like the best money they had ever spent.

Every available car was sold during that first day and orders taken for over 20,000 more.

What everyone wanted was a rakish four-seater, on a 108-in wheelbase, that Ford's in-house stylists had carefully contrived to look like a sporty two-seater. It was available as a hard-top or a convertible with engine options from a gutless 170cu in six, through a 260cu in V8 (derived like most of the rest of the Mustang's running gear from the Fairlane) to a 164bhp 289cu in V8 – plus manual or auto transmissions.

BELOW *Mustang-pony-car for a new generation. Clever marketing by Ford made the rakishly-styled Mustang an overnight success. Steve McQueen drove a Mustang to fame in the now legendary car chase scene in the film* Bullitt.

1965 FORD MUSTANG	
Engine	V8, ohv
Capacity	4.7 litres
Maximum power	271bhp
Chassis/suspension	Platform chassis, coil spring ifs, semi-elliptic rear
Top speed	121mph
0–60mph	8.1 seconds

It was offered at a rock-bottom basic price with minimal equipment but could be loaded up with a vast assortment of profit generating options – and most buyers did load up. Those unable to shrug off old habits went for the autos, but few took the 101bhp six.

With Ford struggling to keep up with demand, especially for the V8s, sales passed 100,000 within four months. They passed a quarter of a million well before the end of 1964 (by which time the smaller six had been dropped and the GT 2+2 'fastback' option added) and the first million within two years.

The Mustang was more than just another car, it was a phenomenon, the fastest selling new car ever and Ford's floodgate to the new generation.

Ford had no hesitation in those less fettered days in selling performance. Options, on top of the power-train choices, included harder suspension (by coils at the front and cart springs at the rear), bigger wheels, higher geared steering and better brakes – all of which the car really needed as standard!

The Mustang could not attain *real* European standards but it was a genuinely sporty car by prevailing American standards, with its bucket seats and floor gearshift.

For a while, the Mustang forged ahead, sharpening up its reflexes and growing in potency – with the early 270bhp Cobra-engined versions good for 120mph/193kph and sub-16-second standing quarters. But then it began to grow out of the simplicity which gave it instant appeal but negligible basic profit margins. By 1967 it was bigger and by 1969, when the Mach I was introduced, it had lost most of its original character. Engine options peaked with the 429cu in 'Boss' engine and 375bhp but no version since has been as close to a real sportscar as the classic original.

1964 LOTUS ELAN

If you believe that what really makes a sportscar is *fun* then this is where you can stop looking. Some sportscars are technically brilliant, some are historically important, several are staggeringly quick. The Lotus Elan is the one with everything. It doesn't have the outright performance of a Ferrari or a Lamborghini, but it doesn't have the pricetag either. It doesn't have the breeding or the name of a Bentley or a Bugatti, but it doesn't have *either* the pricetag or the ever-present responsibility of driving a piece of history. It doesn't always have the reliability of something as mundane as an MG or a Jaguar, but it does have twice the character.

On a sunny summer's afternoon, with the top down and nowhere special to go, it doesn't even have *quite* the raw entertainment of the equally cheap and even less conventional Seven, but if it rains and you're carrying more than a toothbrush and a towel it will get you there reasonably dry and uncrumpled and your luggage (not too much of it, mind you) won't have to come on behind.

It has its faults; if you drive one the way it cries out to be driven you might spend almost as much time underneath it as in it – a small price to pay. The air conditioning involves no more than taking the top down; the only in-car-entertainment is in driving it. Before General Motors took over Lotus early in 1986, Lotus was planning a small, cheap, mass-produced sportscar. Everybody, but everybody, dubbed it 'an Elan for the 'eighties'.

The Elan for the 'sixties (and into the early 'seventies) was a compact, fibreglass-bodied drophead (or, later, coupé) two-seater, powered by various versions of the Ford-based Lotus twin-cam engine. It was shown first at the London Motor Show late in 1962, but didn't reach production until early 1963. Production then didn't necessarily mean complete assembly; a British tax concession of the time (a loophole if you prefer) said that cars bought as 'kits' escaped purchase tax. Lotus was one of many specialist car makers to take advantage of leaving the wheels off and engine out, but was one of the few to survive when the concession disappeared in 1973.

The Elan is a wonderfully simple car. It introduced the classic Lotus backbone chassis, forked at the front to carry the legendary four-cylinder twin-cam engine and coil spring and wishbone suspension, and less

markedly at the back to take a Chapman strut with wide-based lower wishbones and rubber-jointed driveshafts.

The original 1½-litre motor gave 100bhp but only a few were made before the classic 105bhp 1.6-litre unit was introduced, the original engines being recalled and replaced, free of charge. As ever, the bottom-line power grew over the years, with up to 126bhp on offer from 1971 in Sprint versions. There were other changes, like a fixed-head coupé from 1965 and even a slightly bigger +2 sister model from 1967, but they were all Elans.

In many ways, the early ones were the best, like first thoughts, or first impressions. The fibreglass-reinforced plastic body, with its neat pop-up headlamps, never changed much (save for the obvious hardtop and +2 variants) and the biggest first-glance differences between early and late Elans are gradually increasing tyre widths and a bonnet (hood) bulge on the third series.

It is easy to feel at home in an Elan; functional design was Chapman's immutable creed. The car is only just over 12ft/3m long and knee-high, but it is amazingly comfortable even for the biggest driver. Everything works; the stubby gearlever flicks from ratio to ratio just like a switch, the handling is as sharp as a kart on rails and the all-round disc brakes simply stop the car on demand. The balance between soft springs and firm damping give a sweet ride in spite of the low weight and the actual grip would frighten almost any car in the world: point the Elan at corners and it goes round them; simple as that. It won't do more than 110mph/176kph (say 125/200kph with the best engine and more aerodynamic hardtop) but on an average road it will run rings round cars 50mph/80kph faster and ten times the price.

It isn't the *greatest* sportscar in the word perhaps, but if an Elan doesn't tell you what a *real* sportscar is, nothing will.

RIGHT *Colin Chapman had a flair for putting life into his cars, and perhaps none more so than his Lotus Elan. Functional in design and layout, the Elan* combines simplicity with leech-like roadholding and a willing (if occasionally unreliable) twin-cam engine.

1964 LOTUS ELAN	
Engine	In-line, 4-cyl, 2ohc
Capacity	1.6 litres
Maximum power	105bhp
Chassis/suspension	Backbone, coil spring/wishbone ifs, coil spring/Chapman strut irs
Top speed	110mph
0–60mph	8.7 seconds

1966 FORD GT40

Of all the glories that 'total performance' achieved for Ford in the 1960s, perhaps the greatest was not the run of Le Mans wins, or Indianapolis, or even the incalculable spin-off value of vastly increased sales, but one exceptional car – a road car as well as a Le Mans winner – the immortal GT40.

The GT40 was the true measure of how seriously Ford took its racing programme, the car that had to beat Ferrari at the highest levels of sportscar competition. It was an affair of honour; when Ford identified Le Mans as the one and only prize that would bring *worldwide* recognition it tried initially not to beat Ferrari but to buy it. The result would have been Ford-Ferrari road cars and Ferrari-Ford racing cars, but in the end Ford's $15 million offer was not enough to overcome Ferrari's fierce independence and pride.

Instead, in 1963, Ford, with a lot of help from the British racing car manufacturer Lola, began to develop the GT40. Lola had shown a Ford V8 powered, mid-engined GT racing car early in 1963 and that was the car around which Ford's development contract was negotiated. The gestation of the GT40 (named for its planned height of just 40in) was extremely short and in April 1964 the first car was shipped to the USA.

It had the 256cu in, all-alloy, pushrod V8 from the 1963 Indianapolis programme, giving about 350bhp and a theoretical maximum speed of close to 200mph/ 322kph. There were a few teething problems and in fact it took Ford until 1966 to win its covetted first Le Mans, the GT40 having won only two major races up to the end of 1965!

By then the GT40 had grown into the Mark II from early 1965, with 427 V8 power derived from the NASCAR Fords, de-tuned to 'only' 427bhp for endurance racing. Ford Advanced Vehicles in Britain

1967 FORD GT40 (ROAD)	
Engine	V8, ohv
Capacity	4.2 litres
Maximum power	350bhp
Chassis/suspension	Steel monocoque, independent coil spring/wishbone all round
Top speed	165mph
0–60mph	5.0 seconds

RIGHT *The GT40 was developed with one aim in mind – to win the Le Mans 24 Hour Race and beat Ferrari. And win they did, not just once, but four times in a row. Roadgoing GT40s are little different to the racing versions – performance is positively shattering with a 5-seconds 0–60 mph/0–96 kph time.*

also began to build 289cu in GT40s in some numbers from mid-1965, and even built some open cars that year. In all, about 120 GT40s and their derivatives were built and as well as the hugely successful racing types (which went on to win Le Mans four times in a row) Ford also offered genuine roadgoing GT40s, and sold about 31 road cars by 1967.

The first road cars used a 335bhp version of the 289 V8, to give a top speed of 164mph/264kph – with 127mph/204kph in second gear, 142mph/228.5kph in third and 142mph/228.5kph in fourth! The first were little different from the racers save for carpets and door pockets but the later Mark III changed the right-hand gearchange for a central lever and the excellent, fixed 'hammock' seats and adjustable pedals for moveable seats. It also lost a few horsepower, and was not as popular as the earlier car, with only about half a dozen sold.

Even today, driving a GT40 is a remarkable experience. The power and acceleration are truly awesome, with 0–60mph/96.5kph in around five seconds and 100mph/161kph in not much more than ten. Even with the slightly softer road suspension and on wide (but not excessively so) wire wheels, the amount of grip and precision of handling are exceptional, with so much flexible power that it is relatively easy to balance the car on the throttle through fast corners. The steering is super quick, the gearbox is slick perfection, and the only thing that really betrays the car is the massive effort needed to get the best from the big disc brakes.

The roadgoing GT40 really is a very special legacy of 'total performance' – almost certainly the last all-out racing sportscar which could double as such a docile yet shatteringly quick road car; and it was also the Ford that beat Ferrari. At last there was an American sportscar that matched European performance.

1966 LAMBORGHINI MIURA

1966 LAMBORGHINI MIURA	
Engine	V12, 4ohc
Capacity	3.9 litres
Maximum power	350bhp
Chassis/suspension	Mid-engine lightweight platform, independent coil spring/wishbone
Top speed	170mph
0–60mph	6.0 seconds

In the 1960s, when Italian industrialist Ferruccio Lamborghini branched out into the hazardous business of building sportscars, he did so with the intention of beating Enzo Ferrari at his own game. He acted out of a frustration common to many Ferrari owners at the cavalier attitude of Ferrari towards customers who dared find fault with his cars.

Lamborghini was not a man to do things by halves. His substantial fortune was based on building tractors and air conditioning systems. For his badge he chose the bull of his birth sign – and his head-on approach matched it perfectly. He committed himself to building cars to match any Ferrari in performance but without their often unruly temperament or uncompromising ascendancy of engineering over creature comforts.

Against all the odds, he succeeded. His engineering team was young but gifted and his production standards exquisite. His first car, the 350GT, was launched in 1964, with a magnificent 3.5-litre four cam V12 designed by Giotto Bizzarrini. Bizzarrini had just left Ferrari (none too happily) after being closely involved in developing the great GTO and several other racing models. His 602 Lamborghini V12 was a logical progression of his Ferrari work, not a copy. It survives in developed form in today's Countach S.

In 1965 the engine grew to a full 4-litres for the 400GT, introduced at that year's Geneva Show. Alongside the 400GT was a rolling chassis, also with the new 4-litre V12. In this case, it was mounted transversely behind the two-seater cockpit with its five-speed gearbox and final drive cleverly integrated into a modified crankcase. Designed, like the earlier cars, by Gianpaolo Dallara, it was labelled TP400 – for *transversale posteriore* 4-litre. Most people thought it was either a one-off show car or a racing prototype.

They were wrong: Lamborghini never did fall into the financially-perilous racing trap and in 1966 the TP400 re-emerged with a lovely Bertone body as the production Miura. Until then, Lamborghini had only partly fulfilled his dream to upstage Ferrari; with the Miura he beat his rival into the mid-engined supercar league by eight full years.

Simply, he created a car combining near racing standards of performance with luxury appointments

ABOVE *Combining racing car performance and limousine luxury, the Lamborghini Miura is a true Italian supercar in the Ferrari league.*

and an almost limousine comfort.

Dallara's chassis was not the usual tubular affair, but a platform with box section sills, centre and cross members. It was liberally riddled with holes for lightness but immensely strong – a prerequisite for decent road manners, whatever the suspension system. It was complicated and expensive to make, more so because of Lamborghini's insistence on making virtually everything in-house and this more than anything limited the number of Miuras made. Demand, however, always easily outstripped supply.

Not only was the Miura utterly beautiful, it was as quick as it looked. It started as the P400, with 350bhp, and grew with appropriate chassis improvements through the 370bhp P400S of 1969 to the ultimate Miura, the 1971 P400SV, with 385bhp and subtle but unmistakeable aerodynamic tweaks based on a stillborn racing design, the Jota.

In SV form, the Miura would achieve well over 170mph/273.5kph, hit 60mph/96.5kph in under six seconds and 100mph/161kph in 14 seconds. On wishbone and coil spring suspension all round, it combined a supple ride with marvellous roadholding – although it was undeniably nervous around its eventual limits, especially in the early versions, and it did have a tendency to lift its nose at very high speeds. It was also short on luggage space and the interior luxury was offset by a dozen big air intakes woolfing greedily away only inches behind the occupants' heads.

The Miura was a landmark; an engineering *tour de force* which rewarded a skilled driver with staggering performance and lesser mortals with a special symbol of style. Lamborghini sold just 760 Miuras of various kinds up to 1973, shortly after which it was replaced by the even more remarkable Countach – which is still in production.

1967 FERRARI 365GTB4 DAYTONA

The identity of the all-time number one sportscar is a prolonged argument – and, of course, there is no real answer. Sportscars are such a personal thing and there are so many worthy claimants to greatness that trying to single out one is as frustrating as it would be meaningless.

Ask a hundred enthusiasts to list their own all-time top-ten in no particular order, and there is a fair chance that the Ferrari 365GTB4, the Daytona, would be on every list.

The Daytona, more than any other sportscar with the possible exception of the Cobra, has become a popular legend. It takes a real enthusiast to know the genius of Lamborghini or a Bugatti, but a Ferrari can strike a chord in almost anybody – and no Ferrari more so than the classic Daytona.

Even by Ferrari's standards, the Daytona was a milestone: the ultimate expression of the big front-engined V12 bloodline and the pinnacle of one great Ferrari tradition. It was also almost certainly the fastest genuine road car ever to prove its claims against the stopwatch, long past its own production lifetime and even now with few legitimate challengers.

Yet it was a docile and totally civilized Grand Touring car with a restrained elegance that would turn heads anywhere, but never raise eyebrows.

It was unveiled at the 1968 Paris Salon, as a logical successor to the 275GTB4. The designation 365GTB4 represented the capacity of one of its dozen cylinders, the body type *Gran Turismo Berlina* and the number of its cams – four. Later, there would be a tantalisingly small sprinkling of another Daytona, the 365GTS4 – where the S stood for *Spyder*, or open top.

The Lampredi-designed 602 V12 displaced 4390cc and delivered 352bhp at 7700rpm, with 318lb ft of torque at a fairly high 5500rpm. The torque spread, however, was prodigious and the lazy effortlessness of the power delivery gave the car a character all its own.

The beautiful alloy body, with its steeply raked windscreen and high waistline, was designed by Pininfarina and built by Scaglietti. There was no superfluous embellishment; the racing pattern cast magnesium wheels were the Daytona's only small cry for attention; even the Prancing Horse badges were tiny, but such a car could only be a Ferrari.

1967 FERRARI 365GTB DAYTONA	
Engine	V12, 4ohc
Capacity	4.4 litres
Maximum power	325bhp
Chassis/suspension	Multitubular independent coil spring/wishbone all round
Top speed	174mph
0–60mph	5.3 seconds

Under the long bonnet (hood), the heavy V12 was set well back, to produce near perfect weight distribution – helped by the five-speed gearbox and final drive being mounted in unit with the independent rear suspension. It gave the big car – 14½ft and over 1½ tons – staggering performance.

The Daytona would do an honest 174mph/280kph, but it was also perfectly friendly. Effective aerodynamic detailing made it absolutely stable, even at its maximum speed, and its handling was equally protective.

Coil spring and wishbone suspension all round (just like Ferrari's contemporary racers) offered outstanding handling potential to the skilled driver, without demanding any ability out of the ordinary (save a degree of physical strength and stamina for the generally heavy controls).

Below its considerable limits, the Daytona was no more demanding to drive than any big, gentle saloon and perhaps its greatest strength of all was, as its name implied, a real, long-legged Grand Tourer – with the emphasis on the Grand.

In 1974, this last of the front-engined V12 Ferrari line made way for the first of the mid-engined 12-cylinder Ferraris, the 365GTBB – or *Berlinetta Boxer*. The Boxer part gave away the configuration of the car's new flat-12 engine, which had the same, horizontally-opposed layout as Ferrari's contemporary Grand Prix racers. It had the same capacity as the Daytona's V12, the same torque and a little more horsepower.

The Boxer was, and in its latest 388bhp guise still is, a great car, but the Daytona was perhaps the greatest of all.

ABOVE AND LEFT *The greatest Ferrari of all? A totally civilized Grand Tourer, with bite where it counts, the Daytona will probably go down in history as the ultimate Ferrari. Whether in Berlinetta* (ABOVE) *or Spyder* (LEFT) *bodyshell the Daytona is no more difficult to drive than a big saloon car – its aero-dynamics keep it rock steady right up to the 174 mph/ 278.4 kph maximum.*

1968 MORGAN PLUS 8

While any number of small companies worldwide build replicas of classic sportscars from long-gone eras, the Morgan company goes one stage better: it builds *real* sportscars from a long-gone era. That, at least, is the way it seems, but in spite of a basic shape, unchanged since the first four-wheeler Morgan appeared in 1936, and a suspension layout shared with the very first Morgan of 1910, the Morgan Plus 8 successfully combines classic character with modern performance in a way that no one else even approaches.

The Plus 8, launched in 1968 and still going strong, says it all about the Morgan philosophy.

It was introduced because Morgan needed something a bit special to revive its image after the end of its Triumph TR powered Plus 4 series. Having failed miserably to interest buyers in the modern shape of the fibre-glass-bodied Plus 4 Plus coupé, Morgan rightly resigned themselves to the fact that people still wanted a traditional Morgan. This, however, could still be spectacular.

After complex negotiations (and rejection of several alternatives) Morgan arranged to use Rover's recently adopted 3.5-litre development of the small block, all-alloy Buick V8 for its new flagship. By February 1967 they had built a Plus 4 based prototype and by the end of the year the idea was almost ready for production.

In the end, the Plus 8 chassis was slightly longer and wider at the front (dispensing with the unsightly bonnet (hood) bulges of the prototype), and had its rear springs shifted back to ease the axle tramp generated by the V8's power. The whole development programme supposedly cost Morgan about today's price of a single car!

It was an excellent investment; 18 years after the model was introduced, Morgan still has probably the longest waiting list of any car company in the world. Order a new Plus 8 now and you might drive it away in about five years time.

If you did you would find a car of exceptional character and electrifying performance – at least until high-speed aerodynamics take over.

The Plus 8 has changed very little since its introduction. The Z-section ladder chassis still has the famous sliding-pillar and coil spring front suspension, plus a solid axle on semi-elliptic springs at the

ABOVE *Using traditional craftsmanship for the body (hand-beaten aluminium on an ash frame), and allying it to the light-alloy Rover V8, the Malvern-built Morgan Plus 8 is a true sportscar for the 1980s.*

1968 MORGAN PLUS 8	
Engine	Rover V8, ohv
Capacity	3.5 litres
Maximum power	151bhp
Chassis/suspension	Ladder chassis, coil spring/sliding pillar ifs, semi-elliptic rear
Top speed	123mph
0–60mph	6.5 seconds

rear – with lever dampers to complete the 'vintage' specification.

Early cars had a Moss four-speed close-ratio gearbox, remote from the engine. This unit, whose excellent ratios were offset by a very difficult change, was replaced by a four-speed Rover 'box (in unit with the engine) in 1972. At the same time, the car grew a touch wider in track and acquired slightly bigger tyres, with minor bodywork changes to suit. In 1975 an alloy-panelled lightweight version was offered (built, like the steel-bodied car) over a traditional wood frame, but few were sold.

The car was very light anyway, at only 17cwt, helped by the all-alloy engine and the light Rover gearbox. It shed a few more pounds in 1977 when it adopted the latest Rover five-speed gearbox and the 155bhp version of the V8 that went with it. Power output had already varied slightly, from the originally quoted 160bhp, through 151bhp and 143bhp (on a lower compression ratio from 1973). There were other minor changes, notably to wheels and tyres, which standardized 15-inch rims with Pirelli P6 covers early in 1982, and to the steering, with rack-and-pinion as a welcome option from 1983 and, subsequently, a less 'nervous' recirculating ball system as standard.

The biggest change, as an option, came in 1984, when Morgan offered the fuel-injected 190bhp Rover Vitesse engine, to give the Plus 8 even more staggering performance. Where the 155bhp car is good for some 123mph and 0-60 times of 6.5 seconds, the injected Moggie will nudge 130mph and carve the 60mph sprint down to just six seconds.

With a very open-air driving position, a harsh ride on all but the smoothest roads (but superb roadholding and brakes) and a generally 'alive' character, it feels even quicker. Anachronism it may be, but it is fantastic fun.

LEFT *Visually, the Morgan has hardly changed since the 1930s. Driver comfort hasn't changed much either, with a bone-jarring ride over even the smallest bumps – real seat-of-the-pants motoring.*

1969 NISSAN 240Z

It was only a matter of time before the Japanese solved the problem of breaking into the sportscar market. When Nissan did it they did so in the biggest possible way, their 240Z quickly becoming the biggest selling sportscar in the world.

As elsewhere, Japanese ascendancy in the motor industry was based more on making other people's ideas work better than on inventing anything new. Nissan had produced previous sportscars, but anything before the 240Z had only sold in tiny numbers to a specialized market. To Western eyes, most of what went before was idiosyncratic; European and American sportscar buyers brought up on the old-fashioned simplicity of MGs, Austin-Healeys, Triumphs and the like were too ready to mistake clever engineering for unproven novelty.

Japan did make mistakes, but that was not one of them. Their biggest error was, that in spite of their worldwide success, their cars were still peculiarly Japanese – and in particular, most were built to suit the smaller Japanese physique. In saloon cars this was not so obvious, but in first generation Japanese sportscars (of which the Honda S800 was a fair example) big drivers had problems.

Fortunately for Nissan, the man who helped initiate the 240Z programme, as a successor to the MGB-like Fairlady SR3, stylist Albrecht Goertz, was a German, based in New York. He insisted that his car be designed around Western rather than Eastern physiques, even if that made it a pure two-seater rather than the planned 2+2.

His outline design drew on American, Germany and British styling ideas. In 1964 it was translated into a prototype for Nissan by Yamaha, who also built the 2-litre six-cylinder twin-cam engine, but Nissan dropped the whole project after numerous technical problems arose. It was revived in 1966 by Nissan's own engineers, with the more conventional intention of building a car around available running gear – in this case a 151bhp 2.4-litre straight-six engine based on the four-cylinder Bluebird saloon car unit.

It had a unit-construction two-door shell, designed for mass production, with MacPherson strut suspension all round. Brakes were discs at the front, finned drums at the rear, and steering was by rack-and-pinion. A four-speed gearbox was standard for the

USA and the superb, close-ratio five-speed which was optional there was standard elsewhere.

As launched in November 1969, the 240Z was not revolutionary, just a well-honed example of existing technology. A 2-litre version, the Fairlady Z was sold in Japan, but the 240Z's biggest market was the USA, where it was soon labelled as being in a class of its own for its very low price — way ahead of obvious rivals like the MGB and Triumph GT6 in every respect, and much closer to the more expensive E-Type or Porsche.

The 240Z was spiritual successor to the macho European sportscar typified by the 'Big Healeys' — which burgeoning US legislation killed in 1968. It was ready for the rules which killed the Healey.

Most significantly, the Nissan 240Z was always a coupé, never a soft-top, which also let Nissan equip it to the interior standards which Japan considered normal. It was well trimmed, though the seats were none too comfortable, it had a full range of instruments and even a radio. Air conditioning was optional on US-bound cars.

On the road, the flexible, silky smooth engine gave 125mph/265.5kph performance with 0-60mph/96.5kph in under eight seconds and comfortable 120mph/193kph cruising. The handling was crisp and near neutral, with power oversteer on tap and very responsive steering.

Sales boomed and Nissan soon doubled its planned production rate but still took almost three years to catch up with demand.

In 1973 the 240Z was replaced by the 260Z, whose bigger engine did not make up for more de-toxing and more weight. Later Z cars grew bigger and softer and although the current 300ZX Turbo has a style of its own, the 240Z remains the best of all.

1969 DATSUN 240Z	
Engine	In-line, 6-cyl, sohc
Capacity	2.4 litres
Maximum power	151bhp
Chassis/suspension	Unitary construction, MacPherson strut, iars
Top speed	125mph
0–60mph	7.8 seconds

LEFT *Generally regarded as the best of the Nissan 'Z-cars' the 240Z was the first in a long line of Japanese sportscars. With performance to take on E-Types and Porsches, the 240Z proved successful both on the road and in competition.*

1971 DE TOMASO PANTERA

Attractive though the idea is, very few manufacturers have made a success of substituting big, cheap American V8 power with the prohibitively expensive alternative of manufacturing engines from scratch. Even fewer have made the logical progression that the De Tomaso Pantera made in 1970, to the mid-engined format, even though the V8 is an obvious choice for such treatment.

After all, in the mid-1960s and early 1970s big American V8 mid-engines proliferated in European as well as American motor racing – in both Can-Am type sportscars and Formula 5000/Formula A single seaters, Ford, with the Le Mans winning GT40 – the spiritual ancestor of all roadgoing mid-engined supercars – had showed that the idea *could* work on the road, yet most of the big V8 users stuck conservatively with the old front-engined layout.

Surprisingly, as both the basic parameters and most of the hardware were readily and fairly cheaply available from the racing world, no more than one or two tried to follow Ford's lead; they simply left mid-engines to the real supercar builders. Of the handful who tried, the De Tomaso Pantera was the only long-term success.

The Argentine former racing driver, Allejandro de Tomaso, had built some reasonably successful cars before the Pantera, but this soon overshadowed them all. His first mid-engined car was the smaller Vallelunga and in 1966 he launched the evil-handling 4.7-litre V8 Mangusta.

In 1967 he bought Ghia, the firm which styled the Mangusta. When Ford subsequently took over Ghia, Tomaso found an unlikely but enthusiastic ally. The giant US manufacturer saw in the underdeveloped Mangusta the possibility of something better. With its glamorous Italian name and Ford power, its racy

1971 DE TOMASO PANTERA	
Engine	Ford V8, ohv
Capacity	5.7 litres
Maximum power	330bhp
Chassis/suspension	Mid-engine, unitary, coil spring/ wishbone iars
Top speed	160mph
0–60mph	5.6 seconds

BELOW AND RIGHT *The De Tomaso Pantera GTS, styled by Ghia and powered by Ford. Good looks and handling, and a mid-mounted engine make it a car to be reckoned with.*

image might pull buyers into Ford showrooms and closer to more mundane products without Ford having to commit itself to an expensive full-scale sports-car programme.

So, with Ford's help, the mid-engined basics were considerably refined, given an attractive new body evolved by Ghia in Ford's Detroit wind tunnels, and re-launched at the 1970 New York Motor Show as the De Tomaso Pantera, 'Powered by Ford'.

With the weight of Ford backing, and access to many corporate parts bins, it had become a very civilized car. The 5.7-litre V8 and a five-speed ZF transaxle were mounted in a subframe in the back of a steel, unit-construction two-seater coupé shell. It stood on coil spring and wishbone suspension, with ventilated disc brakes all round, and rather larger tyres on the back than on the front – which not only gave it the sporty looks that Ford wanted but also reduced the handling effects of the considerable rearward weight bias.

It was quite a big car, at almost exactly 14ft long. With its robust build and high equipment levels (even air conditioning was offered) it was also heavier than it should have been, not much short of a ton-and-a-half. The standard engine in the L version gave 330bhp at 5,400rpm and 325lb ft of torque at only 3,500rpm, enough for spectacular acceleration to a top speed of around 160mph/257kph.

Even today, it is a format which has remained basically unchanged.

1972 Fiat X1/9

When Fiat introduced the X1/9, in November 1972, they were not by any means the first to explore the mid-engined format for sportscars. By the mid-1960s the layout was essential for racing and by 1972 Ferrari (with the Dino), Lotus, Porsche (with the unloved 914), Lamborghini and Maserati could all offer mid-engined road cars. What Fiat achieved, where even Porsche had failed, was to put the concept into actual mass production, selling large numbers of a sophisticated idea to a market hitherto happy with cheap and cheerful sportscar engineering from the likes of MG, Triumph, Alfa Romeo – even Fiat themselves.

At first, Fiat were as reticent about such a radical change as the surprisingly conservative buyers were. They were talked into the X1/9 project by Bertone, who had come up with the germ of the idea in a typically extravagant but quite workable show-car concept. Their two-seater Runabout appeared at the Turin Show in November 1969, with a 903cc Fiat engine. Apart from silly headlights mounted on its Targa-style roof bar, it is recognisably the basis of the X1/9.

Bertone were struggling to fit a sportscar into the new front-wheel-drive Fiat 128 family. They badly needed to style a replacement for the rear-engined 850 Spyder, but until Nuccio Bertone moved the front-wheel-drive power pack to the other end of the car they were not even come close to solving the problem of the 850's 128-based successor.

Soon after the Turin Show, Bertone built a running 128-based prototype. When Fiat eventually accepted it, the X1/9's long gestation began.

Revealed as a production model in November 1972, it was a two-seater, with limited luggage space in the nose and in a compartment behind the transverse mid-engine. It had a distinctive wedge shape and a removable Targa top which stowed in the front luggage space. The fuel tank was behind the bulkhead aft of one seat and the spare wheel was behind the other. It was a masterpiece of packaging both in cramming so much into so small a space and in keeping the major masses within the wheelbase, contributing to fantastic roadholding.

It used a mildly modified 128 engine, fitted more upright than in the saloons for better access. In single carburettor form the 1290cc overhead-cam four-

1972 FIAT X1/9	
Engine	In-line, 4-cyl, sohc
Capacity	1.3 litres
Maximum power	75bhp
Chassis/suspension	Mid-engine, unitary, independent MacPherson strut all round
Top speed	100mph
0–60mph	12.8 seconds

cylinder unit gave 75bhp at 6000rpm and 72lb ft of torque at 3400rpm – but only a meagre 66bhp and 68lb ft when strangled by US emission regulations.

Nevertheless, when it went on sale in the USA in 1974 (having been launched in Italy in mid-1973) it became a major success. The key was its remarkable handling and roadholding and its sheer style. Its trim was basic, tinny even in places; like the small MGs and Triumphs, its power train was borrowed from a saloon, but at its price nothing approached its style or leech-like grip.

It only offered between 93 and 100mph depending on market, but on 128-based MacPherson strut suspension it gave almost neutral, almost idiot-proof handling, instant steering response, and cornering power way beyond the reach of its mass-produced rivals. Even with 0-60 times of almost 13 seconds, it was often labelled 'a mini Ferrari'.

Fiat were in no hurry to change it. In 1976 it grew bigger bumpers for the USA. A right-hand-drive X1/9 was added in 1977; the British model offered better trim and equipment, including alloy wheels and even a fitted luggage set.

In October 1978 the new Ritmo's 1498cc engine answered criticism that the brilliant chassis deserved more power. The X1/9 1500 had 85bhp; with much better torque and a five-speed gearbox it had far more flexible performance and up to 110mph. US cars had only 65bhp and were heavier – but from 1980 a fuel-injection option (standard after 1982) gave 75bhp – just like the original European 1300!

It wasn't lack of power that eventually hurt the X1/9 most; Fiat's widespread quality control problems of the early 1980s brought a near fatal slump in sales and transfer of much reduced production to Bertone in 1981, since when the car has survived only as a low volume model.

LEFT *Another sleek creation from the Bertone styling studio, that made it through into mass-production is the Fiat X1/9.*

ABOVE LEFT *The distinctive wedgeshape of the X1/9 succeeds where so many other car designs in the same vein failed.*

1972 LANCIA STRATOS

Once the Lancia Stratos had been built, its years of near invincibility in rallying were assured, but it was a minor miracle that the Stratos was built at all. Only two years before the first prototype was shown, at the Turin Show late in 1971, Lancia was all but bankrupt. Had Fiat not taken over the company in October 1969, its long and distinguished history might have ended before the 1970s. Yet without the financial problems and consequent Fiat connection the Stratos would not have happened anyway.

1972 LANCIA STRATOS	
Engine	Ferrari Dino V6, 4ohc
Capacity	2.4 litres
Maximum power	190bhp
Chassis/suspension	Mid-engine monocoque centre with extensions, coil spring ifs
Top speed	142mph
0–60mph	6.6 seconds

ABOVE *The road-going version of the mid-engined Lancia Stratos which dominated the world rally scene for years.*

1972 MASERATI BORA

Another of Fiat's commercial acquisitions was the catalyst for the forerunner of today's rally supercars. In June 1969, shortly before the Lancia takeover, Fiat had acquired a half-share in Ferrari. Fiat extended Ferrari's manufacturing scope (and homologation possibilities) by building the 2.4-litre Dino V6 engine, supplying some of the Ferrari-built mid-engined Dino and fitting many more into their own front-engined Fiat Dino.

After the Fiat takeover, Lancia had a real future, with generous investment in new models and enough backing for a proper rally programme. The front-wheel-drive Fulvia was a prolific winner, and world champion, but by the early 1970s Lancia could see the growing threat from rear- and mid-engined cars like the Alpine-Renault, Porsche 911 and the ultimately abortive Ford GT70.

Lancia competition chief Cesare Fiorio knew a mid-engined car was the solution; in the Ferrari V6 he saw the ideal basis for his car. Thanks to the Fiat connection, the deal was possible (if not universally popular) so all Fiorio needed was a car.

He already had its name and basic inspiration, from a futuristic, Lancia-engined Bertone showcar, seen at Turin in 1970: the Stratos.

The real thing shared only the name, wheelbase and the maker, as Bertone were entrusted with designing not only the body but also the chassis of the new rally car – and then making the 500 units necessary to qualify it for competition. Lancia would complete the final assembly.

Bertone's chassis (their first ever!) used a steel monocoque centre section with sheet, box and tubular extensions at the front and a massively strong rear cage for the transversely-mounted mid-engine, transmission and suspension.

Around this stubby base they built a stunning fibreglass shell. It looked almost as wide as it was long, was exaggeratedly wedge-shaped, and the rake of its beautifully curved screen, swept by one huge wiper, followed the slope of the heavily-louvred nose. The first cars had no superfluous trim; the distinctive (and effective) roof and tail spoilers were only added to later cars. The leather straps on the hinged nose and tail sections (vital for mechanical accessibility)

were there to keep the lightweight panels in line with the rest of the car.

In every respect, the Stratos was an unqualified success. From the start it was a rally and race winner and its eventual tally included four Monte Carlo Rallies and a hat-trick of world championships. Its career might have been even longer except that by 1978, marketing needs put the Fiat name to the fore, with the Abarth 131.

ABOVE *Power comes from the Ferrari Dino engine sitting behind the driver.*

RIGHT *The glassfibre body of the Stratos was styled and built by Bertone.*

1972 MASERATI BORA

Like Ferrari, Maserati started out reluctantly as a road car manufacturer, and like Ferrari only really went into production at all as a way of paying for its primary interest, motor racing.

Enzo Ferrari had a long career in racing, as a driver and a manager (with Alfa Romeo), before he became a manufacturer in his own right immediately before World War II. When he started building Ferraris after the war, he quickly, if a little cynically, cashed in on roadgoing cars as a source of income. It took Maserati a little longer.

Maserati was a racing car manufacturer (a highly successful one) from 1926. Some of their racing sportscars were usable on the road but that was incidental. The first Maserati intended for the road appeared in 1950, after the Maserati brothers had sold the business to the wealthy industrialist and racing enthusiast, Omer Orsi.

The two-door A6 coupé of 1950 was introduced not out of choice but of necessity, to help offset mounting losses for the racing time. It took Maserati another seven years to get serious about road car production – still basically for racing finance – with the lovely, six-cylinder, twin-cam 3,500, built with various body styles until 1964.

Thereafter, Maserati built quite a mixture of road cars, many of them excellent, but somehow never seeming to generate the charisma of a Ferrari or a Lamborghini.

In many people's eyes, the best Maserati of all came at a time when the company was going through an even deeper crisis than usual. It was the V8-engined Bora, introduced at the Geneva Show in March 1971, widely acclaimed but often overlooked in the supercar stakes, although it stayed in production, against the odds, until 1980.

Like other new generation supercars, it was mid-engined, in this case with a truly excellent V8 of Maserati's own making and developed from their successful 4.5-litre sports racing cars of the mid-to late 1960s.

It was a light, compact, all-alloy unit with twin overhead cams and fed by four twin-choke down-draught Weber carbs. It started life at 4.7-litres, which gave 310bhp at 6,000rpm, and an even more impressive 340lb ft of torque. It grew later to just over 4.9-litres, adding another 20bhp and becoming even

ABOVE *The Maserati Bora, like many supercars of its day, is mid-engined and developed from Maserati's racing expertise. Its main drawback is the Citroën-derived braking system which has little 'feel'.*

1972 MASERATI BORA	
Engine	V8, 4ohc
Capacity	4.7 litres
Maximum power	310bhp
Chassis/suspension	Mid-engine, unitary, coil spring/ wishbone iars
Top speed	157mph
0–60mph	6.2 seconds

more willing at low revs – helped by five perfectly chosen gear ratios in a 'box mounted, racing style, behind the final drive.

All this sat in a tubular subframe at the back of a steel unit-construction two-door coupé shell, by master-stylist Giugiaro. It was properly equipped, even to the extent of standard air conditioning, electric windows and automatically adjustable seats and pedals.

The Bora was quite capable of exploiting all its near-160mph/257kph performance. On coil spring and wishbone suspension it had near perfect handling balance and exceptional grip even by these standards – although exploiting the higher reaches demanded a degree of skill and a slice of bravery.

If it had a fault it was in the braking system. In 1968 Citroën had taken over Maserati during one of its periodic crises. Citroën gained a Maserati-developed V6 for its SM saloon (also used in a slightly modified Bora shell as the supposedly 2+2 Merak) and Maserati gained Citroën's electro-hydraulic braking system. This was hardly a fair swap; the Bora's disc brakes were fine, but the button on the floor where the pedal should be was a strictly on-off affair with no feel and no place in an otherwise great car.

If the Bora had not been as good as it was, it might only have survived a couple of years. In 1973 the Citroën association ended and during the oil crisis of that time the company all but folded. Production actually stopped until 1976, by which time Maserati had been taken over by Allejandro de Tomaso – a man with a powerful survival instinct. The Bora continued until 1980; de Tomaso has lasted a little longer and with his help the greatest days of all for Maserati's road cars might still be to come.

1974 Lamborghini Countach

Ferrucio Lamborghini had a way with words; no name could have been more appropriate for his first V12 mid-engined supercar than Miura – the name of a particularly brave and pure-bred fighting bull. For a while though, Lamborghini was at a loss for a suitable name for the Miura's even more sensational V12-engined successor.

According to legend, local workers solved the problem for him the first time the prototype of the new car was wheeled out in public. They took one look at the sleek, futuristic, swing-up door device and exclaimed, simply: *Countach*! This is a word from the expressive local Piedmontese dialect and the nearest printable translation is something to the effect of 'Wow!'.

So, Countach the new car was.

Although it uses essentially the same V12 engine as the Miura, it is a very different car indeed. Without any argument, it is quite the most spectacular-looking production car in the world. More than 15 years after the LP500 prototype was unveiled on the Bertone stand at the Geneva Show in 1971, the Countach *still* looks futuristic! Over the years it has grown even more dramatic with the gradual addition of aerodynamic aids and more massive modern rubber on the road to deal with increased horsepower.

The original designation, LP, states the biggest change from the Miura, which first appeared as the TP400. Both cars were mid-engined, but where the Miura's TP mean *transversale posteriore* (rear, transverse), the Countach's LP means *longitudinale posteriore* (rear, in line). The difference did not simply amount to turning the big alloy engine through 90°. The Miura had a clever gearbox and final drive built into its crankcase; the Countach uses a more conventional arrangement with its five-speed gearbox on the forward end of the block, bringing the gearbox between the occupants and the gearlever to the driver's hand with no additional linkage. Less conventionally, drive is fed back by a shaft running through the sump, to a final drive at the back of the engine.

The Countach did not go into proper production, as the LP400, until 1974, by which time it had undergone several changes from the prototype. The engine had returned from 5-litres to the Miura's 4-litres, and 375bhp at 8,000rpm; the planned monocoque chassis

RIGHT *Little more than a thinly-disguised racing car, the Lamborghini Countach offers stunning performance. The sleek alloy bodyshell hides a tubular spaceframe chassis. Rear visibility is negligible through the tiny rear screen – but you would probably be looking ahead anyway at 170 mph/272 kph!*

gave way to a fantastically complex and highly effective multi-tubular spaceframe, with welded-on alloy panels. Also, the originally uncluttered shape sprouted its first tweaks, with both NACA ducts and airboxes by the rear quarters for cooling – which had proved to be a major problem area. It retained the dramatic door opening arrangement by which the doors swung up and forward in an arc around their top leading corner, counterbalanced by hydraulic struts.

The fully adjustable suspension was by coil springs and wishbones at the front, and coil springs, wishbones, top and trailing links at the back. The brakes too, were virtually to racing specifications, with large ventilated discs and four-pot calipers. Like the rest of the car, they were well up to the expected performance.

The Countach was shatteringly fast (though not as fast as the maker's claims of 190mph/306kph) and at over 170mph/273.5kph its handling and roadholding were everything that even the most demanding driver could hope for. It had firm suspension with almost no body roll and, now that it has tyres to match the chassis ability, has grip racing standard.

Changes began in 1978 with the much better shod Countach 400S, which also had considerably wider wheel arches to suit, plus the option of a large rear aerofoil – announcing the Countach's even more aggressive look. The next change came in 1982 with the Countach LP500S, which in spite of its designation originally had a 4.8-litre version of the V12, with a claimed 400bhp. Finally the Countach has gained four-valve cylinder heads which puts it firmly back among the latest generation of Ferraris and Porsches for performance.

Common to this class of car, the Countach could, of course, offer more in the way of comfort, petrol consumption and noise level. This, however, can be overlooked in favour of its stunning performance.

1986 LAMBORGHINI COUNTACH QUATTROVALVOLE	
Engine	V12, 4ohc, 48v
Capacity	5.2 litres
Maximum power	455bhp
Chassis/suspension	Multitubular spaceframe, coil spring iars
Top speed	190mph
0–60mph	4.5 seconds

1977 Aston Martin Vantage

Walk around the outside of an Aston Martin Vantage and you may be struck first by the sheer size of the car; at over 15ft long and more than six feet wide, it is big by any standards, and it weights the best part of two tons. Its size is matched by an undeniable elegance, a timeless elegance that makes it a difficult car to date, a solid, muscular elegance that is more than skin deep.

It seems crouched, ready to pounce. The deep front air-dam, below a blanked-off radiator grille, almost touches the ground; the huge bulge of the bonnet could only hide something horribly potent. It sits low, wide and square on massive sculpted wheels and squat, low-profile tyres.

Look closer and you will see a purity of line and excellence of fit that could only be achieved by traditional hand craftsmanship; you can literally see the depth of the paint – dozens of coats, hand-buffed to a finish as lustrous as Chinese lacquer and as perfect as any Rolls-Royce.

Open one of the heavy doors and everything inside is utter luxury. There are acres of deep, wool-pile carpet, edged in leather. The sumptuous 2+2 seats – far more limousine than sportscar – are leather too, and so is virtually all the other interior body trim. Over the door cappings and the dash is beautiful burr walnut, but overriding the luxury is the same air of purpose. The steering wheel and gear lever are small and chunky, a fly-off handbrake is down by the driver's seat. The instruments are classically plain, comprehensive and placed exactly right. It is a driver's car.

Under the bonnet, four cam covers and a giant air-box top an all-alloy V8 which almost fills the substantial space available. On one cover is a small brass plate bearing the name of the one man at the factory who assembled this particular engine.

For many years, while Aston Martin told his name, they omitted to tell how much power his handiwork had wrought, preferring, like Rolls-Royce, to call it 'adequate'. Now we know that the 5.4-litre engine as used in its standard form in the basic V8 saloon (latterly with Weber-Marelli fuel injection) gives a quoted 305bhp, but as modified for this sybaritic hot-rod Vantage it thumps out no less than 375bhp, with enormous torque all across the rev range.

Fed surely onto the road through an appropriately robust manual gearbox, limited-slip diff and those wide tyres, it hurls the big car forward with a blood-curdling howl of sound but less apparent fury than a stopwatch would suggest.

In reality, its size, luxury and apparently advancing years apart, the Vantage remains one of the fastest cars in the world. In the right circumstances, not necessarily wide open spaces, it will thunder up to 170mph/273kph and in spite of its huge bulk will reach 60mph/96.5kph in just five seconds – with the acceleration, incredibly, growing even more vigorous as car and engine get into their stride.

It is not just dragstrip performance either; the engine is wonderfully responsive, with no hint of temperament – just that sleeping giant power. Its chassis, though designed in the 1960s and unashamedly built for comfort, is as good as any Italian exotic. The steering is heavy in spite of power assistance, but supremely accurate and informative. The ride is firm, almost harsh, and the tyres are noisy and nervous over bad surfaces, but almost impossible to unstick at any speed in any corner except deliberately. The Vantage forgives any indiscretion save the truly unforgiveable – just as an impeccably bred English gentleman should. Even in stopping its two-ton bulk from the wrong side of 150mph/241kph it makes no fuss at all; it does that, as everything else, with an ease so understated as to be almost contemptuous.

If you need to ask how much it costs, or how far it goes on a gallon, you can't afford it. In the end, there is only one word to sum up what this fabulous motorcar has; style.

ABOVE *The interior of the Aston Martin Vantage exudes class.*
RIGHT *The timeless grace of the* Vantage *makes it look as fresh now as it was when first produced in 1977.*

1985 ASTON MARTIN VANTAGE	
Engine	V8, 4ohc
Capacity	5.4 litres
Maximum power	375bhp
Chassis/suspension	Platform chassis, coil spring independent all round
Top speed	170mph
0–60mph	5.0 seconds

1978 BMW M1 Coupé

After World War II, BMW, a company whose pre-war reputation revolved primarily around its sporting excellence, was crippled. The majority of its assets were irretrievably stuck on the wrong side of what Winston Churchill was about to dub the 'Iron Curtain'. The best of the pre-war designs had been doled out piecemeal as war reparations to the Allies – with Bristol in England taking the lion's share as the basis of its own new marque.

BMW was reduced to building what the parlous German domestic market needed most: cheap, basic, economy cars, reduced finally to the lowest denominator, a tiny bubblecar built under licence from Iso in Italy. Almost all that BMW had left after the war was a tradition and spirit.

Not until the late 1950s could the company again translate these qualities into something more tangible, with its first small sporting saloons of the post-war period.

BELOW *The M1 was developed to help BMW enter into racing, but changes in the racing regulations made it obsolete. The M1 is a superb road car – even with only 277 bhp as opposed to the 500 bhp the racing versions would have used, the car can still top 160 mph/256 kph on unrestricted roads.*

ABOVE RIGHT *The racing pedigree of the M1 shows through on the road. Softer spring to improve the ride comfort do nothing to upset the car's natural poise and stability.*

By the mid-1960s, with the coming of the 2,000 series cars, and the later coupés, BMW's image was painstakingly rehabilitated, and amply shown off by its prolific racing successes, in every category from saloon cars to Formula Two – and even, finally, in winning the Grand Prix World Championship with the Brabham team.

The only thing BMW still lacked was a front-line sports racing car which, like Ford's GT40, might sell in limited numbers as a roadgoing flagship.

In 1972, BMW unveiled a remarkable, gull-winged, mid-engined coupé, the BMW Turbo, on the show circuit. It was never intended for production, but in 1978 a car with most of the Turbo's style and character *was* unveiled as a production reality.

It was called, simply, the M1 – the M-Style logo being BMW's way of saying 'Motorsport'.

Strangely, the car had been developed to BMW's ideas by Lamborghini, who were to build it in the sort of numbers that were perfectly reasonable for them but much too small for BMW itself.

The car, powered by BMW's potent 24-valve, 3.5-litre twin-cam straight-six motor, was less radical and more practical than the show-going Turbo coupé. It had conventional doors and striking, but not excessive styling by the ubiquitous Giugiaro.

1978 BMW M1 COUPÉ	
Engine	In-line, 6-cyl, sohc, 24v
Capacity	3.5 litres
Maximum power	277bhp
Chassis/suspension	Mid-engined, space frame, coil spring/wishbone iars
Top speed	160mph
0–60mph	5.8 seconds

It was openly admitted that it was intended first as a racing car (with production limited to numbers appropriate to homologation requirements) but the production run was to include road cars, fully trimmed and well equipped.

Even before the M1 was announced, however, Lamborghini's own near-terminal commercial problems ended their involvement, and the car was eventually built in Germany. Unfortunately, by the time the M1 was in production, changes to international racing regulations had rendered it obsolete. It did race against open opposition, with only limited success, but BMW contrived some far more conspicuous racing exposure for their potential lemon, in the guise of the Procar series. In 1979 and 1980, racing M1s provided a supporting event at selected Grand Prix races. Alongside healthy numbers of private entries, BMW entered six works cars for the fastest Grand Prix qualifiers – a brilliant publicity exercise and a great spectacle with these 200mph/322kph supercars, but doomed to failure by the convoluted politics of driver contracts.

So, the majority of the 450 or so M1s built between 1978 and 1980 made outstanding road cars. Where racing engines could boast 500bhp (as much as 850bhp with turbocharging), the fuel injected production engine gave a perfectly adequate 277bhp and comfortable 160mph/257kph performance.

Even on softer springing and road tyres, the M1 retained much of its racing poise. Its handling combined inherent understeer with easily power-induced neutrality, or even oversteer – progressing to a more naturally tail-out stance at much higher speeds.

If bureaucracy had rendered the M1 something of a failure in its intended racing guise, nothing has taken away its brilliance as a road car and a perfect symbol of BMW's triumphant return.

1981 DE LOREAN GULLWING COUPÉ DMC-12

When John Z. De Lorean was arrested by FBI agents on charges of drug-trafficking, in October 1982, his dream of a world-beating sportscar seemed finally over. In 1984 De Lorean was cleared of the drug charges and since then he has often spoken of starting again to build his 'ethical car'. So far, however, all that remains of his dream is a vast number of unanswered legal and financial questions and a small number of De Lorean DMC-12 sportscars.

Both the commercial story and the car itself were more the stuff of Hollywood than of Detroit; and both will be remembered as failures. Unfortunately so, because if De Lorean's methods were suspect, his aim, to build a new generation of safety-conscious sportscar, was worthy.

The bare bones of the convoluted commercial story are that De Lorean was a respected, if flamboyant, former General Motors top executive. Having outlined his plans, he eventually persuaded the British government to back his venture to the tune of several hundred million dollars, to manufacture his technically advanced car in depressed Northern Ireland. He set up his factory near Belfast and, with a lot of help from Lotus and Colin Chapman, adapted his fairly unworkable original designs to produce a more viable car. Viable, that is, in engineering terms, because early in 1982, after endless delays and scandals, the company collapsed and the questions began. De Lorean had built a little over 5,000 cars in all, of which about 4,000 went to the USA. Ironically, some sold at well over cost after the company's collapse, where only months earlier they could hardly be sold at all.

They were exciting cars, and but for all the problems might have developed into something good, but any appreciation of the car as it exists is not much more than a look at a final prototype.

De Lorean's original intentions, dating from the mid-1970s, were to build a rear-engined, Ford V6-powered, two-seater coupé, with many high-tech features. A light composite material was to be used for the chassis, clad in a body of unpainted stainless steel, styled by Giugiaro, and based on the Tapiro, an exercise he completed for Porsche in 1970. Its gullwing doors were one seeming contradiction to its safety conscious intentions.

In the end, a new body moulding process, with

1981 DE LOREAN DMC-12	
Engine	P-R-V V6, sohc
Capacity	2.8 litres
Maximum power	156bhp
Chassis/suspension	Rear-engine, backbone, coil spring independent all round
Top speed	135mph
0–60mph	8.2 seconds

different materials, was developed by Lotus, who also made the rear-engined design workable by giving the De Lorean a backbone chassis. The stainless steel cladding and gull-wing doors were retained and pilot production started in mid-1980.

The car now featured the all-alloy 2.8-litre Peugeot-Renault-Volvo V6 engine, which, with fuel injection delivered 156bhp and 173lb ft of torque, through a five-speed gearbox. The production suspension used coil springs and unequal length arms at the front, with semi-trailing arms and upper and lower links at the rear. The brakes were ventilated discs all round and the car was a lot heavier than it was supposed to be, largely due to De Lorean's insistence on trimming it to Detroit limousine standards, with leather upholstery, power everything, a built-in stereo system and even air conditioning as standard.

Nevertheless, the DMC-12 went well enough in a straight line, partly because of a fairly respectable drag coefficient. The few European examples (including a handful of right-hand-drive cars) would do 135mph/216kph and 0-60 in a little over eight seconds, but strangled US models with maybe 30bhp less could hardly get out of their own way, 110mph/176kph wasn't enough for a supposed sportscar, even if it was twice the national speed limit.

Thanks to Lotus, the handling was better than it had any right to be, but not as good as a real sportscar should be. Larger rear tyres subdued the inherent oversteer but the car still hadn't quite made up its mind whether it was a Lambo or a limo.

It was a wasted opportunity; with more attention to the nuts and bolts and a lot less hype it could have been good enough to give Detroit the shake-up that John Z. undoubtedly intended.

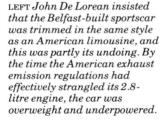

LEFT *John De Lorean insisted that the Belfast-built sportscar was trimmed in the same style as an American limousine, and this was partly its undoing. By the time the American exhaust emission regulations had effectively strangled its 2.8-litre engine, the car was overweight and underpowered.*

BELOW *The everlasting car? The stylish, stainless steel bodyshell of the De Lorean, with its futuristic gullwing doors, provided the basis for the time machine in the film* Back to the Future.

1985 MG EX-E

Since the mid-1960s and the steady growth of restrictive. supposedly safety-oriented legislation, the traditional sportscar has been pushed further and further into the background; but, contrary to many opinions, it hasn't disappeared yet. It may be restricted by relatively low production levels and consequently high manufacturing costs to either the smaller specialists or the true giants, but it is still with us; even though the hot hatchback and the sporty coupé have become the surrogate sportscars of the 1980s, there is still, conspicuously, a future for the real thing. It may never be quite so simple, cheap or cheerful as in the golden days between the wars and through the 1950s, but so long as there are enthusiastic drivers,there will always be cars which fit our broad definition of the sportscar.

Somehow, it seems particularly appropriate to look at the sportscar's future through a car shown off by one of the greatest names of the past: MG.

MG, creators of the T-series, the Midget, the MGB and several entire generations of sportscar enthusiasts, had at one time seemed consigned to a future as no more than an evocative model badge on 'sporty' saloons within the British Austin-Rover range; but at the Frankfurt Motor Show late in 1985 they showed, in sensational style, that neither they nor the sportscar were finished yet.

The prototype that they showed was dubbed the MG EX-E and it created as much of a stir in 1985 as many predecessors have in the past.

The sleek, high-tech body is made of a self-coloured, injection-moulded plastic and covers a stiff, bonded-aluminium spaceframe. It is strictly a two-seater and has superb low-drag aerodynamics. The mid-mounted engine and five-speed transmission of the prototype are derived from the Austin-Rover Group's successful four-wheel-drive Metro 6R4 rally car and like that car the EX-E offers permanent all-wheel drive, with a sophisticated viscous coupling system and limited slip differentials front and rear.

The EX-E has variable rate power steering, an anti-lock system for its four-wheel ventilated disc brakes (common now on high performance saloons, but a rarity on sportscars), variable, cockpit adjustable ride-height for optimum aerodynamic performance, and even electronic proximity warning devices for low speed manoeuvering. Most of its high-

RIGHT AND ABOVE RIGHT Although only a concept development car, Austin-Rover Group's MG EX-E gives a taste of the sort of sportscars we are likely to be driving in the future. Ultra-low, sleek bodystyles, with computer- *controlled everything is the norm. Instrumentation as we know it is replaced by head-up displays projected on to the windscreen – a development currently being used on fighter aircraft.*

198? MG EX-E	
Engine	V6, 4ohc, 24v
Capacity	3.0 litres
Maximum power	250bhp
Chassis/suspension	Mid-engine, bonded aluminium spaceframe, four-wheel drive
Top speed	—
0–60mph	—

technology dynamic features are microchip-based and there are further looks into the future in card-key entry and service systems, road condition monitoring and in-dash navigation aids. Its sumptuously finished cockpit also features sophisticated but workable electronic instrumentation and controls which mark the EX-E as a real car of the future and not just a show special.

Although the rally Metro's all-alloy, 3-litre, four-valve-per-cylinder V6 engine is detuned in the EX-E from over 400bhp to a more docile 250bhp or so, it still offers enough power to promise supercar levels of performance without temperament. Part of its appeal for the rally car was that a big, normally aspirated engine would be both more responsive and more reliable than a smaller, more highly stressed turbo engine – and those are just as important in the MG application.

So far, the futuristic MG is just that, a possibility for the future, but there is little reason to doubt projected performance figures of approaching 170mph/ 272kph and 0-60mph/96kph in only five seconds and the car's chassis specification, on paper at least, seems more than good enough to handle all this urge. What's more, its stunning good looks speak for themselves, and that more than anything else may prompt the car's originators to take the next vital step, into building running prototypes.

Whether or not the EX-E ever becomes a production reality, it has served its purpose as a pointer to what is possible for the sportscar in a technological age where enthusiasm still lives.

1985 PONTIAC FIERO

Apart from the evergreen Corvette and a few low volume specials and replicas, America hasn't had much to offer by way of sportscars since the mid-1960s. Perhaps the change of public attitudes that followed Ralph Nader's scathing attack on the Chevy Corvair in *Unsafe at Any Speed* gave the big US manufacturers the final excuse. Privately, they may have been glad of a reason to shun the sportscar business even more totally than they had in the past. In pure sales terms it would hurt them very little to leave the low volume specialist market to the Europeans (who always had them beaten anyway), and latterly to the Japanese.

And even if you had expected a sportscar for the 1980s from the USA, it is highly unlikely that you would have dreamed of it being mid-engined, plastic-bodied – and coming from Pontiac.

Yet with the Fiero, introduced in 1983, the least likely GM division produced a car that was at once stylish, innovative, admirably functional and – in its chassis at least – quite capable of taking on many of Europe's and Japan's best.

It was based on a steel inner shell, with a prominent backbone, on which all the mechanical bits append to make a completely driveable rolling chassis. This is then clothed in an all-plastic outer shell, attached to machined locating pads to ensure perfect panel fit.

It was clever, pretty and, as launched, a frustrating disappointment to real enthusiasts, because Pontiac had failed to go the whole way. They had launched the mid-engined coupé as a sporty commuter car rather than a sportscar, with an old and asthmatic 91bhp, 2.5-litre, four-cylinder, cast-iron engine that left it barely able to get out of its own way. With this engine, the dynamic abilities of the Fiero were wasted. It struggled to achieve 100mph or to reach 60mph in much less than 12 seconds even in manual gearbox form, and such figures hardly matched the appeal of the sporty two-seater's looks.

The cure came within a year, as Pontiac gave the Fiero a rather more exciting fuel-injected 2.8-litre V6. It was just as suitable for the mid-engine location but, in the GT version (which also has slightly stiffer springing than the base model, minor styling changes and an optional rear wing), it offered almost 50 per cent more power, up to 140bhp at 5,200rpm,

1986 PONTIAC FIERO GT	
Engine	V6, ohv
Capacity	2.8 litres
Maximum power	140bhp
Chassis/suspension	Mid-engine, backbone/inner shell, coil spring ifs, Chapman strut irs
Top speed	127mph
0–60mph	8.0 seconds

ABOVE AND LEFT *American dream – or nightmare? In the Pontiac Fiero, General Motors at last have a car to take on the sportscars of Europe and Japan. Mid-engined and plastic-bodied, with superb handling, the Fiero embodies all the latest in sportscar technology, but throws it all away with its outdated under-powered engine.*

and an equally useful 170lb ft of torque.

The Fiero was still no lightweight, at well over a ton, but at least it could now deliver the sort of performance its looks promised. In GT form its top speed went up to over 125mph/200kph and the 0-60 time came down to a far more respectable 8 seconds – both figures comfortably better than US versions of the very similar looking and only slightly cheaper Toyota MR2, which is generally accepted as the standard setter in the small sportscar class.

The Fiero GT, which sits on wider alloy wheels and low profile tyres, can also give the MR2 a run for its money in terms of handling, roadholding and ride, which is no mean achievement.

Suspension is by unequal length wishbones at the front and a Chapman strut arrangement with lower wishbones at the rear, with coil springs, telescopic dampers and anti-roll bars at both ends. Being a heavy car with shortish suspension travel, the Fiero's ride is necessarily firm and the rear weight bias is noticeable near its limits, especially on lifting suddenly from the throttle.

The steering, while feeling sharp enough, is slower than the sportscar norm but there is enough built-in understeer to make the Fiero inherently very safe for all but the clumsiest driver. Its all-round disc brakes are also very competent except for a tendency to fade a little after repeated hard use – another reflection of the car's weight.

Again like the MR2, one big area where the Fiero succeeds in bringing small sportscars into the 1980s is in comfort and build quality. It has an excellent driving position (with a tilting steering wheel option for anyone who still thinks entry is difficult in spite of the large doors) and very good visibility except for the inevitable three-quarter rear problem.

1985 TOYOTA MR2

Until 1985, only the Fiat empire had been brave enough to offer the mid-engined format on a mass-produced small sportscar. They had done it twice; once successfully, with the pioneering and highly regarded X1/9, and once disastrously, with the slightly larger Lancia Beta Monte Carlo: not a bad car but a failure.

There was no doubting the theoretical advantages of the mid-engined layout, at least not when it was properly sorted out, and it had few drawbacks other than making luggage space a problem – which was not the biggest consideration with two seats.

The layout had already become virtually indispensible at the grown-up end of the supercar market, and if for no better reason than emulating big-brother you might have expected *somebody* to build another mid-engined small car. Strangely though, what little was left of the mass-produced sportscar industry in the mid-1980s (when the hot hatchback had become the almost universal sportscar surrogate), remained almost laughably conservative. What little creative instinct remained seemed more directed at creating replicas of what had gone than designs for what might be.

Nevertheless, if you had had to say where a new mid-engined sportscar might come from, you would more likely have named one of those small European specialists than a Japanese giant.

And then the car which re-wrote the script for all other small sportscar builders in the mid-1980s came from the biggest of them all, Toyota: steady, uninspiring Toyota who hadn't even looked at the sportscar market for 20 years.

Toyota's MR2 was a winner from the moment it was revealed in 1985. It is what the Lancia might have been, a bigger S1/9 with more power, more room and more refinement. In typically Japanese style, it invented nothing new but perfected much that already exists.

The 1.6-litre twin-cam four-cylinder engine is mounted transversely between the cockpit and rear axle line, driving through a sweet, close-ratio five-speed gearbox, which, for once, isn't ruined by a linkage to the rear.

This 16-valve, injected engine is a free-revving gem (derived from the front-wheel-drive Corolla hatchback). It peaks with 122bhp at 6,600rpm, with exceptional smoothness and throttle response throughout the rev range. The straightline performance is comfortably ahead of the old X1/9, at 122mph/195.2kph and 0-60mph/96kph in only eight seconds, but the MR2's real excellence is in its roadholding, handling, brakes and overall dynamic feel.

Judged on those criteria, it is in a class of its own in this price sector and has caused the few remaining makers of 'conventional' mass-produced sportscars all manner of headaches.

On MacPherson strut suspension, it has all the flair, instant response and outstanding roadholding

BELOW *There is nothing new under the sun, and it is the Japanese car giant Toyota that has bought the mass-produced mid-engined sports coupé to the world's attention again with their MR2.*

1986 TOYOTA MR2	
Engine	In-line, 4-cyl, 2ohc, 16v
Capacity	1.6 litres
Maximum power	122bhp
Chassis/suspension	Mid-engine, unitary construction, MacPherson strut iars
Top speed	122mph
0–60mph	8.0 seconds

BELOW AND OVERLEAF *The power plant for the MR2 is a 1.6 litre twin-cam unit, mounted transversely just behind the cockpit. The mid-engine layout gives the car near-faultless handling and ride.*

of many true supercars – more, in fact, than most, plus the near-faultless ride comfort of a far bigger car.

It has most of the comfort and equipment levels of a much bigger and more expensive car too; not for the Japanese that notion that sportscar drivers will settle for second best when it comes to accommodation. Unlike the X1/9, the MR2 is only available as a hardtop – albeit with a large, removable glass sun-roof.

It is roomy, comfortable, with all the clear instrumentation and well-thought-out controls, of a proper sportscar, plus such refinements as in-car-entertainment, electric windows, central locking and other features more typical of an up-market hatch-back.

It looks marvellous, stops on the proverbial six-pence, and it even has an acceptable amount of luggage space. More than any car since the original X1/9, it has redefined the rules for small sportscar excellence – and at a time when the very idea of the sportscar was in danger of disappearing. Surely this time the competitors can't simply sit back and ignore the challenge.

1986 ASTON MARTIN ZAGATO

For a company that has been so many times to the brink of extinction, Aston Martin lacks nothing in public self confidence. In 1960, during one of its brief spells of relative stability (this one following the considerable achievement of winning both Le Mans and the World Sports Car Manufacturers' Championship in 1959), Aston introduced its greatest road-legal, semi-competition car, the lovely DB4GT Zagato.

Its voluptuous, lightweight body, built over a light, strong, tubular frame, housed a 314bhp version of Aston's 3.7-litre twin-cam straight-six engine. It gave the short-wheelbase car 150mph/241kph-plus performance, but it was not an easy car to drive and most were used only for racing, where they were overshadowed by the Ferrari 250GTO, which was no great disgrace.

In 1985, Aston, healthy again and brimming over with enthusiasm, announced a new association with Zagato. Their planned new model would be the company's fastest road car ever; in fact, with an uprated version of the Vantage engine in a smaller, lighter car, it would be one of the fastest cars in the world.

At the outset, the only tangible evidence of Aston's intentions was several artists' impressions and a welter of words in the press -- including projected numbers such as 187mph/301kph and sub-five-second 0-60 times. These would make the second generation Aston Martin Zagato not just *one* of the fastest production cars in the world, but *the* fastest -- quicker even than Ferrari's latest Testarossa or GTO, or the Lamborghini Countach QV.

Yet it would be a conventional, front-engined car, frankly described as an adapted Vantage. Even in the

wake of the mid-engined Nimrod sports racing cars, Aston Martin was not prepared to take the plunge for the road.

More cynical observers took the 'believe-it-when-you-see-it' stance, while Aston Martin started taking substantial deposits on the strictly limited production run of 50 cars – all on the strength of little more than a promise.

By August 1985, however, every car was spoken for and, incredibly, in April 1986 Aston Martin showed not one interim dummy, but three fully-trimmed running production cars at and outside the Geneva Show. They were built and trimmed by Zagato in Italy, with alloy and re-inforced polyester bodies on rolling chassis shipped from Britain.

The original 1960s Zagato was a hard act to follow in terms of outstanding looks, but the 1986 Vantage Zagato stole the show. Built on a much modified Vantage floorplan, the Vantage Zagato was strictly a two-seater coupé, with a traditional Aston Martin grille shape cleverly incorporated into the smooth, moulded nose, between four, big, rectangular headlights. Only a hefty bonnet (hood) bulge (imposed by retaining carburettors on the Vantage engine) intruded into otherwise notably smooth lines. This did not spoil an impressive drag coefficient.

Suddenly, the Vantage Zagato in the flesh opened disturbing possibilities for the cynics that Aston's big-number claims might be more than hype. For one thing, the car was significantly smaller than the Vantage (no slouch itself) and it had a far better drag coefficient. Its claimed 425bhp from the modified engine (with higher compression, improved breathing and more extreme camshafts) was a good 50bhp more than the Vantage but perfectly credible. According to Aston, this engine in a Vantage shell, stripped to match the Zagato's weight, if not its aerodynamic excellence, had already managed 175mph/ 281.5kph and 0-60mph/96.5kph in 4.7 seconds – the latter in first gear!

As with any supercar in this stratospheric performance league, few owners are likely to come any closer to the genuine top speed than reading properly calibrated test track figures in the 'legitimate' motoring press.

Whether or not the Zagato can match its claims, it is unlikely that any of the 50 examples will follow in the original Zagato's wheeltracks as a full-time racer. It is far more likely that they could eventually match the old car's status as a highly prized classic, and perhaps even compete with Jaguar in the American market.

1986 ASTON MARTIN VANTAGE ZAGATO	
Engine	V8, 4ohc
Capacity	5.4 litres
Maximum power	432bhp
Chassis/suspension	Platform chassis, coil spring/ wishbone ifs, De Dion rear, Watts
Top speed	187mph
0–60mph	4.7 seconds

LEFT *This high-performance version of the Vantage engine allows a top speed of 187mph.*

FAR LEFT AND BELOW *Probably the ultimate in exclusivity the 1986 Zagato is Aston Martin's most powerful, fastest and most stylish model to date.*

1986 CHEVROLET CORVETTE

To American car enthusiasts, the Corvette long ago ceased to be just another sports car and became more of an institution. It is no longer just any American sports car, it is *the* American sports car, the one that any fan will defend to the death against puny European hardware, the one that can beat Porsches in the Sports Car Club of America stock racing classes and one of the few American sports cars which has built up any kind of European following, in a market where the traffic across the Atlantic is almost entirely in the opposite direction.

The Corvette survives because it has kept its integrity while moving with the times and although the nameplate has had its ups and downs it has always managed to come back – to the extent that its long-term future will probably be as a separate marque within the General Motors empire.

Since the 1953 shaky start of the underpowered little roadster with the wheezy six-cylinder engine and the hopeless automatic transmission, there have only really been four distinct restyles. The last of them, in 1982, brought the shape right up to date with the clean, uncluttered lines which survive on to the 1986 car.

It was the introduction of V8 power and a manual gearbox in 1956 which really got the Corvette off the mark as a serious sports car, and since then it has had a formidable list of big and small block V8 options. The weakest was the mid-1970s small block which could only muster a rather feeble 165 bhp, but at the other end of the scale, in 1970, at the height of the musclecar age, there was the 460 bhp 7.4-litre big block. The same year also saw the most potent of the smaller engines, with a very impressive 370 bhp. The same 350 cu. in./875 c.c. capacity survives in today's small block model and with multi-point fuel injection it gives a very useful 240 bhp – a sure sign that performance is making something of a comeback in

the US markets of the mid-1980s.

Better still, the latest Corvette is a car which can make full use of that power, with chassis performance which will give a lot of supposedly superior European cars a fair run for their money. Its glassfibre and reinforced-plastic body sits on a steel chassis whose all-round independent suspension uses transverse glassfibre leaf springs front and rear. Until recently the car was almost universally condemned for having a ride that was too firm for its own good, but it was softened up quite markedly for 1986, to the point where it is now firm but forgiving. The overall effect is helped by superb seats and interior appointments including electronic instrumentation with a mixture of analog and digital readouts.

Chassis refinement runs to a limited slip differential as standard, a four-speed manual gearbox with overdrive on no less than three of the ratios, and ABS anti-lock brakes. There are only 2½ turns of the wheel from lock to lock, with perhaps a shade too much power assistance for some tastes, though the steering is very precise.

On the road, the lazy, torquey engine gives pretty rapid progress by any standards, with 0–60 mph/ 0–96 kph times down below six seconds and a top speed in the order of 150 mph/240 kph – given enough road. The motor revs slowly by European standards but it has both excellent response and a lovely growl,

and of course, with all that stump-pulling, low down torque it has incredible flexibility.

The handling tends heavily towards understeer, easily neutralized by lifting off the power and with power oversteer fairly easily on-tap – but it is not a car whose limits should be explored by the unwary, all that weight takes a little catching once it does let go.

More than ever perhaps, the Corvette is a true sports car which can mix it with the best of them, and there is little reason to believe that it won't still be carrying the banner for a long time to come.

1986 CHEVROLET CORVETTE	
Engine	V8, ohv
Capacity	5.7 litres
Maximum power	240bhp
Chassis/suspension	Steel chassis, GRP body, tl/ wishbone ifs, tl/multiple link irs
Top speed	151mph
0–60mph	6.5 seconds

BELOW *The Chevrolet Corvette is a mighty entrant in the sports car stakes, with stylish handling and a quick* 0–60mph/0–96kph start. *It is a formidable rival to the European competition.* INSET *The small-block, powerful V8 engine.*

1986 MAZDA RX-7

D rive a Mazda RX-7, and the uncanny smoothness of its engine confirms something out of the ordinary about this attractive Japanese coupé. In fact, the RX-7 is not just out of the ordinary, it is unique among sportscars in its choice of engine.

Where every other sportscar in the word uses the traditional reciprocating piston engine, the Mazda uses the brilliantly simple Wankel rotary engine, an engine that offers wide-ranging benefits but enough technical problems to have restricted it to a handful of production applications.

Dr Felix Wankel's engine, which basically comprises a three-sided rotor following a four-stroke cycle within an outer casing, was developed during the 1950s by Wankel and the German car and motorcycle maker NSU. The engine solved the problem of converting the energy of burning fuel directly into rotary motion, but there were serious practical problems with sealing the rotor tips and with excessive fuel consumption.

NSU never really did solve the problems themselves, although they did make several Wankel-engined cars, the first of them a sports version of the NSU Sport Prinz, introduced in 1963.

By this time, Mazda too were committed to building rotary-engined cars, having entered a licensing agreement with NSU in 1961. The first Mazda rotary was shown in 1963, just weeks after NSU's first, but like the NSU it still had problems. Part of Mazda's solution was to try multi-rotor engines, and they eventually settled on the twin-rotor format used in today's RX-7. Their first rotary-engined production car, the 110S coupé, went on sale in 1967. Mazda has continued rotary engine development ever since, alone after NSU abandoned the format in 1977.

ABOVE *Mazda's latest RX-7 coupé is powered by the turbine-smooth, Wankel rotary engine. Only Mazda have persevered with the rotary, and it has finally paid off with a powerful smooth-running, twin-rotor unit that endows it with performance akin to that of a Porsche 924S. Even more*

1986 MAZDA RX-7	
Engine	Twin-rotor Wankel rotary
Capacity	2.6 litres
Maximum power	148bhp
Chassis/suspension	Unitary construction, MacPherson strut ifs, multi-link irs
Top speed	133mph
0–60mph	8.5 seconds

remarkable is that the rotary engine does this with an engine of just over 1.3 litres, yet delivers performance similar to a 2.4-litre engine. To get round this apparent disparity, the capacity of the rotary engine has to be multiplied by 1.8 to give an equivalent cylinder capacity.

By the end of 1978, Mazda had built over one million rotary-engined cars and launched the first RX-7; since then, the RX-7 has achieved exceptional sales success in both Europe and America and overcome all the Wankel's inherent problems save its excessive thirst. Between 1978 and 1985, Mazda sold almost half a million RX-7s, comfortably outselling its most obvious rival, the Porsche 924. Late in 1985 they launched the second generation RX-7, aimed this time at Porsche 944 territory; it had new body styling, a clever new suspension system and a 2.6-litre version of the trusty twin-rotor engine – giving 148bhp at 6,500rpm and 135lb/ft of torque at only 3,000rpm for superb flexibility and smoothness.

Like its predecessor, the latest RX-7 is very well equipped for a sportscar, with such standard fittings as an electric sunroof, electric windows, an up-market stereo system, air-conditioning for the US market and much more; yet it still behaves like a true sportscar. Top speed is almost 135mph in European spec, or almost 130mph even for the USA, with 0-60mph times in the region of 8 seconds, with sparkling mid-range performance. In deference to keeping the free-revving engine in one piece, a buzzer indicates its 7,000rpm limit, well before tip-seal damage is likely to occur.

The new suspension is excellent. The front uses MacPherson struts with lower A-arms, coil springs and an anti-roll bar, but the real novelty is at the back, which is a multi-link system with floating hubs, coil springs and an anti-roll bar – with telescopic dampers all-round.

The main feature of the 'Dynamic Tracking' rear suspension is variable geometry, which allows a small degree of initial toe-out during cornering (for very precise turn-in) changing to a degree of toe-in, which helps neutralize oversteer. It is even more complicated than it sounds, but it works. Coupled with adjustable damping rates and superb variable rate power steering, it gives the RX-7 very high levels of grip (especially in the wet), very precise responses and even a reasonably good ride.

In sticking with the rotary-engined concept, Mazda have evolved not only a unique sportscar, but also a thoroughly competent one, which went one stage further early in 1986 with the introduction of an even more potent turbo version. The only problem which still remains is heavy fuel consumption, but that never seems to have bothered sportscar buyers unduly.

1986 RELIANT SCIMITAR SS1 Ti

When the small English car-maker Reliant introduced their distinctive little plastic-bodied Scimitar SS1 two-seater early in 1985, they were reviving a breed of car which most people thought had died with the last MG Midgets and Triumph Spitfires many years before. They were bringing back the affordable small sports car, not quite mass-produced in the big corporate sense, but a legitimate production model and much more than the usual run of the kit-car market.

Reliant was the perfect company to launch such a car. It had long experience of building relatively short-run models with glassfibre bodies and 'bought-in' running gear. Reliant even has a worldwide reputation for designing cars and setting up entire manufacturing plants for countries such as Israel,

An Italian-styled British sports car, the Reliant Scimitar has proved popular in the United States. Princess Anne probably gave sales a boost when she was caught speeding in her Scimitar!

India and assorted Mediterranean and Caribbean countries which need rugged, straightforward cars in relatively small numbers. Reliant's bread-and-butter models, using their own excellent lightweight engines, are three-wheel saloons and small vans taking advantage of British tax concessions, plus limited numbers of four-wheel derivatives.

For many years, Reliant also built the larger, glassfibre-bodied, Ford-engined Scimitar sports car, which started life as a coupé and grew into the unique Scimitar sporting estate, to which a drophead model was eventually added. For better or worse the new Scimitar˙ spelled the end of development for the previous model but took nothing from the old car except its name. It was based on an engine size midway between Reliant's own four-cylinder and the 2.8-litre Ford V6 of the big Scimitar, and launched with a choice of two engines, a rather flaccid 69 bhp 1.3-litre four-cylinder Ford engine, or the 96 bhp, 1.6-litre Ford four-cylinder from the Escort XR3.

Its fabricated steel chassis with independent suspension all round, by wishbones and coil springs at the front and semi-trailing arms and coil springs at the rear, was excellent, but the looks of its Michelotti-designed body, with integral bumpers and pop-up headlights, were widely criticized. Virtually every reviewer thought the car could handle more power.

At least the bolted-on glassfibre panels made the SS1 very distinctive and kept insurance costs low, and it did have the biggest of all advantages for a sports car – it was a full convertible.

In mid-1986, Reliant solved the power problem by offering the Scimitar in Ti form, with a 135 bhp version of the Nissan Silvia 1.8-litre four-cylinder turbo engine, plus the five-speed gearbox that went with it. This excellent engine fitted into the SS1 with virtually no other changes but it completely transformed the car's performance and made it a sports car worthy of the name. The 0–60 mph/0–96 kph acceleration time came down from over 11 seconds for the 1.6-litre car to barely 7 seconds – quick by most standards. Top speed went up from not much better than 105 mph/168 kph to comfortably over 125 mph/ 200 kph. It was a stunning transformation.

Yet the chassis handles it with great character. There is a tendency towards wheelspin and power oversteer but the car is so predictable and easy to drive that every ounce of performance can be exploited by even reasonably competent drivers. It gives the mid-engined Toyota MR2, the car which re-defined the mid-1980s sports car market, a good run for its money and is markedly cheaper – if admittedly less refined. With a mixture of disc and drum brakes in a very lightweight package it stops exceptionally well and everything about it, from its compact size to its exceptionally responsive engine,

1986 RELIANT SCIMITAR SS1 Ti	
Engine	Nissan, 4-cyl, in-line, turbo
Capacity	1.8 litres
Maximum power	135bhp
Chassis/suspension	Fabricated steel, GRP body, coil spring/wishbone ifs, trailing arm irs
Top speed	125mph
0–60mph	7.0 seconds

make it a very rapid car from point to point on everyday roads. And, of course, when the sun shines the top comes off, which is still one of the real tests of a true sports car.

Perhaps the critics are right and the SS1 should have been styled by the new wave of English stylists, rather than in Italy, but as a drivers' car it is a worthy successor to the sports cars of old.

1986 RENAULT ALPINE GTA V6 TURBO

Renault might not be the most obvious name for a sports car builder but the giant French car company, with its reputation for competent hatchbacks and attractive but not particularly inspiring saloons, nowadays has a turbocharged rear-engined flagship which can give almost any medium-range sports car a run for its money.

The Renault Alpine GTA V6 Turbo is designed by Renault's own engineers and built around Renault running gear in the small and specialized Alpine workshops at Dieppe. Alpine has had a long association with Renault which started in the mid-1950s, when Alpine's founder, former racing driver Jean Redélé, built the first Alpine, a rallying coupé, around Renault 750 parts.

Over the years, the Alpine name became associated with most of Renault's racing and rallying efforts, and in 1970 they became officially responsible for the whole of Renault's competition programme, the greatest achievement in sports racing terms being the team's dominant win in the 1978 Le Mans 24-hour race. The Alpine name was also used on several Renault road cars, as the Renault performance badge yet until the mid-1980s, the Alpine marque was far better known for racing than for its road cars.

It was only with the introduction of the V6-engined Renault-Alpine early in 1984 that Renault began to think of selling a real sports car worldwide. By mid 1986, the car was available in both left- and right-hand drive, for most world markets. Top of the range was the very rapid V6 Turbo.

Unusually for a current sports car, but like the Porsche 911 which is one of its most obvious direct rivals, the GTA is rear-engined. The engine is positioned behind the rear axle-line of the neat backbone chassis. The glassfibre-reinforced monocoque body shell is a reasonably spacious 2+2 seater which even offers a fair amount of baggage space for two people and very good standards of interior trim and equipment. Yet its sleek lines make it one of the most aerodynamic of all production cars – although the wide wheels of the Turbo version do detract a little from the normally-aspirated car's extraordinary efficiency.

The most potent engine is the 2.5-litre V6 with a single overhead camshaft on each cylinder bank and a Garrett turbocharger. This smooth, free-revving unit gives a very healthy 200 bhp with a big spread of torque; coupled to a five-speed gearbox with perfectly chosen ratios it gives the GTA quite exceptional performance, with a top speed of over 150 mph/240 kph and 0–60 mph/0–96 kph acceleration times of less than 6½ seconds.

In general, the Renault is a very capable car and much more practical for everyday use than most exotics, one of its few obvious running faults being that the front baggage compartment has to be opened to gain access to the fuel filler cap.

Its handling is generally, but not always, taut and predictable, with coil springs and double wishbone suspension all round and very precise rack-and-pinion steering, which manages without power assistance thanks to the fairly light front end weight. On the wide tyres of the turbo version, there is a very high level of cornering grip and the suspension, unusually for a French car of any kind, is stiff enough to keep body roll well under control.

What the GTA does lack to some extent is straight line stability at very high speeds in windy conditions, and although the car is always safe, it demands some concentration to drive it in a hurry. There is also a definite degree of turbo lag, which tends to make for exciting progress when driving quickly on twisty, damp roads. Furthermore, the weight of the engine behind the rear axle is always noticeable around the car's very high limits – in much the same way as a Porsche 911.

The Alpine is something very special, having brought a major manufacturer firmly into the exotic sports car market. It is a spectacular car to look at, and is even more spectacular to drive.

RIGHT *The Turbo version of the Alpine, Renault's venture into sports cars, using the Alpine name it has made famous in motor racing. The Alpine GTA is a great car, proving that even the mass production manufacturers can produce classic sports cars if they try.*

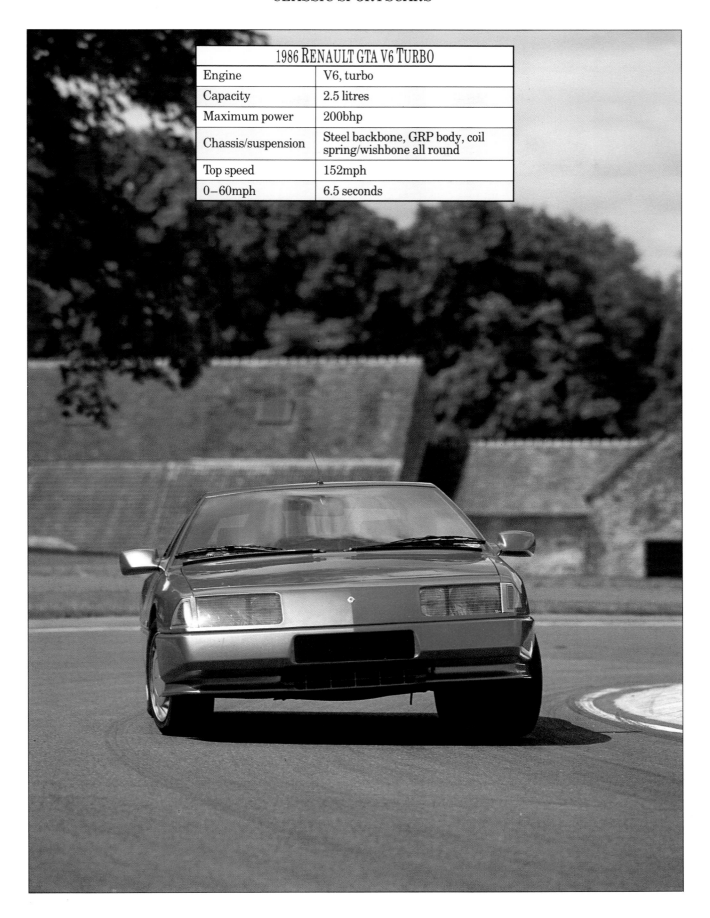

1986 RENAULT GTA V6 TURBO	
Engine	V6, turbo
Capacity	2.5 litres
Maximum power	200bhp
Chassis/suspension	Steel backbone, GRP body, coil spring/wishbone all round
Top speed	152mph
0–60mph	6.5 seconds

1986 TVR 390iSE

In a market where smaller specialist sportscar makers have come and gone with frightening regularity, only three or four have survived with any sort of distinction. Morgan and Panther have continued to make a reasonable business out of selling nostalgia, either real or contrived, and TVR has soldiered on with cars of no great pioneering spirit but a legacy of steady, solid development and real character.

The TVR company itself was started in the late 1950s by an enthusiastic special-builder, Trevor Wilkinson, from whose Christian name it took its title. Since then, the small but hugely enthusiastic maker from the famous English seaside funfair town of Blackpool has been through numerous changes of ownership, each of them in turn shrugging off its own financial crises with varying degrees of success.

Concurrent with the frequent commercial changes, the TVR car has developed from Wilkinson's early Ford and Coventry-Climax-engined Granturas, with more and more power, constantly revised and refined chassis and running gear, and just a few fundamental changes of body style. The cars have always just about kept pace with the rest of the world, without ever really changing from Wilkinson's original concept.

Today, TVR is probably stronger than it has ever been, partly due to a long period of stable and efficient management but even more to the continuing success of the angular body style cars which saw the company into the 1980s on the early Tasmin. In coupé and open variants (the latter by far the more popular), the shape has variously used Ford four-cylinder engines, Ford V6 engines of up to 3-litres (though the best of all was the Capri 2.8 injection unit) and, since 1982, the mighty, Buick-based Rover 3.5-litre V8, which, in

RIGHT AND OVERLEAF *The stylish simplicity of the TVR 390iSE gives more than a hint of the potential performance from the 3.9-litre, Rover V8-derived engine. A real driver's car, its immense power means the TVR needs more than a little care to prevent the rear end stepping out of line – especially in wet driving conditions.*

1986 TVR 390iSE	
Engine	Rover V8, ohv
Capacity	3.9 litres
Maximum power	275bhp
Chassis/suspension	Multi-tubular backbone, coil spring/wishbone iars
Top speed	150mph
0–60mph	5.5 seconds

190bhp fuel-injected form topped the range as the TVR350i until early 1985.

Then TVR went a large step further, by dropping an injected Rover V8, enlarged to 3.9-litres, into their excellent tubular backbone chassis, to create a cut-price supercar chaser – the 390iSE.

Set well back under the beautifully finished fibreglass shell, this heavily modified all-alloy engine with a claimed 275bhp and 270lb ft of torque turned the TVR convertible from merely quick to staggering. Even hampered by a frustrating lack of traction, the 390iSE would hit 60mph in about 5½ seconds, accompanied by the most glorious noises from the flexible, instant-action V8. And the power went on and on, with 100mph/161kph available in less than 15 seconds and a top speed – given a long enough run – over over 150mph/241kph.

Good as the chassis was, the lusty engine had more than enough power to catch out a lead-footed driver, especially on slow corners and in a low gear – or anytime in the wet if discretion was cast aside. Treated with respect, however, the 390iSE responded with enormous amounts of grip, without allowing

any real time for relaxation as the heavy steering fed back steady streams of information in the form of small twitches and suppressed kicks. The ride itself was rock steady, however, with hard springs but excellent damping and body isolation.

In fact, the car was remarkably comfortable for a convertible – or more accurately a semi-Targa-top. The seats are deeply shrouded within the well-trimmed cockpit and the big central tunnel gives unbeatable lateral support – plus the familiar high-sited TVR gearchange.

The TVR roof is an object lesson in simplicity, a rigid central panel which clips easily in and out between the top of the steeply-raked windscreen and the rear, folding hood (top), which flips up and down in one simple action. When it is up it is waterproof and solid; down, it is commendably free from buffeting.

The TVR has many similar assets, with just enough slightly rough edges to remind the driver, if he should need reminding, that this is not just another soulless, mass-produced design from the big batallions; it is a car of character.

1987 CADILLAC ALLANTE

In most ways, the Cadillac Allante's inclusion here under the label of 'sports car' is something of a cheat, but in another way it deserves to be included as an illustration of the way the market may be headed in the future in the biggest of all markets, the USA.

The Allante doesn't have particularly sparkling performance by the best European sports car standards, and it isn't particularly high-tech, even though it does use clever electronic analog instruments and anti-lock brakes. It is a sporty two-seater with a soft top and Italian styling, and it typifies a change of direction which many observers see as only the beginning of pastures new for the greatest of American 'quality' car builders. It is what you might call a significant model.

There were several good reasons behind the birth of the Allante, principally the growing prestige of European sporting luxury cars such as Mercedes and Jaguar in the American market in recent years, and their steadily-increasing prices relative to domestic models. There was also a new corporate structure for Cadillac itself, which recently lost its own manufacturing facilities within the General Motors empire, but was compensated by the new freedom to shop around for its major engineering elements. Fortunately, Cadillac has engineering management with the vision to take advantage of such circumstances.

So, enter the Allante, late in 1986. It is an open two-seater, sleekly styled with a high waistline, steeply-raked windscreen and a wide, low look. It has a high-quality convertible top and a detachable aluminium hardtop which should spend the summer months in the garage. It is built on a shortened version of Cadillac's Eldorado platform chassis, with that car's MacPherson strut front suspension with lower arms and trailing links, plus Chapman strut rear suspension with lower wishbones and a transverse glassfibre leaf spring. The chassis goes all the way to Italy for its Pininfarina clothing, mostly in steel but with a few aluminium panels, and then back to Detroit for its running gear.

That too comes largely from the Eldorado, with a fuel-injected version of the alloy-block 4.1-litre V8, upgraded to give 170 bhp – a rather paltry specific output by European standards where a 4-litre engine would be looking for somewhere nearer 250 bhp to be worthy of being called sporty, but not bad when you realise that power has to go through the front wheels only. The engine is mounted transversely and drives through an uprated four-speed automatic transmission – sticking with automatic is another sign that Cadillac hasn't quite gone all the way to thinking of the Allante as a sports car.

On the other hand the Allante has all-round disc brakes with the most sophisticated Bosch ABS anti-locking system as standard, as well as quick ratio rack-and-pinion steering and surprisingly taut suspension – certainly a change from the previous Cadillac norms.

In terms of performance, the Allante, as befits a car weighing almost a ton and a half and with just 170 bhp on tap, only claims a top speed in the region of 120 mph/192 kph and 0–60 mph/0–96 kph in a little under 9½ seconds, which is well behind most European alternatives. The handling and ride are perhaps more European than American, though, helped by specially developed wide, low-profile Goodyear tyres, another area where Cadillac can exert a lot of corporate clout.

It is still difficult to pigeonhole the Allante as a sports car or otherwise, but it is without doubt an interesting pointer to the way American auto makers feel they can go now that 'soft-top' isn't quite such a dirty word as it was at the height of safety lobby power. Cadillac see the Allante as an ultra-luxury specialist car for enthusiastic drivers; many people see it as a glimmer of hope for a new breed of sporty American cars.

RIGHT *The Cadillac Allante is a classic example of the luxury sedan manufacturer's idea of a sports car – an ultra-luxury specialist two-seater with soft top and sporty Italian styling. Yet Cadillac refuses to abandon automatic transmission in favour of the classic sports car stick-shift.*

1987 CADILLAC ALLANTE	
Engine	V8, ohv
Capacity	4.1 litres
Maximum power	170bhp
Chassis/suspension	Platform, Macpherson strut, Chapman strut/wishbone/tl irs
Top speed	120mph
0–60mph	9.3 seconds

The
World's Fastest Cars

GERMANY

The German claim to be the true home of the fast car rests on much the same arguments as Italy's. The *autobahn* idea was originally tried during the 1920s, and not, as many people believe, only after Hitler came to power in 1933. An inner-city motorway, the Avus autobahn, was opened in Berlin in 1921 and, surprisingly, the German railway system built a section of autobahn near Bonn in 1928 for use by the public. The success of these early experiments showed Hitler that such a fast road system was feasible, cost effective and, for the military machine that he was building, vital for the rapid deployment of men, materials and equipment.

Since the turn of the century the German education system has placed great emphasis on technical training and research. The automobile received proper attention, fittingly so in the country of its real origin, and this was reinforced by the nature of the people who designed and built German cars. Among them are numbered innovative personalities like Gottlieb Daimler, Karl Benz, Ferdinand Porsche (who was actually an Austrian) and Felix Wankel. These men brought to their automotive genius that special Teutonic stubbornness recognized in so many aspects of German life, a special ability to grind away at problems until they have been surmounted, even if it should take years of effort.

I first noticed this characteristic during the first ot many contacts with the Daimler-Benz company in Stuttgart. During 1967, I was taking photographs in the Untertürkheim factory and being shown around by one of the management. I commented on the high proportion of hand-finishing work in the typical Mercedes-Benz car compared to its nearest British counterpart and on the workers' obviously intense application to their work. The whole factory was literally humming with effort. I was quietly informed that the company knew exactly what was expected from everyone involved with the production of its cars and if that meant, for instance, a 30% increase in the inspection staff then that was what happened. The executive went on to describe the Swabian worker as the best in the world, especially for car manufacture; hard working, loyal, self critical and determined to make the best car possible. There was a degree of arrogance in his attitude but it was a benign arrogance, very much like that to be found at Rolls-Royce! In fact it is actually pride, a feature common to all great engineers whatever their nationality.

Germans do not particularly expect life to be easy (although this attitude has begun to change in the last few years) but in my own experience the majority of Germans take life, work and pleasure very seriously. They work hard at all of them! Efficiency is the path they follow and when it comes to making a fast car they make that too as efficient as they can. Each major German manufacturer approaches this important task in his own way as can be seen later.

One final, vital factor, at least over the last 30 years, that has created Germany's present strength as a car manufacturer is its willingness to reinvest profits in research and

Germany is one of the very few places in the world where unlimited speeds are still allowed on public roads — though even in Germany that freedom is now threatened. A road system designed for high speed transit and a legislature which has not condemned speed itself have allowed German manufacturers to develop unashamedly fast luxury cars such as the BMW 635CSi shown here.

development. The German industry has shown that it will pay top salaries for top men and these are the sort of men who help Germany produce world beating cars. The German driver works his car hard and expects total reliability, which has made sure that only the most durable of cars succeeds in this very demanding market place.

I have already offered reasons why Germany might justifiably consider itself to be today's real home of the fast car. In this chapter I will begin to look at the cars themselves and describe a selection of the fastest German production models and their capabilities.

At the time of writing there are no fewer than 35 different models available from German manufacturers which will exceed the base-line 125mph. Most are available in all European markets and in the USA, but specifications — even availability — do vary with local requirements and most of these descriptions will be based on home market models, which are, of course, the most typical.

PORSCHE

PORSCHE 959

Porsche have the unique distinction among the major German makers of being able to claim, accurately, that *all* its models will exceed 125mph! Where better to start then, than with a look at the very latest Porsche model, the 959, which goes on sale in 1985. The first astonishing feature about this Porsche is its price. In Britain, the three model range has a starting price of £111,000, or about twice the cost of either a Ferrari Boxer or an Aston Martin Vantage, with a similar equivalent price in the USA! The three types offered will be a luxury roadgoing version, a sporting model and a pure competition vehicle. The price of the sports and competition types increases by leaps and bounds over the price of the 'basic' luxury model, with the cost of the racing version running comfortably into the telephone number league.

The technical specification of the 959 would not be out of place on a NASA space project. Its body is made of Kevlar, a material more usually found in the bodies of endurance racing or Grand Prix cars. This immensely strong, light and corrosion-resistant material has been formed into a wind-cheating shape with a very impressive aerodynamic drag coefficient, or Cd, of only 0·32 yet weighing only 1,226·5lb. The 959's styling continues the recognizable Porsche theme that can be traced back to the introduction of the 356 series, over 35 years ago. In the writer's eyes it is one of the best looking of all Porsches. The Kevlar body is mounted on a galvanized steel chassis that carries racing type suspension with dual wishbones at front and rear. Twin dampers are fitted all round, and those at the front incorporate dual springs. The driver can adjust both ride height and spring rates from the cockpit even while the car is on the move.

On the 959, Porsche fit magnesium wheels with hollow spokes, which allow the wheel and tyre assembly to be monitored constantly for punctures or structural failure. Not only will a drop in tyre pressure due to a puncture be registered but any crack in the wheel material will also cause a loss of pressure and can also be noted instantly by the driver. The tyres are secured to the wheel rims and in the event of a puncture should give the driver time to slow and stop the 959 with complete safety.

The four-wheel-drive system is electronically controlled, to give optimum traction to the car by varying the front-to-rear drive balance automatically at all road speeds. In typically Porsche fashion this fail-safe arrangement has a manual override to allow the driver to select his own setup should he feel that conditions warrant it.

The mid-engined 959 uses a refinement of Porsche's existing 935/936 racing engines that have been so successful throughout the world in recent years. It is a twin turbocharged 2.85-litre flat-six unit with an intercooler. The cylinder heads feature four valves per cylinder and water cooling. The engine

S P E C I F I C A T I O N	
MODEL/TYPE	PORSCHE 959
ENGINE	FLAT-6, 2,850CC, TURBO
HORSEPOWER	400BHP PLUS
TRANSMISSION	6-SPEED 4-WD
CHASSIS	KEVLAR/STEEL
BRAKES	4-WHEEL DISC
TOP SPEED	190MPH PLUS
ACCELERATION 0–100MPH	UNDER 8 SECS
PRODUCTION SPAN	1985 →

block itself however is air cooled. This engine's power output is rated at a minimum of 400bhp and the 959 will accelerate from zero to 62mph in 4.9 seconds, with a top speed of over 190mph! As with all previous Porsche engines the unit has enormous potential for further development in terms of both performance and refinement, and over the next few years will undoubtedly reach quite staggering power outputs.

Porsche intend to build 200 examples of this car and a further 20 pure competition models will be prepared for racing, by the factory and by selected private owners. All the cars will be left-hand drive and each and every 959 will undoubtedly be sold even before Porsche start to build them!

The 959 is the fastest and most expensive car Porsche have ever offered for the road. Although the shape is clearly related to the 911, the car owes more allegiance to the 935 racers.

PORSCHE

PORSCHE 911 TURBO

In descending order of performance the Porsche line-up continues with the 911 Turbo model, which is known as the 930 in North America. This car can accurately be described as the current ultimate expression of the 911 concept, that was introduced way back in late 1964. Progressive improvements over the years have upped the 911's power output from 130bhp to 300bhp! Any doubts, however, as to whether the 911 chassis could really cope with 300bhp had already been allayed by even more powerful racing derivatives and the 911 Turbo has all the necessary refinements to enable it to handle this massive amount of power with ease.

Nevertheless, experience suggests that only a really capable driver, used to handling large numbers of horses, can utilize the remarkable potential of this machine to the full. Over the years, together with the substantial power increases, Porsche have improved the roadholding of their rear-engined cars to the extent that now even with so much horsepower it is both easier and safer to use all the available performance. However, in the case of the 911 Turbo in particular, it would be a very foolish driver indeed, especially on wet, twisty roads, who did not treat his car with a deal of respect. Full throttle in the middle of a wet corner is a sure recipe for landing in the ditch!

Like all the 911 models, the Turbo retains some aspects from its past, in particular, its instruments and heating. As with all air-cooled cars the efficiency of the 911's heating and ventilation system varies with the engine speed — slow running in traffic means that little heat is supplied but fast, high-revs use supplies almost too much heat and finding the best compromise is not easy. The instrumentation of the 911 series lags behind the best examples of today's cars; with the exception of the speedo and rev-counter, the other dials and switches are scattered about the dash, and to a new driver they do not fall to hand easily.

A Porsche, however, is not just about decent heating and instrument layout, it is about quality of construction, value for money, sheer performance and fun. The 911 Turbo may be flawed, but its virtues outweigh its faults by a very wide margin. A top speed of over 160mph, acceleration from zero to 62mph in just 5·4 seconds, fuel consumption of 23·9mpg at a steady 75mph, together with the car's incredibly stable resale value really do put the Porsche 911 Turbo into a very special category.

S P E C I F I C A T I O N	
MODEL/TYPE	PORSCHE 911 TURBO
ENGINE	FLAT-6, 3,299CC, TURBO
HORSEPOWER	300BHP @ 5,500RPM
TRANSMISSION	4-SPEED MANUAL
CHASSIS	STEEL MONOCOQUE
BRAKES	4-WHEEL DISC
TOP SPEED	160MPH
ACCELERATION 0–60MPH	5.4 SECS
PRODUCTION SPAN	1981 →

Although introduced as long ago as 1975 and based on a series which dates from 1964, the Porsche 911 Turbo is still the fastest accelerating car of any in series production. Its understated, almost mundane looks belie truly stunning performance. Porsche pioneered the use of aerodynamic wings on road cars and, with a car as quick as the Turbo, they are not simply for show.

PORSCHE 911 CS

For about two-thirds of the price of a Turbo there is a Porsche which, to my mind, offers even better value for money. It is the 911 Carrera Sport, with a top speed only about 10mph down on that of the Turbo, at 152mph, better fuel economy, with 31·4mpg at 75mph and a slightly longer 0–62mph acceleration time of 6·1 seconds. The Carrera Sport is more drivable in all conditions than the Turbo, being less nervous in its manner of going. Its five-speed gearbox (compared to the Turbo's four-speed unit) gives a better spread of ratios, and the car feels better balanced on its improved 1985 suspension. This Porsche model must be *the* car to lay away, like a good wine, except that it is so much fun to use that it would be very difficult to put it into storage!

Like its 1973 predecessor the original 911 Carrera, the 1985 version is an instant classic of its type. Some time ago I drove from Los Angeles to New York in a factory prepared Carrera. By comparison with today's car its suspension was firm to the point of being harsh, there was a complete lack of body sound damping, so the car was pretty noisy, but oh, how it went! Crossing Kansas I came across a 47-mile straight road, an empty road, devoid of traffic, people, even birds. I opened up the Porsche and ran flat out for the whole length of that road. The speedometer needle went right off the scale, at 160mph, and stayed there, speeding up on the down slopes, holding the speed on the upgrades and flat sections. The Carrera was as stable as could be; the steering remained positive, without any suggestion of lightness and at the end of the long straight the brakes came on with complete conviction, stopping the car without drama.

S P E C I F I C A T I O N	
MODEL/TYPE	PORSCHE 911 CS
ENGINE	FLAT-6, 3,164CC, OHC
HORSEPOWER	231BHP @ 5,900RPM
TRANSMISSION	5-SPEED MANUAL
CHASSIS	STEEL MONOCOQUE
BRAKES	4-WHEEL DISC
TOP SPEED	152MPH
ACCELERATION 0–60MPH	6.1 SECS
PRODUCTION SPAN	1984 →

The 911 Carrera Sport may not have quite the top speed or the shattering ultimate acceleration of the Turbo, but without even minimal turbo-lag it is even more responsive to the throttle. This makes it more idiot-proof at and around its very high limits but with quite enough power to reward the highest levels of driver skill.

PORSCHE 928S

After the introduction of the 924 model in 1975, rumours soon began to circulate that it would not be long before Porsche would bring out a super-sports coupé, incorporating all that they had learnt with this, their first front-engined car. Enthusiasts were not to be disappointed, as the new 928 broke fresh ground for Porsche.

All previous Porsche cars except the 924 had been either rear-engined or mid-engined, so the 928 was a new departure with its front-mounted V8. This engine featured an alloy block with the pistons running directly in the cylinder bores without the usual benefit of steel liners, and hydraulic tappets. The 928 also offered the option of an automatic gearbox, made by Daimler-Benz. Like the standard five-speed manual transmission, this unit as used on the 928 was located at the rear of the car in unit with the differential. This feature (which was shared by the 924) provided the 928 with near perfect 50/50 front-to-rear balance, with obvious benefits in ride, handling and braking.

Early road test comments waxed lyrical over the car, its performance and its overall dynamic qualities but suggested that an anti-lock braking system (ABS) could well be applied to the 928 and more performance would not be unwelcome. They also, in the main, went on to declare the automatic gearbox as much better suited to the 928 than the manual component, as it appeared to match the character of the car so perfectly — a surprising comment perhaps, in view of the very sporting nature of Porsche products.

With the S model, which followed soon after, and now the 928S Series 2, it would appear that the original criticisms, minor though they were, have been dealt with. The 1985 928S is generally regarded as one of the very best two-seater high performance cars of all time. Many ordinarily cynical road-testers have gone into raptures over the car, their only criticism being that their bank balance wouldn't allow them to own one!

Technical details of the 928S Series 2 give some idea of the immense care and attention to detail that Porsche lavish in ensuring that lovers of fast cars continue to feel this way about the model. The fuel-injected V8 engine has a compression ratio of 10.4:1 to give excellent thermodynamic efficiency with low fuel consumption and the car's superb aerodynamic shape helps in achieving consumption figures of 26.9mpg at 75mph, even with the four-speed automatic 'box. A peak of 310bhp is developed at 5,900rpm and maximum permitted engine speed is 6,500rpm. The 0–62mph time is a very quick 6.2 seconds and the top speed is 158mph. The Porsche 928S Series 2 is a very fine automobile, albeit a rather expensive one, but ownership costs are reduced to quite reasonable levels largely because the servicing intervals are now 12,000 miles.

S P E C I F I C A T I O N	
MODEL/TYPE	PORSCHE 928S
ENGINE	V8, 4,664CC, SOHC
HORSEPOWER	310BHP @ 5,900RPM
TRANSMISSION	5-SP/4-SP AUTO
CHASSIS	STEEL MONOCOQUE
BRAKES	4-WHEEL DISC
TOP SPEED	158MPH
ACCELERATION 0–60MPH	6.2 SECS
PRODUCTION SPAN	1980 →

The 928S is widely regarded as a 'softer' Porsche although the 911 types make most cars look relatively tame. The 928 is just different, a great state-of-the-art car in its own right, largely free of the 911's aggressive image.

PORSCHE

PORSCHE 944 TURBO

Early in 1985 Porsche announced their latest high performance car, the long awaited 944 Turbo model. The body styling is very little different from the non-turbo 944 and the price was expected to be between that of the 911 Carrera and the 911 Turbo. The 944 Turbo's front-mounted four-cylinder engine produces a claimed 220bhp, enough to propel the car to a top speed of 152mph and cover the 0–62mph run in 6.3 seconds. Fuel consumption should be better than that of the 911 Carrera, but no details had been announced at the time of writing. The car's turbocharger is water cooled, and both an intercooler and engine oil cooler are fitted, displaying again the attention to detail which is a recurring feature of the Porsche way of doing things.

The improvement in performance over the standard 944 can be quickly gauged from a top speed of 137mph, 0–62mph in 8.4 seconds for the 'ordinary' car and very similar fuel economy, which helps to balance the substantial difference in price. On each model of 944 certain common features remain: low-drag aerodynamics, a good balance between performance and fuel economy, high top speed, good handling, steering and braking, remarkably high levels of build, fit and finish — together with an understated appearance that appeals to the appreciative enthusiast.

S P E C I F I C A T I O N	
MODEL/TYPE	PORSCHE 944 TURBO
ENGINE	4-CYL, 2,496CC, TURBO
HORSEPOWER	220BHP @ 5,800RPM
TRANSMISSION	5-SPEED MANUAL
CHASSIS	STEEL MONOCOQUE
BRAKES	4-WHEEL DISC
TOP SPEED	152MPH
ACCELERATION 0–60MPH	6.3 SECS
PRODUCTION SPAN	1985 →

When the Porsche 944 *(below)* **was introduced in 1982 it helped bridge a gap between the relatively low-powered 924 and the quick but very expensive 928, which was really more of an executive express. It combined what were essentially the 924's mass-produced shell, with some modification, and half the 928's V8 engine. This 944 Turbo** *(left)***, introduced in 1985, takes the car a step further towards 911 performance and the best of all worlds.**

PORSCHE 924

At the bottom of the Porsche performance car list is the 924 coupé, which was introduced by Porsche in 1975, after Volkswagen had commissioned them to design a sports coupé to be built and sold under their own name but then decided to drop the whole project. Porsche could not bear to see what they considered to be an excellent car go to waste and so they undertook to make it themselves. The 924 quickly established itself as a very good introduction to Porsche motoring, in spite of the fact that its four-cylinder engine came originally from the Volkswagen commercial van, a fact which was always noticeable when running at high revolutions, where the unit sounded strained and harsh.

However, as with all Porsches, the 924 has received constant refinement, becoming better with each year of production. Today the 924 is still a marvellous first step towards Porsche motoring pleasure and even at its 1985 price is still very good value for money.

As a group all the Porsche models give quality of handling precedence over ride quality and to some people they may appear to be harsh because of that, but with the kind of performance that a Porsche offers this must be the right compromise for the buyer.

The idea that Germany *may* bring in speed limits for its autobahn system makes it interesting to contemplate the future of a company such as Porsche, which builds nothing *but* high performance cars. Perhaps we can take hope from the fact that the best market for Porsche cars is still the USA in spite of a 55mph national speed limit.

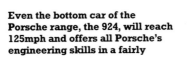

Even the bottom car of the Porsche range, the 924, will reach 125mph and offers all Porsche's engineering skills in a fairly inexpensive package. Unlike several earlier Porsche efforts at producing a low-priced model, the 924 is a notable sales success.

PORSCHE

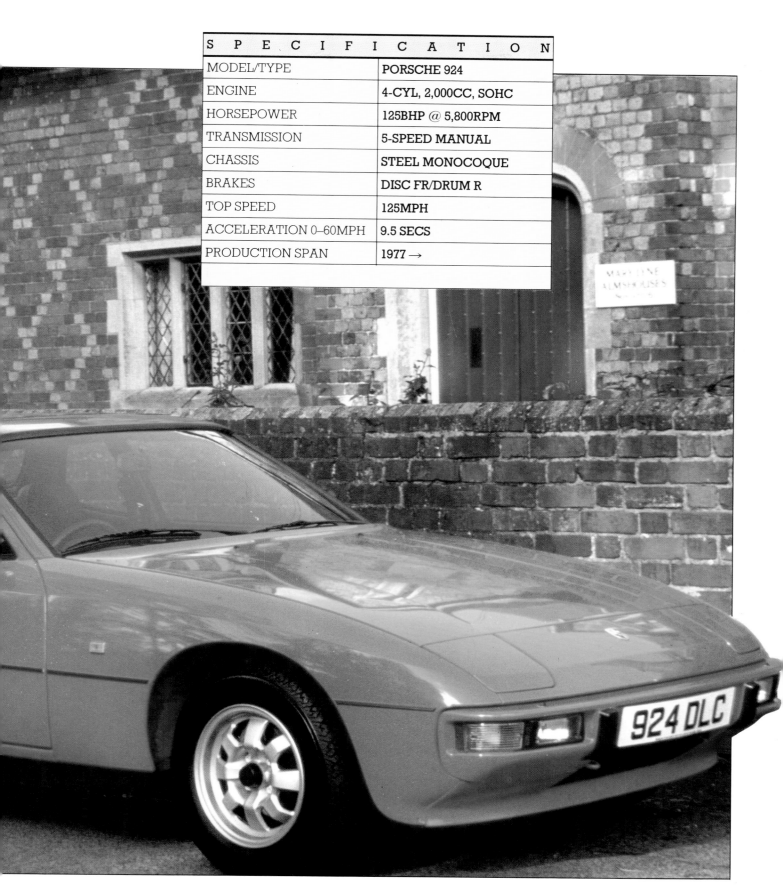

S P E C I F I C A T I O N	
MODEL/TYPE	PORSCHE 924
ENGINE	4-CYL, 2,000CC, SOHC
HORSEPOWER	125BHP @ 5,800RPM
TRANSMISSION	5-SPEED MANUAL
CHASSIS	STEEL MONOCOQUE
BRAKES	DISC FR/DRUM R
TOP SPEED	125MPH
ACCELERATION 0–60MPH	9.5 SECS
PRODUCTION SPAN	1977 →

BMW

In recent years BMW have advertised their cars as 'The Driving Machines' and from 1985 as 'The ULTIMATE Driving Machines'. As an owner of two BMWs that well fit this description I can only agree with the factory but add that until the 1985 models, BMWs had to be driven hard to realize their full potential but were notorious for being tail-happy when going fast in wet conditions. For years, published road tests almost always made mention of this characteristic but my own experience suggests that it is only apparent when driving on or about the limits of any BMW's adhesion, certainly at very high speeds and more obviously in bad weather conditions. In those circumstances, as with any car, the driver must be on his toes and alert if he does not intend to land in the ditch!

BMW's subtle differences from their German rivals in this sector of the market, Porsche and Mercedes-Benz, may have something to do with the fact that the BMW plant is in Munich, in Bavaria, while the others emanate from Stuttgart. A BMW is not so clinical as a Mercedes-Benz, nor so quirky as a Porsche, in fact a BMW has a distinct flavour of the Italian in its nature. It is that flair, combined, of course, with German design and engineering qualities, that makes the Munich cars so appealing. Sit in a BMW (especially after sitting in an equivalent Mercedes-Benz) and the first impression is of luxury, with well upholstered, comfortable seats, beautifully presented instruments, and excellent carpeting that cossets the driver and passengers so that they feel they are in a car made by humans and not by robots.

BMW M635CSi

The current top of the league among BMW's performance cars is the M635CSi coupé. For 1985 this new model has received a series of major improvements over the previous, and already excellent, 635CSi machine. The new in-line 3,453cc six-cylinder engine has duplex-chain-driven double overhead cams, four valves per cylinder and a compression ratio raised to 9.6:1, instead of the previous 9.3:1. Maximum power is now 286bhp but the new engine is both lighter and more fuel efficient than the earlier unit. At 75mph, consumption is 32.1mpg for the manual gearbox version, which is a remarkable figure. Digital engine electronics controlling the ignition and fuel supply systems have been programmed to give optimum timing and fuel metering under all conditions of speed, engine temperature, air temperature, barometric pressure and other variables. For such a large car with this kind of performance the M635CSi's paltry appetite for fuel is astonishing.

An ABS, anti-lock braking system, is fitted as standard, increasing the braking performance of the car and allowing it to be utilized at maximum efficiency while retaining full steering effect at the same time.

The ultimate driving machine? BMW Motorsport division's engine and suspension modifications turn the already rapid 635CSi into the incredible M635CSi *(below)*. The heart of the matter is a 286bhp 24-valve version of the superb BMW straight-six engine *(opposite)*.

S P E C I F I C A T I O N	
MODEL/TYPE	BMW M635CSi
ENGINE	6-CYL, 3,453CC, SOHC
HORSEPOWER	286BHP
TRANSMISSION	5-SPEED MANUAL
CHASSIS	STEEL MONOCOQUE
BRAKES	4-WHEEL DISC
TOP SPEED	158MPH
ACCELERATION 0–60MPH	6 SECS
PRODUCTION SPAN	1984 →

One particularly interesting feature of all the big BMWs is the availability of the ZF four-speed automatic gearbox, with its three ranges of operation. With this unit, a small switch selects either 'E', for economy, wherein the car assumes a high set of overall ratios, giving excellent fuel consumption but slightly slower acceleration, 'S' for sports-type driving, where there is a change to a lower set of overall ratios for more rapid acceleration, and a third position allowing the gearbox to be used effectively as a manual transmission. With this gearbox, the M635CSi can improve on its fuel consumption figures quite appreciably, to register 32.5mpg at a steady 75mph and no less than 41.5mpg at 56mph, while top speed is 158mph!

The big BMW coupé is smooth, so very smooth to drive — quiet and comfortable enough for four large adults to cover hundreds of miles in a day and not feel distressed at the end of the journey. The BMW's steering and braking are more than capable of handling any road situation, and even visibility for the driver, often a bugbear with coupés, is excellent. Heating, which used to be less than good, is now very much improved, as is the ventilation system. For customers who have to have four decent seats in their coupé, plus all the dash and glamour of a really fast car there is not much that can hold a candle to the M635CSi BMW. At a price in Britain of £32,195, close to, say, a Porsche 928S or a Ferrari Mondial, it is out on its own as a four-seater — nothing else even comes close to its combination of comfort, safety, style and performance.

BMW

BMW M535i

In order to meet the challenge of the new 16-valve Mercedes-Benz 190E 2.3 in the smaller car sector, BMW have introduced their M535i. On paper it has more than enough in its specification to face up to, even to beat, the small Mercedes. A new 3,430cc single-overhead-cam fuel-injected straight-six engine develops 218bhp and gives the BMW a 33bhp advantage, plus a top speed of 143mph. Acceleration from zero to 62mph is also better than that of the Mercedes, with a time of 7 seconds against 7.5 seconds. Even the current price is comfortably less, by nearly one third. Rear seat accommodation is much more generous, with proper legroom for two adults, where the rear quarters of the 190E are rather cramped.

There is a choice of three different gearboxes for the M535i buyer, the BMW five-speed with overdrive unit, a close-ratio Getrag five-speed, or the ZF triple-range switchable automatic box, which is my own preference. Braking is by four-wheel ventilated disc units, with ABS anti-lock control. Power-assisted steering is also standard and in use it is really excellent. Handling is of a very high standard for such a heavy car, with no more of the dreaded BMW habit of snapping into instant oversteer if indiscreet use is made of the throttle. Now, the car remains well under control at all speeds. Like the M635CSi, the M535i is a car for covering long distances, at high speeds in safety and comfort.

S P E C I F I C A T I O N	
MODEL/TYPE	BMW M535i
ENGINE	6-CYL, 3,430CC, SOHC
HORSEPOWER	218BHP
TRANSMISSION	5-SP/4-SP AUTO
CHASSIS	STEEL MONOCOQUE
BRAKES	4-WHEEL DISC
TOP SPEED	143MPH
ACCELERATION 0–60MPH	7.1 SECS
PRODUCTION SPAN	1984 →

M-style engineering and cosmetic packaging turn BMW's originally rather staid 5-series saloon into the road-burning 143mph M535i, a **Bavarian wolf in wolf's clothing. In this guise the comfortable five-seater will seriously embarass many out-and-out sportscars.**

BMW

BMW B9

The rapid Alpina C-cars are based on the 3-series BMW, the German manufacturer's small saloon, for owners who want more performance in the same compact package — yet they are far more than just another tuned BMW.

Alpina, the most respected of the many companies which tune and otherwise modify BMWs, is based in the village of Buchloe — not far from BMW's own headquarters in Munich. The company was established in 1965 by Burkard Bovensiepen, a large, amiable man who is a wine connoisseur as well as being a car manufacturer — the only manufacturer in the world officially sanctioned by BMW to produce versions of its cars, sold worldwide as Alpina BMWs. For many years, Alpina and BMW have co-operated closely in developing both road and racing cars, with many impressive wins including the prestigious European Touring Car Championship.

Unlike most, Alpina do not simply bolt on more engine power, but completely re-engineer the basic car with modified suspension, brakes, aerodynamics and interior fittings. Alpina offer virtually any level of modification desired on any of BMW's range and the 3-series based C-cars are the company's biggest sellers. The first was the C1, based on the BMW323i but with a much modified version of the 2,316cc six-cylinder engine. An increase in power output from 150 to 170bhp gave substantially improved performance, matched by very effective suspension changes.

The C2, the newly introduced successor to the C1, is even quicker, with a top speed of 133mph with the close-ratio five-speed Getrag sports gearbox and will accelerate from zero to 60mph in 6.6 seconds. With the 'overdrive' manual gearbox and a higher final drive, the C2 will top 140mph — but at the expense of some of its sparkling acceleration. The excellent four-speed ZF automatic gearbox is an interesting third option.

This level of performance is achieved by using a 2,490cc engine derived from the BMW525 Eta, with special Alpina cylinder head and crankshaft (both based on 323i parts) and Bosch LE Jetronic fuel injection. This is good for a supremely smooth and flexible 185bhp but the C2 is also capable of averaging some 25mpg — helped substantially by the Alpina-designed aerodynamic additions, notably the deep front air-dam. To cope with the extra urge, Alpina also fit progressive rate suspension with Bilstein gas-filled shock absorbers, a limited-slip differential and 195/50 VR16 Pirelli tyres on handsome Alpina alloy wheels. Surprisingly, an ABS anti-lock system is not deemed necessary on the servo-assisted all-disc brakes — which are standard 323i components.

Among the many companies which tune BMWs for road and track use, Alpina is probably the best known — and in racing terms **the most successful. Their C1, and C2, which replaced it recently, are both based on the compact 3-series.**

S P E C I F I C A T I O N	
MODEL/TYPE	ALPINA BMW C2
ENGINE	6-CYL, 2,492CC, SOHC
HORSEPOWER	185BHP @ 6,100RPM
TRANSMISSION	5-SP/4-SP AUTO
CHASSIS	STEEL MONOCOQUE
BRAKES	4-WHEEL DISC
TOP SPEED	133MPH
ACCELERATION 0–60MPH	6.6 SECS
PRODUCTION SPAN	1985 →

BMW

BMW 745i

Before leaving the really fast current BMWs, mention must be made of a car available only in Germany, the 745i, a 3.5-litre turbocharged 7-Series car. Luxuriously appointed, with an on-board computer, ABS braking, very high levels of trim and equipment, this car is a match for anything else on Germany's high speed autobahns. I tried one on a recent visit to Munich, in the most awful winter weather conditions, with heavy snow and bad visibility, but even so the car impressed greatly. The engine's performance was sensational; completely free of the dreaded turbo-lag, it urged the big, heavy car up to seemingly impossible speeds, yet without any fuss or excessive noise. The ABS braking system handled the very slippery conditions with ease and safety, and the steering further emphasized the overall excellent nature of the car. It is so good as to make the possibility of the appearance of the new 700 series, which *will* be sold outside Germany, something really to look forward to.

On a lower rung of the BMW performance ladder the 735i and the 528i might appear at first to be poor relations for the cars already mentioned, but although somewhat lacking in outright speed they are still cars of very acceptable performance. Their special attraction lies in their lower prices and less prohibitive insurance costs, which for many people may balance out their relative lack of go.

Many German car enthusiasts place BMW second to the cars from Mercedes-Benz but I am happier to think of the Munich cars as simply different, not inferior. Their blend of good looks, performance and attractive interiors, with the normal German qualities of good design and construction, make them a favourite alternative to the Stuttgart cars.

The flagship of the BMW fleet is the large, luxurious 7-series saloon. The turbocharged 745i tops the range in Germany and offers 150mph transport in the grand manner. In other European markets, the normally aspirated 735; (*above and right*) is the quickest of the 7-series.

S P E C I F I C A T I O N	
MODEL/TYPE	BMW 745i
ENGINE	6-CYL, 3,430CC, TURBO
HORSEPOWER	295BHP
TRANSMISSION	4-SPEED AUTO
CHASSIS	STEEL MONOCOQUE
BRAKES	4-WHEEL DISC
TOP SPEED	150MPH
ACCELERATION 0–60MPH	7 SECS
PRODUCTION SPAN	1982 →

S P E C I F I C A T I O N	
MODEL/TYPE	BMW 735i
ENGINE	6-CYL, 3,430CC, SOHC
HORSEPOWER	218BHP
TRANSMISSION	5-SP/4-SP AUTO
CHASSIS	STEEL MONOCOQUE
BRAKES	4-WHEEL DISC
TOP SPEED	135MPH
ACCELERATION 0–60MPH	7.4 SECS
PRODUCTION SPAN	1982 →

S P E C I F I C A T I O N	
MODEL/TYPE	BMW 528i
ENGINE	6-CYL, 2,788CC, SOHC
HORSEPOWER	184BHP
TRANSMISSION	5-SP/4-SP AUTO
CHASSIS	STEEL MONOCOQUE
BRAKES	4-WHEEL DISC
TOP SPEED	127MPH
ACCELERATION 0–60MPH	8.7 SECS
PRODUCTION SPAN	1983 →

MERCEDES·BENZ

Turning to the fastest cars from Mercedes-Benz themselves, however, I must admit to a sneaking regard for the products. Over the last 15 years I have had a professional relationship with the company, and never fail to be impressed when I drive their cars. At the same time, however, I must admit that I have yet to own one! The reason is strictly personal. I actually find it difficult to be enthusiastic about perfection, when, as in the case of Mercedes-Benz cars, it translates to a clinical coldness, an unappealing machine-like efficiency. There is no denying, however, that Mercedes-Benz cars are among the best mass-produced cars available in the world today.

I have selected three cars from Untertürkheim to represent Mercedes-Benz and these are the 380SEC, the 500SEL and the 500SL.

MERCEDES-BENZ 380SEC

The 380SEC is a superb four-seater coupé, well able to carry four adults far and fast, with excellent economy of operation. Its 3,839cc V8 engine produces 204bhp at 5,250rpm, and 225lb ft of torque at 4,000rpm. Maximum speed is 133mph and the 380SEC can maintain this speed all day if necessary! Its 0–62mph time is very good, at 6.4 seconds, but the overall fuel consumption is only average, at 22mpg. In appearance the 380SEC rivals the very good looks of the BMW 635CSi and is without doubt one of the most handsome Mercedes-Benz cars ever made.

In my eyes, the 380SEC is so good looking that anyone thinking about adding any of the increasingly prevalent aftermarket body styling appendages should really think very carefully before changing the standard car's beautifully balanced appearance.

With the elegant 380SEC coupé, Mercedes-Benz show that it is possible to combine performance with style and still retain a strong marque identity—even though the functional simplicity which characterizes the marque is interpreted by some as blandness.

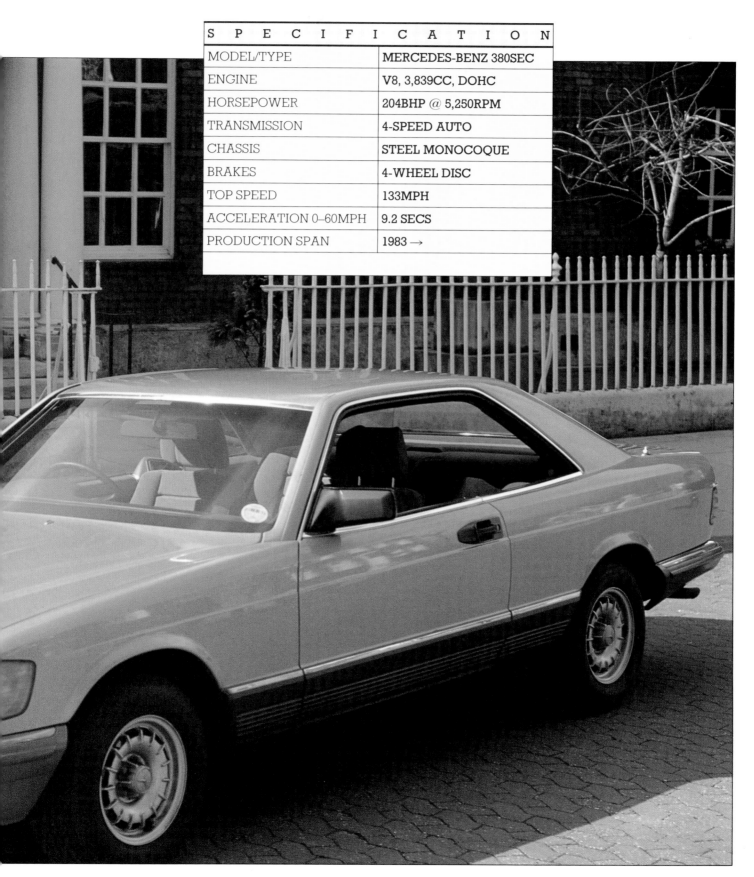

S P E C I F I C A T I O N	
MODEL/TYPE	MERCEDES-BENZ 380SEC
ENGINE	V8, 3,839CC, DOHC
HORSEPOWER	204BHP @ 5,250RPM
TRANSMISSION	4-SPEED AUTO
CHASSIS	STEEL MONOCOQUE
BRAKES	4-WHEEL DISC
TOP SPEED	133MPH
ACCELERATION 0–60MPH	9.2 SECS
PRODUCTION SPAN	1983 →

MERCEDES·BENZ

MERCEDES-BENZ 500SEL

The 500SEL is slightly cheaper than the 380SEC and uses a 4,973cc V8 engine, producing 231bhp at 4,750rpm, which gives the 3,649lb car a top speed of 140mph. The 'S-class' Mercedes-Benz has been one of the most desirable mass produced cars of recent years and the longer-bodied SEL is even more admirable in all respects.

Until the S-class cars came along I thought Mercedes-Benz were without a really good looking model in their range but with the S cars all that has changed. Having looked closely at a number of body styling exercises on Mercedes-Benz models over the last two years I still think that the standard shape is unequalled for looks and proportions.

Fuel consumption for the 500SEL is very slightly better than for the 380SEC, at an average of 23.6mpg and for such a large car it is surprisingly easy to drive quickly. It appears to shrink as the miles fly past, allowing the driver to place the car very accurately on corners. Brakes are discs all round, those at the front are internally ventilated and ABS comes as standard. The transmission is the excellent Mercedes-Benz four-speed automatic and the differential is a limited-slip unit. Suspension is independent all round, with the front having anti-dive characteristics and the rear incorporating anti-squat control.

Mercedes-Benz seats may provide rather a surprise to most people sitting in one of these cars for the first time, as they appear to be both plain and very hard! However, they are anatomically correct in their design and very comfortable even over very long distances. A trip from Nairobi to Mombasa, for instance, through the Tsavo Game Park, over rutted murram tracks in a 280SE left the author feeling no worse than a drive across town.

Irrespective of performance and price, the 500SEL is one of today's great automobiles.

S P E C I F I C A T I O N	
MODEL/TYPE	MERCEDES-BENZ 500SEL
ENGINE	V8, 4,973CC, DOHC
HORSEPOWER	231BHP @ 4,750RPM
TRANSMISSION	4-SPEED AUTO
CHASSIS	STEEL MONOCOQUE
BRAKES	4-WHEEL DISC
TOP SPEED	140MPH PLUS
ACCELERATION 0–60MPH	7.6 SECS
PRODUCTION SPAN	1984 →

The Mercedes-Benz 500SEL is a big car by any standards, but 231bhp and exceptional aerodynamics add up to 140mph performance coupled with surprisingly good fuel economy.

MERCEDES-BENZ

MERCEDES-BENZ 500SL

Mercedes-Benz have always prided themselves on offering a fast convertible that lacked nothing in comfort and whose amenities in no way compromised high performance. The 300SL was a classic example of this type of vehicle and the 'SL' label has come to be applied to many fine sporty convertibles from Mercedes-Benz, a tradition which the latest 500SL continues. The all-alloy 4,973cc V8 engine uses fuel injection, transistorized ignition and hydraulic tappets and produces 231bhp at 5,000rpm. A four-speed automatic gearbox is fitted, as is a limited slip differential. Suspension is as on the 500SEL model and the braking system is also similar.

The 500SL's top speed is 137mph and its 0–62mph time is 7.6 seconds. Fuel economy is an average of 26.5mpg, which makes the 500SL a remarkably economical performance car.

With increasingly restrictive legislation demanding even better crash protection, particularly for the American market, the drophead sportscar came close to extinction in the 1970s but, happily, cars like the 500SL show that the breed has not been stamped out yet.

S P E C I F I C A T I O N	
MODEL/TYPE	MERCEDES-BENZ 500SL
ENGINE	V8, 4,973CC, SOHC
HORSEPOWER	231BHP @ 5,000RPM
TRANSMISSION	4-SPEED AUTOMATIC
CHASSIS	STEEL MONOCOQUE
BRAKES	4-WHEEL DISC
TOP SPEED	137MPH
ACCELERATION 0–60MPH	7.6 SECS
PRODUCTION SPAN	1983 →

AUDI

For many years, Audi made low priced, sensible cars, for the family that aspired to a BMW but couldn't afford one. They were well made in the German manner, rather lacking in character but making up for that by being so well put together and finished. Gradually, Audi's cars became bigger, faster and more sought after by an increasingly prosperous middle class in Europe.

Ten years ago the drive from Cologne to Frankfurt could be undertaken in just under two hours but it took an expensive, fast car to do it. I recently did the same journey in an Audi 80CD and very comfortably took 25 minutes off that time. As a practical measure of the improvement in the current crop of everyday cars this sort of comparison of journey times is of more value than any test track measurement.

Currently there are six Audi cars that can easily exceed 125mph, the 100CD, 200ST, 200T, Quattro, 200 Quattro and the new Quattro Sport. They are all excellent cars but I have zeroed in on the fastest, the 155mph Quattro Sport, not only because it *is* the fastest but also because it incorporates all the latest technology coming out of Audi's base at Ingolstadt. It is also the most expensive car Audi has ever offered to the public, if only a very limited public!

AUDI QUATTRO SPORT

The Audi Sport's capabilities take it out of the merely fast into the super-fast, super-expensive class of car, although it has more than a passing similarity to the more mundane Audi GT coupé. By no means a beautiful car, some have labelled the Sport downright ugly. It sits on a wheelbase that is two inches shorter than that of an Austin Rover Metro, giving the car a short, squat appearance, emphasized by a longer nose to accommodate the intercooler for the turbo unit.

The engine, a new five-cylinder unit, is a benchmark for any turbo installation and marks another step in the progress of

S P E C I F I C A T I O N	
MODEL/TYPE	AUDI QUATTRO SPORT
ENGINE	5-CYL, 2,133CC, TURBO
HORSEPOWER	300BHP @ 6,500RPM
TRANSMISSION	5-SPEED MANUAL
CHASSIS	STEEL/GRP/KEVLAR
BRAKES	4-WHEEL DISC
TOP SPEED	155MPH
ACCELERATION 0–60MPH	5 SECS
PRODUCTION SPAN	1985 →

extracting usable power by means of the exhaust-driven blower. After the introduction of this engine, Audi upped its power in 1980 from 115bhp on carburettors to 130bhp using fuel injection. Use of the turbocharger increased this to 200bhp, with the works rally cars enjoying the benefits of up to 350bhp. This new car has a reliable 300bhp at 6,500rpm even in standard form. Current rally cars have 450bhp, with another 50bhp to come for next year.

The engine installation in the Quattro Sport represents the fourth generation of Audi turbo refinement with its twin overhead camshafts operating four valves per cylinder. The engine, in alloy, is nearly 50lb lighter than the previous cast iron-block engine and is the first all-alloy Audi engine to be offered to the public.

The interior may *promise* to be able to accommodate four people, but in practice the Sport is strictly a two-seater and

there is no way that even two small children can be carried in comfort on the rear seats. The body, which is made by Bauer, has boot and roof sections of aluminium reinforced glassfibre, with other body parts using Kevlar material.

One very distinct difference from other Audi models is that the Sport must have the aerodynamic qualities of a house brick, yet sitting on its 225/50VR 15 Pirelli P7 tyres the Sport has all the charisma of the Ferrari GTO.

Never noted as the smoothest of engines, the 2,133cc five-cylinder Audi unit in its latest guise is surprisingly silky, almost as smooth as a BMW six. Real power starts to come in at over 3,000rpm when the familiar turbo 'whoosh', sounding like an astonished gasp from an unsuspecting passenger, takes over. There is also some extra noise from the transmission but its shift quality is not affected and it remains smooth and positive. The brakes are ventilated discs all round and have selectable ABS anti-lock capability. Audi have found that ABS is not necessarily desirable in all driving conditions and in some circumstances can be dispensed with to advantage, so they give a Sport driver the option.

Ride quality is firmer than previous Quattros, to the point where it could almost be described as harsh but, if anything, the roadholding of this car is appreciably better. Steering is also improved to the point where the Sport is easier to drive really fast, much faster than last year's Quattro and with greater relaxation.

Anyone with the equivalent of £60,000 to spend on a car, a two-seater remember, that is in the forefront of the latest technology, with the reliability and durability that comes from German engineering, and which is as safe as any car manufacturer can make it, should look no further than an Audi Quattro Sport.

The stubby and purposeful-looking Audi Quattro Sport (*below left and previous page*) takes the four-wheel drive format of the original Quattro (*below*) a stage further, in a short-wheelbase derivative designed primarily (though not entirely successfully) for rallying.

AUDI

AUDI 2005T

For the fast car buyer who must have a full five-seater with all the basic advantages of an Audi, the Audi 2005T model may be an ideal choice. The larger 200 body style gives sumptuous accommodation for five large adults with every possible comfort, and the driver has near-sportscar performance to keep him happy. The 2005T has a top speed of 143mph, will accelerate from zero to 60mph in 8.2 seconds and offers overall fuel consumption of just over 19mpg — and this maker's quoted figure for top speed is probably more than a little on the conservative side. The beautifully finished Audi 2005T has only two small causes for criticism. Firstly, it is very expensive within its class and secondly it shares a characteristic with most other Audi's of being too cold and clinical. That however is the price to be paid for a near perfect automobile. If I had to transport five adults a long way in a hurry and in considerable comfort then I can think of few better alternatives than the Audi 2005T.

Vorsprung durch Technik—ahead through technology—is the Audi slogan and the 2005T is an excellent example of the company's advanced engineering and stylish packaging.

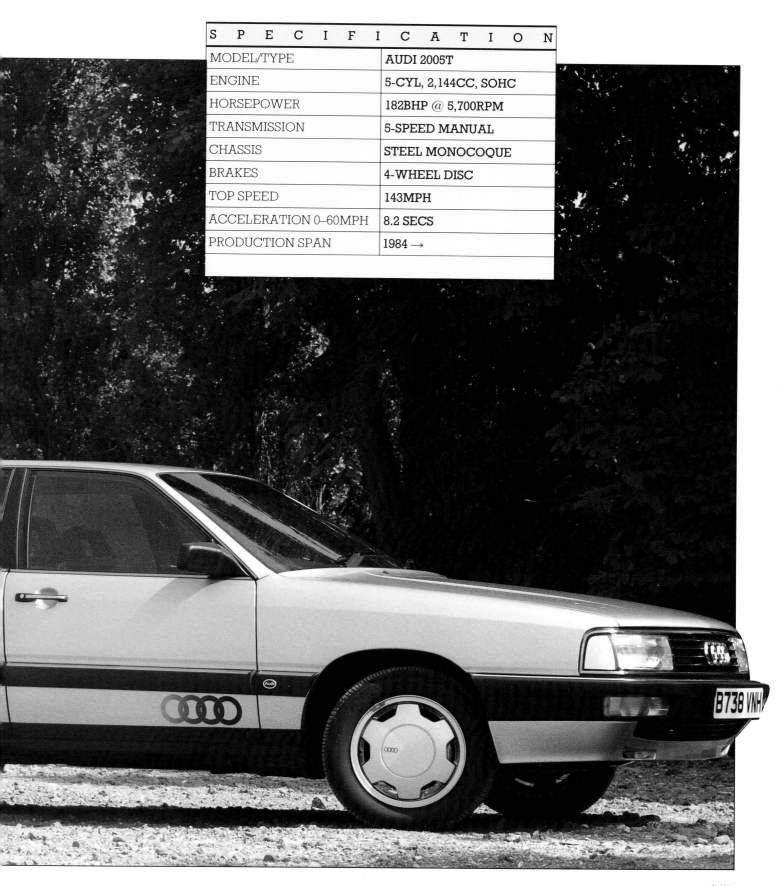

S P E C I F I C A T I O N	
MODEL/TYPE	AUDI 2005T
ENGINE	5-CYL, 2,144CC, SOHC
HORSEPOWER	182BHP @ 5,700RPM
TRANSMISSION	5-SPEED MANUAL
CHASSIS	STEEL MONOCOQUE
BRAKES	4-WHEEL DISC
TOP SPEED	143MPH
ACCELERATION 0–60MPH	8.2 SECS
PRODUCTION SPAN	1984 →

OPEL

OPEL MONZA GSE

My final selection from the ranks of German fast cars is the excellent but often underrated Opel Monza GSE, which is considerably cheaper than many of its rivals and tremendous value for money. The Monza is a striking looking car that is very well made, most fully equipped, has really excellent road manners and is safe and fast at the same time. The hatchback GSE is able to carry four adults and all their luggage over long distances in great comfort. It is powered by a 3-litre straight-six overhead cam engine developing 180bhp at 5,800rpm and an equally impressive 183lb ft of torque at 4,200rpm. Bosch LE-electronic fuel injection and electronic ignition are fitted and give impressive smoothness and power.

Either a five-speed manual or a four-speed automatic transmission can be ordered with this engine and both options allow the full performance potential to be exploited. With the five-speed manual gearbox, top gear gives 25.5mph per 1,000rpm, a factor that contributes a great deal both to lack of fuss at high speed and fuel economy — which is an impressive 30mpg at 75mph. Four-wheel disc brakes are fitted and these are ventilated at the front and solid at the rear, assisted by a servo and regulated to prevent rear-wheel lock-up in emergency operation.

Light alloy wheels help brake-cooling and enhance the overall appearance of this car, whose top speed is 133mph with the manual gearbox and 130mph with the optional automatic. Its acceleration times are equally good, for the 0–62mph dash the manual takes only 8.2 seconds and the auto-equipped car is just two seconds slower.

With this line-up of fast, or very fast, cars Germany can certainly claim to be the home of some of the fastest cars in the world. It remains to be seen whether the possibility of a national speed limit ever materializes, and if it does what effect it will have on the type of car which German manufacturers build. There are already several short sections of autobahn that are speed restricted, including a notorious downhill stretch between Cologne and Frankfurt that is particularly dangerous in the wet, and in 1975 the government did establish a 50mph overall speed limit to conserve fuel after the Arab/Israeli war. Enormous pressure from the motoring public and from Germany's domestic car makers had the restriction lifted within three months.

It is still difficult to see either an overall speed limit being imposed, or German fast cars slowing down!

S P E C I F I C A T I O N	
MODEL/TYPE	OPEL MONZA GSE
ENGINE	6-CYL, 2,969CC
HORSEPOWER	180BHP @ 5,800RPM
TRANSMISSION	5-SPEED MANUAL
CHASSIS	STEEL MONOCOQUE
BRAKES	4-WHEEL DISC
TOP SPEED	133MPH
ACCELERATION 0–60MPH	8.2 SECS
PRODUCTION SPAN	1984 →

The Opel Monza GSE is the top of General Motors' European range and maintains Opel's longstanding reputation as makers of cars with flair. The GSE's smooth fuel-injected straight-six gives the big, well-equipped fastback coupé sparkling performance at remarkably low cost.

Italy has long been the home of several famous makers of fast cars, albeit in small numbers, as befits any hand-made product. The very names of these manufacturers, Ferrari, Lancia, Maserati, Lamborghini and Alfa Romeo, conjure up an image of speed and high performance. The rather prosaic name of Fiat can now be added to this list in view of their recently announced Turbo Uno model.

I might reasonably begin this look at Italy by considering Lancia, a company older than all but Fiat of this group of makes and with a proud heritage of building and racing fast cars. In the last 20 years Lancia have suffered badly in the market place, despite enormous financial help from their current owners, the Fiat company. The Lancia has been an engineer's car, and their designers and chief engineers have been household names among Lancia owners. Vincenzo Lancia himself took an enormous pride in his company's products, and right up to his death in 1937, at the early age of 56, he would insist on evaluating on the road every single Lancia model, be it a prototype, research or pre-production car. If it did not at first meet his own very critical standards, the car simply didn't go on to the next stage in its development.

Although a fine racer himself in his early days, Vincenzo believed that sheer horsepower alone was not the way to make a fast car for a customer. Balance was the most immediate obvious feature in all Lancias that were built in Vincenzo's day. Although with the passage of time this characteristic was allowed to become less important, especially after the Fiat takeover, up to the end of the Vincenzo Lancia period all the Turin cars offered the best possible balance between roadholding and horsepower. Chassis performance was essential to the Lancia way of doing things.

It was always possible to find engines with more power per cc than a Lancia from other Italian makers, in particular from Alfa Romeo, and as most people are more instantly impressed by horsepower than by road abilities, Lancias began to appear as less than appealing cars. However, since the end of World War II Lancia models have emerged that must be considered real high performers by any standards.

They include cars like the B20 GT, one of the very first mass production cars properly to qualify for the title of Gran Turismo (and to my mind one of the most beautifully shaped cars of all time). It was also a car with a very honourable record in GT-class racing, scoring a second place in the Mille Miglia in 1951, winning the 1952 Targa Florio, the 1953 Liège–Rome–Liège, the 1954 Monte Carlo Rally and, as late as 1958, winning the Acropolis Rally. Then came the under-financed D50 Grand Prix racing car, which, with more financial backing might have seriously challenged the W196 Mercedes-Benz racing record. Various factory and Zagato-bodied Appias, Fulvias and Flaminias followed.

All were wonderfully responsive cars, lovely to look at and to drive, well engineered but they never really caught the

public's imagination enough to slow Lancia's slide into insolvency. The spectacular Stratos came too late and in any case was not really a proper Lancia in the strictest sense but a Ferrari-engined special built to go rallying, which it did very successfully. In truth, it was more a Fiat exercise than a Lancia one.

To give some idea of the addictive qualities of the marque I can do no better than recount the words of Pininfarina, who after he had styled the lovely Flaminia coupé and had driven thousands of test miles in it, said 'When I die, I want to drive to Paradise in the Flaminia'.

LANCIA THEMA

At last, after years of hovering on the edge of extinction, the name Lancia can again be linked to a car with real performance pretentions, the turbocharged Thema. With a body styled by Giugiaro in co-operation with Lancia's in-house design office, this four-door car looks as ordinary as the Lancias of old. Spectacular body shapes have *never* been the way Lancia have sold their cars (and perhaps that is why they very nearly went out of business). Clean, modern, almost anonymous, would be a good way to describe the Thema's styling but, as always with Lancia, it is what is *under* the bodywork that is important.

The engine of the fastest Thema is a 2-litre four-cylinder, turbocharged, fuel-injected unit delivering 165bhp through a five-speed gearbox. This engine has two counter-rotating balance shafts to smooth out the four-cylinder roughness. The fuel injection is by the Bosch LE-2 Jetronic system, aided by Magnetti Marelli Microplex microcomputer ignition control, which features an 'overboost' arrangement allowing the driver to select, for very short periods, a delay in the turbo wastegate opening which has the effect of increasing torque from a normal 188lb ft to 210lb ft.

The ZF power-assisted rack-and-pinion steering has variable rate characteristics, lowering the ratio at low speeds, to help in parking manoeuvres, and quickening up at higher speeds for more sensitivity. Self-levelling rear suspension and ABS braking are also offered on the turbocharged Thema.

Lancia claim a top speed of 135mph for the car, with a 0–60mph acceleration time of 7.1 seconds. Accommodation for four adults is generous and, in the BMW manner, very luxurious. At speed the old, strained, Fiat 2-litre engine note is absent in the turbo car, but there *is* some wind noise.

Slightly slower than the turbo, at 130mph, is the normally aspirated V6 Thema. It is also a little quieter and requires fewer gearchanges when pressing on fast. This latest Lancia has all the right qualities to restore the marque to its former glories but there is no doubt that the road ahead for the Turin manufacturer is going to be a long hard slog.

S P E C I F I C A T I O N	
MODEL/TYPE	LANCIA THEMA
ENGINE	4-CYL, 1,995CC, TURBO
HORSEPOWER	165BHP @ 5,500RPM
TRANSMISSION	5-SPEED MANUAL
CHASSIS	STEEL MONOCOQUE
BRAKES	4-WHEEL DISC
TOP SPEED	135MPH
ACCELERATION 0–60MPH	7.1 SECS
PRODUCTION SPAN	1985 →

Lancia has rarely resorted to styling excesses to sell its cars, preferring instead to rely on fine engineering—a policy which in the past has caused the company more than its share of financial crises. The turbocharged Thema, styled under the direction of Giugiaro and the fastest Lancia for many years, is no exception

ALFA-ROMEO GTV-6

The next oldest of these Italian car makers is Alfa Romeo, which, like Lancia, has been teetering on the edge of financial disaster. Also like Lancia, Alfa have a marvellous background in making high performance cars. At the moment they have but one car that qualifies for inclusion in this book, and that is the GTV6. This car follows on from a long line of very fine 2 + 2-seater GT coupés that goes back to the superb little Bertone-styled Giulietta of the early 1950s. The three-door hatchback GTV6 is powered by the latest in a range of fine Alfa Romeo engines, a 2,492cc all-alloy V6 (of 60° included angle) with twin overhead camshafts, producing 160bhp at 5,600rpm. Bosch L-Jetronic fuel injection is used, together with electronic ignition. A five-speed manual gearbox is mounted at the opposite end of the car, in unit with the differential, and the long gear linkage can sometimes give a less than perfect change.

The GTV6's suspension is rather different from many other fast cars. It is independent at the front, by wishbones and with torsion bars supplying the springing medium, while an anti-roll bar controls sway in cornering. At the rear, however, a de Dion axle is used, with coil springs and an anti-roll bar. This design of axle is not fully independent in the true sense of the word but has the enormous advantage of keeping the rear wheels perpendicular to the road surface at all times, retaining a full tyre contact patch with all the virtues that that gives.

Brakes are disc all round, the fronts having ventilated rotors. Steering is by rack and pinion, without any assistance, and in use none is necessary. The wheels are 15 × 6in light alloy components and the tyres are 195/60HR 15. With the excellent balance achieved by virtue of having the transmission located at the rear of this front-engined car, the GTV6 has wonderful handling qualities. Although the Alfa Romeo has no more power than many of its competitors, it performs as well (and sometimes better) as them because of its balance, road grip and dynamic handling qualities. Above all, it remains very fine value for money in its class.

The Alfa Romeo GTV6 is a car of real character, for better or worse. The attractive coupé has a fabulous V6 engine, exceptional roadholding and handling, a dreadful gearchange and a typically Italian driving position—best suited to long arms and short legs. All the GTV6's shortcomings however are trivial alongside its sheer *brio*.

S P E C I F I C A T I O N	
MODEL/TYPE	ALFA-ROMEO GTV-6
ENGINE	V6, 2,492CC, OHC
HORSEPOWER	160BHP @ 5,600RPM
TRANSMISSION	5-SPEED MANUAL
CHASSIS	STEEL MONOCOQUE
BRAKES	4-WHEEL DISC
TOP SPEED	127MPH
ACCELERATION 0–60MPH	8.1 SECS
PRODUCTION SPAN	1983 →

FERRARI

Like Porsche, Ferrari's cars are all capable of more than 125mph and several of them will beat this arbitrary figure by a very large margin. The two most recent, and to date fastest, Ferraris are the Testarossa and the GTO. Both names recall great Ferrari cars from the recent past and Ferrari have used them appropriately enough again on two machines that incorporate all the latest in high performance technology.

Ever since 1950, when Ferrari properly started to make and supply customer cars, as opposed to purely competition machinery, they have given pride of place to their engines. In the vast majority of cases these beautifully crafted power units have followed the overhead-cam V12 layout and plainly show the great influence that Enzo Ferrari himself has on the design philosophy of his company, even though he is now well into his 80s and the customer side of the business is owned by Fiat. As

an ex-racer and racing team manager, his thirst for engine performance dominates his thinking on the Ferrari customer cars. It is not, however, quite as overwhelming as in the past, when the quality of design and performance of a Ferrari road-car engine was streets ahead of the rest of the car, which could often be described as no more than ordinary.

With the coming of 'science' into the closed shop of racing car design nearly 30 years ago, with Lotus's late founding-genius Colin Chapman in the forefront, Ferrari have been forced to take more heed of the other dynamic aspects of their racing cars. As with so many developments at Maranello, these have filtered down to keep their road cars in the vanguard of high performance vehicles. For the record, Ferrari probably make more of the components of their own cars than any other car maker in the world.

FERRARI

FERRARI GTO

Ferrari make no bones about the new GTO and describe it in their own literature as 'The Fastest Ferrari road car ever Built'. The GTO, which stands for *Gran Turismo Omologato,* is powered by a 2,855cc 32-valve V8 engine with twin turbochargers and developing a massive 400bhp at a typically Ferrari engine speed of 7,000rpm. The turbo system and its ancillaries use much of the technology developed on Ferrari's turbocharged Grand Prix cars. For instance, Weber-Marelli IAW electronic injection and ignition are used, with each bank of cylinders having its own separate system. The transmission is entirely designed and made by Ferrari, and the single composite unit comprises the five-speed gearbox, clutch and limited-slip differential.

Four-wheel ventilated disc brakes are fitted but ABS is not deemed necessary. Suspension follows the Grand Prix car

The Ferrari GTO, introduced in mid-1984, amply underlines Ferrari's continued commitment to ultimate performance—having finally overtaken the legendary front-engined V12 Daytona as the fastest ever Ferrari road car.

layout, being independent all round and with coil springs and Koni dampers providing the springing medium. Slightly different wheel sizes are employed at front and rear, being 16 × 8in front and 16 × 10in at the rear, while Goodyear NCT tyres are supplied as standard fittings.

The body styling is very similar, but not identical, to the 308GTB Ferrari, and extensive use was made of wind tunnel testing to achieve a very aerodynamic shape. To meet racing homologation requirements, as its name implies, only 200 GTOs will be made and prices will be very high, at over £75,000 in Britain for example.

On the performance front, the 'off-the-shelf' GTO is reckoned to be good for 189mph and acceleration is equally stunning, with 0–62mph possible in under 5 seconds. As it is obvious that the standard 400bhp can easily be uprated to as much as 600bhp, even more shattering performance can be anticipated from the competition versions which are this car's *raison d'etre*.

S P E C I F I C A T I O N	
MODEL/TYPE	FERRARI GTO
ENGINE	V8, 2,855CC, TURBO
HORSEPOWER	400BHP @ 7,000RPM
TRANSMISSION	5-SPEED MANUAL
CHASSIS	STEEL TUBULAR
BRAKES	4-WHEEL DISC
TOP SPEED	190MPH PLUS
ACCELERATION 0–60MPH	4.9 SECS
PRODUCTION SPAN	1985 →

FERRARI TESTAROSSA

The next Ferrari carries the name of one of the most beautiful competition cars ever to race, the Testarossa, or Red Head. This name was given to the car because its cam covers were painted red instead of the more usual black. In the year of the original car's introduction, 1958, it won the 1,000km of Buenos Aires, the Sebring 12 hours, the Targa Florio and Le Mans. During the next year, success followed success for this lovely looking machine and so it is no surprise that Ferrari have seen fit to restore the name to their latest high performance car in 1985. The power comes from a 4,942cc flat-12, four-valve-per-cylinder engine mounted amidships in the car, and on top of the transmission. This impressive powerhouse produces 390bhp at 6,300rpm, to give the 1985 Testarossa a top speed of 181mph and acceleration from 0 to 62mph in 5.8 seconds.

The stunning body, like its predecessor, is from the studios of Pininfarina and, also like the earlier car, is like nothing else around today. The new radiator position, in the middle of the car instead of in the more usual place at the front, has been accommodated successfully in the body styling and although the car has its critics, to my mind Pininfarina have done an excellent job. The car is also very aerodynamically stable at all speeds, continuing the outstanding abilities of all recent Ferrari GT models.

The Testarossa's interior continues the constant improvement in driver and passenger accommodation that Ferraris have shown in the last few years and at the speeds that this car is capable of only the best ergonomics could be deemed as right. Noted journalist and former Ferrari team driver, Paul Frére, testing the new Testarossa, commented on the excellent roadholding and ride, the steering and braking performance, but added that the Ferrari trait of placing more emphasis on the engine than the chassis still remains in this latest Ferrari. Much as things change, they still remain the same, especially at Maranello!

By Ferrari standards, the styling of the new Testarossa is wildly extravagant but, as ever, the real story lies under the skin—in this case centering on the 5-litre 'boxer' engine with its red crackle-finish cam covers that give the car its name, Red Head.

FERRARI

FERRARI 308 GTB QV

I will only mention briefly the other Ferrari cars, not because they only warrant a few words, far from it, but because compared to the two new cars they are actually very well known and no long description is necessary. The 308 model comes in two styles, the GTB and the GTS, the former a coupé, the latter a spyder. Both use the latest 2,926cc four-valve V8 engine which develops 240bhp at 6,600rpm and gives the official designation Quattrovalvole, or QV. Both models can reach 158mph and accelerate from zero to 62mph in 7.3 seconds, while the spyder is slightly more expensive than the coupé.

S P E C I F I C A T I O N	
MODEL/TYPE	FERRARI 308 GTB QV
ENGINE	V8, 2,926CC, OHC
HORSEPOWER	240BHP @ 6,600RPM
TRANSMISSION	5-SPEED MANUAL
CHASSIS	STEEL TUBULAR
BRAKES	4-WHEEL DISC
TOP SPEED	158MPH
ACCELERATION 0–62MPH	7.3 SECS
PRODUCTION SPAN	1984 →

SPECIFICATION	
MODEL/TYPE	FERRARI TESTAROSSA
ENGINE	FLAT 12-CYL, DOHC
HORSEPOWER	390BHP @ 6,300RPM
TRANSMISSION	5-SPEED MANUAL
CHASSIS	TUBULAR STEEL
BRAKES	4-WHEEL DISC
TOP SPEED	181MPH
ACCELERATION 0-62MPH	5.8 SECS
PRODUCTION SPAN	1985 →

S P E C I F I C A T I O N	
MODEL/TYPE	FERRARI 308 GTS QV
ENGINE	V8, 2,926CC, OHC
HORSEPOWER	240BHP @ 6,600RPM
TRANSMISSION	5-SPEED MANUAL
CHASSIS	STEEL TUBULAR
BRAKES	4-WHEEL DISC
TOP SPEED	158MPH
ACCELERATION	N/A
PRODUCTION SPAN	1984 →

S P E C I F I C A T I O N	
MODEL/TYPE	FERRARI MONDIAL QV
ENGINE	V8, 2,926CC, SOHC
HORSEPOWER	240BHP @ 6,600RPM
TRANSMISSION	5-SPEED MANUAL
CHASSIS	STEEL MONOCOQUE
BRAKES	4-WHEEL DISC
TOP SPEED	149MPH
ACCELERATION 0–60MPH	6.4 SECS
PRODUCTION SPAN	1982 →

FERRARI MONDIAL QV

The Mondial model also comes in two similar body styles, and carries the same engine as the 308. Its top speed is 149mph and it will accelerate from 0–60mph in 6.4 seconds. As with the 308 spyder, the open-topped Mondial Cabriolet is rather more expensive than the coupé.

FERRARI 400i

The last Ferrari which I would mention is the 400i model, a full four-seater two-door car that is powered by a 4,823cc fuel-injected V12 engine. This car has the usual classic, ageless Pininfarina styling and despite being in production for many years still looks as up to date as any other performance car. It is one of the great classic cars of the modern era.

The supremely elegant 400i *(top right)* **offers 150mph-plus Ferrari motoring for four and was the first Ferrari ever to offer automatic transmission. The Mondial Cabriolet** *(opposite)* **provides wind-in-the-hair motoring for a privileged few and its cockpit** *(above)* **combines leather-trimmed luxury with straightforward, strictly functional controls. The hardtop version of the Mondial is shown on pages 50–51.**

S P E C I F I C A T I O N	
MODEL/TYPE	FERRARI 400i
ENGINE	V12, 4,823CC, SOHC
HORSEPOWER	315BHP @ 6,400RPM
TRANSMISSION	5-SP/3-SP AUTO
CHASSIS	STEEL MONOCOQUE
BRAKES	4-WHEEL DISC
TOP SPEED	152MPH
ACCELERATION	N/A
PRODUCTION SPAN	1982 →

The Ferrari 308GTB, styled by Pininfarina, was originally introduced in 1975 with a glass reinforced plastic body, but within a couple of years it reverted to a metal shell, under which now lurks a 240bhp four-valve V8 which is unmistakably Ferrari *(previous page).*

Like Lancia and Alfa Romeo, Maserati have had a long and often financially difficult history in fast car production. The company was founded by the five Maserati brothers, Carlo, Bindo, Alfieri, Mario and Ernesto in 1926 and their early cars were tough, hand-built, sensible machines for the competition driver. Always short of money really to develop their ideas, the brothers soldiered on until they were forced to sell out to the Orsi industrial combine in 1938, with Omer Orsi taking over as managing director. The company is now owned by the Argentine Alessandro De Tomaso who has continued the policy of building high quality, durable cars of high performance. One of the nicest touches about Maserati, even after several changes of ownership, is that the factory address still commemorates one of the brothers, Alfieri — the engineering genius of the family.

I would like to mention just two of their cars, the Merak SS and the Khamsin, as I feel that these are the two that embody all the finest qualities of the Maserati marque.

MASERATI

MASERATI MERAK SS

The Merak was first shown at the 1975 Geneva Auto Show. As with all Giugiaro-styled cars, it is very good looking, from every angle. Fit and finish of the bodywork are good rather than excellent and like all Italian cars, whatever their cost, any lapse in maintenance, cosmetic or mechanical, very soon shows itself. Some neglected five-year-old Meraks look ten times their age, while equally old models that have received regular loving attention look almost new.

Any mid-engined 2+2 car loses out in two major respects over more conventional, front-engined models, in accessibility to the engine and in a definite lack of real luggage carrying capacity. In these failings, however, the Merak is no better or worse than any similar car, and in one other respect the Merak is outstandingly good for a mid-engined car; unlike most, its three-quarter rear view vision is good, as the usual blind spot is much reduced by the use of the flying buttress rear window arrangement devised by Giugiaro.

The Merak SS's engine is a 2,965cc V6 with double overhead camshafts driven by a duplex chain. This engine produces 208bhp at 5,800rpm on three Weber twin-choke carburettors — two are 42DCNF31s and the third is a single 42DCNF32. This is enough to carry the car to a top speed of 143mph. However, there is one drawback to this engine, on driving the Merak at maximum revs for any length of time an alarming drop in registered oil pressure is noticed. This may be due to the all-alloy engine flexing, allowing the main bearings to release pressure, with dire effects on engine life. The maker's handbook simply recommends that the engine shouldn't be run at maximum speed for extended periods but there is no rev-limiting device to guard against this problem.

The lack of a modern fuel-injection system shows up in temperamental cold starts and fussy driving habits until the engine is fully warmed up. Fuel consumption averages out at about 18mpg, so that even with the 18.7-gallon tank only about 350 miles are possible between refills.

On the road, the Merak behaves like any good mid-engined car. It is stable, with a reasonable amount of understeer at all times, its ride is choppy at low speeds, improving with an increase in speed to become acceptable. Braking is by the Citroën high-pressure system and really isn't well suited to such a high performance machine, as its over-sensitivity hardly makes for smooth, fast progress.

The driving compartment is comfortable, with enough room for two average-sized adults, but the heating and ventilation systems are no better than poor, taking a very long time to warm up and then control of the heat is difficult and the ventilation almost non-existent! Air-conditioning is available as an extra, and is almost a necessity. The Merak is not a cheap car and is really for Maserati-lovers only, as there are certainly better value cars of similar performance on the market.

**Somehow, the Maserati name has never had quite the same *cachet* as Ferrari, but the Neptune's trident badge of the city of Bologna has nonetheless graced some superb cars.
The Maserati Merak SS (*opposite and previous page*) was introduced in 1975, the year in which Citroën, who had rescued the Bolognese company in 1968, relinquished control to Allesandro de Tomaso. Under de Tomaso's management, Maserati has made a remarkable recovery and for once in its troubled history can face the future with real confidence.**

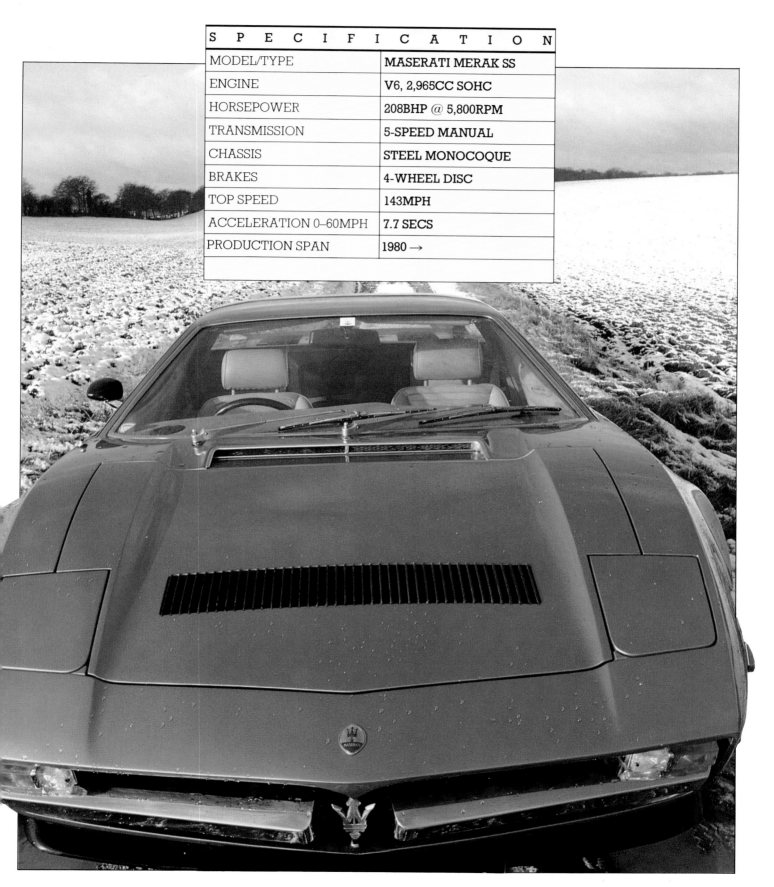

S P E C I F I C A T I O N	
MODEL/TYPE	MASERATI MERAK SS
ENGINE	V6, 2,965CC SOHC
HORSEPOWER	208BHP @ 5,800RPM
TRANSMISSION	5-SPEED MANUAL
CHASSIS	STEEL MONOCOQUE
BRAKES	4-WHEEL DISC
TOP SPEED	143MPH
ACCELERATION 0–60MPH	7.7 SECS
PRODUCTION SPAN	1980 →

MASERATI KHAMSIN

The Khamsin model is the final embodiment of the great front-engined, high-speed Maseratis, like the Mexico and the Mistral. As a design, it is now nearly 12 years old and many aspects of the car show this fact very clearly. The handsome body houses a front-mounted 4,700cc V8 engine, with double overhead cams, driven by a duplex chain. This power unit breathes through four Weber 42DCNF41 carburettors and produces 280bhp at 5,500rpm.

The Khamsin body although officially described as a 2+2 is really only a two-seater, as rear leg and head room are minimal at best. Accommodation for two, however, is comfortable, although the seats are covered in rather slippery leather, which, together with a strange lack of lateral support makes for less than positive driver location. The steering and seats are adjusted hydraulically, and the steering column can be adjusted for both length and rake by this system. The body styling is tasteful and the car is very well finished. The Khamsin is also very reasonably priced for a car that will reach 160mph and accelerate from 0 to 60mph in 6.5 seconds.

MASERATI

S P E C I F I C A T I O N	
MODEL/TYPE	MASERATI KHAMSIN
ENGINE	V8, 4,700CC DOHC
HORSEPOWER	280BHP @ 5,500RPM
TRANSMISSION	5-SPEED MANUAL
CHASSIS	STEEL MONOCOQUE
BRAKES	4-WHEEL DISC
TOP SPEED	160MPH
ACCELERATION 0–60MPH	6.5 SECS
PRODUCTION SPAN	1978 →

Although the Bertone-styled Maserati Khamsin, introduced in 1974, is now growing somewhat long in the tooth, it must still be regarded as a classic example of the traditional big front-engined supercar.

LAMBORGHINI

LAMBORGHINI COUNTACH S

Lamborghini is the relative newcomer among the classic Italian makes, but its engineering is second to none and its Countach S is arguably the most dramatic of all fast cars. It has one of the most outrageously extrovert bodies any car has ever been given. Standing still, it really does *look* as if it is doing 200mph! Although it is by no means a practical car, the Countach S makes the biggest automotive statement of any car on the road today. One problem for any owner of a Countach S, however, is that he must expect to be stopped fairly regularly by the police just because the car looks too fast for its own good!

What's more, it *is* fast; very fast. The 4,754cc double overhead cam V12 engine is rated at 375bhp at 7,000rpm. This gives the car a top speed of 174mph, accelerating it to 100mph from rest in 12.9 seconds! The car's performance really does match its appearance. It can stop too, with massive disc brakes all round, which will deliver 1.1g deceleration, stopping the car from 30mph in under 28 feet. Fuel consumption is only an average of 16mpg but with all this performance on hand who worries about the fuel bills?

If you've got it, flaunt it! The dramatic Lamborghini Countach S most certainly has it and isn't exactly shy about admitting it . . .

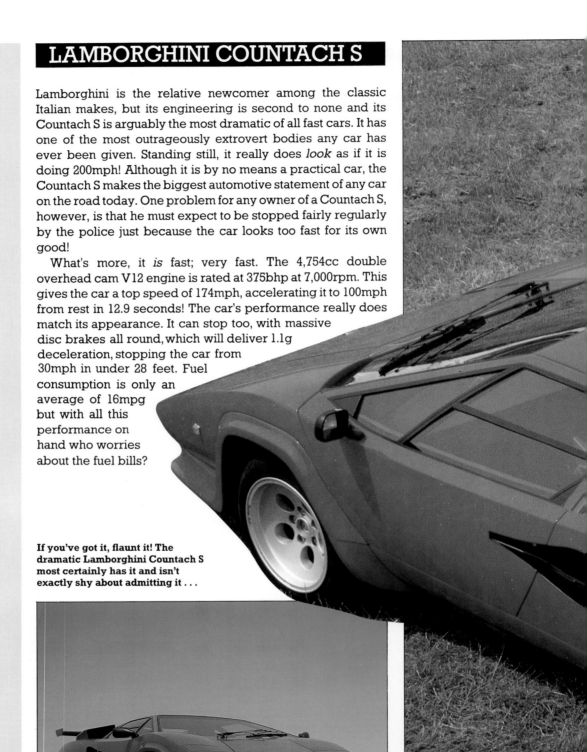

PYK 98Y

S P E C I F I C A T I O N	
MODEL/TYPE	LAMBORGHINI Countach S
ENGINE	V12, 4,754CC, DOHC
HORSEPOWER	375BHP @ 7,000RPM
TRANSMISSION	5-SPEED MANUAL
CHASSIS	STEEL MONOCOQUE
BRAKES	4-WHEEL DISC
TOP SPEED	174MPH
ACCELERATION 0–60MPH	4.8 SECS
PRODUCTION SPAN	1976 →

FIAT

My last selection for these ranks of fast Italian cars comes from Fiat, and it is the unexpectedly rapid Uno Turbo model. This car, which was launched in Rio during the weekend of the Brazilian Grand Prix in April 1985, has a turbocharged 1.3-litre engine with water injection and 105bhp, which gives the little hatchback a claimed top speed of 125mph and a zero to 62mph time of 8.3 seconds. It can also claim an overall fuel consumption of some 32mpg!

No price has been decided on but sales will begin late in 1985 and the Uno Turbo should be a welcome addition to the growing ranks of small, really fast cars.

With the exception of this forthcoming Fiat, really fast Italian cars are invariably exotic and very expensive, but for his money the buyer gets not only high performance but that other sought-after quality, exclusivity. There are some places in the world where Porsches seem as common as Volkswagen Beetles — just take a look at southern California for instance. Even in California though, the sight of a Ferrari Testarossa or a Lamborghini Countach S is a very rare treat.

Despite the imposition of speed limits (which few Italian drivers observe) Italy still makes very fast cars and makes them better than ever before; long may it continue to do so.

The boxy Fiat Uno Turbo may look like a fish out of water in this hallowed company of supercars but the mixture of small hatchback and turbo power adds up to a few surprises for 'real' sportscar drivers.

S P E C I F I C A T I O N	
MODEL/TYPE	FIAT UNO TURBO
ENGINE	4-CYL, 1,301CC TURBO
HORSEPOWER	105BHP @ 5,750RPM
TRANSMISSION	5-SPEED MANUAL
CHASSIS	STEEL MONOCOQUE
BRAKES	4-WHEEL DISC
TOP SPEED	125MPH
ACCELERATION 0–62MPH	8.3 SECS
PRODUCTION SPAN	1985 →

GREAT BRITAIN

Great Britain has always had its share of the fast car market, from Napiers before World War I, Bentleys after it, and Jaguars, Aston Martins, Bristols and AC Cobras since. Unlike those of many other countries, the British fast car industry has been heavily handicapped by speed limits, high insurance premiums and by the lack of a really rich mass of population wanting, and able to buy, expensive fast cars. However, in today's world and in spite of speed limits, there are more fast cars available to the British consumer than at any time in the country's motoring history. They range from the very expensive to the affordable. I will comment on thirteen (out of a list of several more) in this chapter.

Tackling them in alphabetical order, I will start with two Aston Martin models, the Lagonda and the Vantage. Both are very expensive, as befits hand-made vehicles. The Lagonda is priced at £65,999 on its home market, or almost twice the price of a Porsche 928. The Vantage costs £52,494, and both cars, even at these prices, are in considerable demand by customers all over the world. They combine the twin advantages of being rare items to be seen on the road and of having very high performance.

The best of British? Wind in the hair performance or exclusive elegance are both available from Aston Martin with the Vantage (*left*) or the strikingly individual and very rare Lagonda (*below*).

ASTON MARTIN LAGONDA

The Lagonda has a 5,340cc double overhead cam V8 engine breathing through four Weber 42DCNF90/100 carburettors. The Aston Martin factory in the small town of Newport Pagnell does not quote horsepower figures but the German ministry of transport requires all cars sold in the Federal Republic to disclose their power outputs and for that requirement Aston Martin have quoted a figure of 390bhp, which must be close to the mark.

Transmission from the front-mounted engine is via a Chrysler Torqueflite automatic gearbox to a chassis-mounted limited-slip differential. Front suspension is by the classic unequal length wishbone, coil-spring and damper set up, with an anti-roll bar. The rear suspension is self-levelling and features a de Dion axle. Steering is by power-assisted rack and pinion and brakes are ventilated disc units all round. The Lagonda uses 15 × 6in alloy wheels fitted as standard with the superb Avon Turbospeed 235/70 VR 15 tyres.

The car's instruments use digital LED displays and cover all possible information that the driver may need. The Lagonda weighs 4,622lb, has a top speed of 143mph and takes just 20.8 seconds to reach 100mph from a standstill. The William Towns-designed body is striking in appearance and certainly has looks in keeping with the price. The whole car exudes luxury and high performance

This classic power unit was introduced in 1970 and by 1972 it had replaced the long-serving six-cylinder unit as the standard Aston Martin engine. Most specialist manufacturers looking for more horsepower tend to turn to big, easily available American V8s but it is typical of Aston Martin's integrity that they looked to their own drawing boards and came up with an engine which powers not only their road cars but also the company's Nimrod Group C racing sportscar.

Tickford is Aston Martin Lagonda's advanced engineering and styling arm and even the lines of the stunning Lagonda saloon, originally styled by Bill Towns, can benefit from the Tickford touch.

S P E C I F I C A T I O N	
MODEL/TYPE	ASTON MARTIN Lagonda
ENGINE	V8, 5,340CC, SOHC
HORSEPOWER	N/A
TRANSMISSION	3-SPEED AUTO
CHASSIS	STEEL
BRAKES	4-WHEEL DISC
TOP SPEED	143MPH
ACCELERATION 0–60MPH	8.9 SECS
PRODUCTION SPAN	1980 →

ASTON MARTIN

ASTON MARTIN VANTAGE

The Aston Martin Vantage is a sports coupé in the old style, big, very fast, very expensive, constructed in the finest materials, and very beautifully finished. The car uses the same hand-built V8 engine as the Lagonda but with high-performance camshafts and bigger Weber 48IDF 3/150 carburettors increasing both power and torque. The gearbox is the ZF five-speed manual model which is heavy in operation but otherwise superb. Wheel sizes are also uprated compared to the Lagonda, to 15 × 8in and standard tyres are 275/55 VR 15 Pirelli P7s.

The Vantage is shatteringly fast, with a 168mph top speed and acceleration from 0 to 100mph in 11.9 seconds. Don't ask about fuel consumption which averages only 9–10mpg; in this league, such calculations never come into the equation. For such a large car, the Vantage is, surprisingly, really only a two-seater. Space for passengers in the back is, at best, minimal. Agility on twisty roads is obviously limited by sheer size, the car being much more suitable for long high-speed journeys preferably by unrestricted motorway.

The Aston Martin Vantage is the ultimate example of the traditional British sports coupé and if it is ever dropped from production by the powers-that-be at Newport Pagnell it will be sorely missed, even by those who will never be able to afford to buy one.

The Aston Martin Vantage (*inset*) and the drophead Volante (*below*) both look, and indeed feel, big, but their lusty V8 engines — all built **by hand and each bearing its builder's name on a brass plate — make them two of the fastest cars in the world.**

S P E C I F I C A T I O N	
MODEL/TYPE	ASTON MARTIN Vantage
ENGINE	V8, 5,340CC, SOHC
HORSEPOWER	N/A
TRANSMISSION	5-SPEED MANUAL
CHASSIS	STEEL
BRAKES	4-WHEEL DISC
TOP SPEED	168MPH
ACCELERATION 0–60MPH	5.2 SECS
PRODUCTION SPAN	1978 →

Next on the list are three cars from the Bristol Car Company, the Britannia, the Beaufighter and the Brigand—all named after famous Bristol aircraft from the company's earlier days. Although Bristol now use American V8 engines, the big, luxuriously appointed and extremely quick cars are in reality archetypally British. They are thoroughly conventional, even a little old fashioned in overall concept, but what they lack in high technology or advanced thinking they more than make up for in engineering quality.

This is a logical result of a background in aero engineering, where fundamental change is slow but quality is everything. Aircraft were Bristol's forté up to the end of the war in 1945, when the Bristol Aircraft Company sought new employment for suddenly redundant production capacity and opened a car division—which had been under consideration even during the war.

The first Bristol car, launched in 1947, was based on much-improved prewar BMW six-cylinder engines and chassis, rights to which Bristol had acquired as wartime reparations. Bristol's main improvements to the BMW engines were in the use of superior materials—unavailable in prewar Germany as high-grade metals were already being diverted to military use.

With these first cars, the Bristol reputation for performance with quality was born. The Bristol has never been a slavish follower of fashion, never for instance changing its shape simply to attract a fickle buying public. The cars are made by hand, slowly and at a rate of only three a week. They are bought and driven, usually with some verve, by real enthusiasts. Packard used to use the slogan 'Ask the man who owns one' and every Packard owner by implication became an unpaid salesman. Bristol might use the same words; every single Bristol owner I have ever met loves his car (or sometimes cars) and cannot wait to start selling the virtues of the make to anyone who will listen.

From the BMW-engined models, Bristol developed their own, classic, hemi-headed straight-six engine and this, in superbly developed chassis, was used until 1961. Then, having rejected the option of building their own V8 engine as being too expensive for three cars a week, Bristol began its association with American power which continues in the superb cars described here.

BRISTOL BRIGAND

The most expensive of the current Bristol range is the Brigand, a turbocharged two-door four-seater saloon whose sleek lines date back to 1978 and the introduction of what was then known as the 603 saloon. At a price in Britain of £52,692, the Brigand costs a few pounds more than the thoroughbred Aston Martin Vantage and not much less than the normally-aspirated version of the Bentley Mulsanne—each of which uses its own

design and make of V8. This is not to imply that the Bristol is in any way inferior, in fact at least one magazine road-tester has described the Bristol as being, overall, the best car in the world, at any price.

That, as with any car, is open to endless argument, but with a top speed of 150mph and the ability to reach 60mph from rest in under six seconds, the Brigand is not as quick as the Vantage (but then nor is much else) but will comfortably outrun the 'ordinary' Mulsanne.

Part of the Bristol's strength lies in its chassis performance, where the engineering quality is really evident, and although it will give best place to many modern supercars, its ride and handling are quite exceptional for such a luxurious, spacious saloon.

S P E C I F I C A T I O N	
MODEL/TYPE	BRISTOL BRIGAND
ENGINE	CHRYSLER V8, TURBO
HORSEPOWER	N/A
TRANSMISSION	CHRYSLER AUTO
CHASSIS	BOX SECTION STEEL
BRAKES	4-WHEEL DISC
TOP SPEED	150MPH
ACCELERATION 0–60MPH	5.9 SECS
PRODUCTION SPAN	1984 →

Although many other Anglo-American hybrids have been hastily conceived and appropriately short-lived, the 140mph Bristol Britannia saloon **shows that a marriage of the best British engineering and an American mass-produced power unit can result in a genuine classic car.**

design and make of V8. This is not to imply that the Bristol is in any way inferior, in fact at least one magazine road-tester has described the Bristol as being, overall, the best car in the world, at any price.

That, as with any car, is open to endless argument, but with a top speed of 150mph and the ability to reach 60mph from rest in under six seconds, the Brigand is not as quick as the Vantage (but then nor is much else) but will comfortably outrun the 'ordinary' Mulsanne.

Part of the Bristol's strength lies in its chassis performance, where the engineering quality is really evident, and although it will give best place to many modern supercars, its ride and handling are quite exceptional for such a luxurious, spacious saloon.

S P E C I F I C A T I O N	
MODEL/TYPE	BRISTOL BRIGAND
ENGINE	CHRYSLER V8, TURBO
HORSEPOWER	N/A
TRANSMISSION	CHRYSLER AUTO
CHASSIS	BOX SECTION STEEL
BRAKES	4-WHEEL DISC
TOP SPEED	150MPH
ACCELERATION 0–60MPH	5.9 SECS
PRODUCTION SPAN	1984 →

Although many other Anglo-American hybrids have been hastily conceived and appropriately short-lived, the 140mph Bristol Britannia saloon shows that a marriage of the best British engineering and an American mass-produced power unit can result in a genuine classic car.

BRISTOL

S P E C I F I C A T I O N	
MODEL/TYPE	**BRISTOL BEAUFIGHTER**
ENGINE	**CHRYSLER V8, TURBO**
HORSEPOWER	**N/A**
TRANSMISSION	**CHRYSLER AUTO**
CHASSIS	**STEEL BOX SECTION**
BRAKES	**4-WHEEL DISC**
TOP SPEED	**150MPH**
ACCELERATION 0–60MPH	**5.9 SECS**
PRODUCTION SPAN	**1984 →**

BRISTOL BEAUFIGHTER

The most glamorous of the Bristol range, if such a term is appropriate, is the turbocharged Beaufighter, which shares the same version of the Chrysler hemi as the Brigand saloon. The Beaufighter however is a much more distinctive and rather angular car, distinguished by its flamboyant targa-type top, with a substantial roll-hoop and a lift off centre section.

The car was styled by Zagato and introduced as the 412 Convertible, later known as the Convertible Saloon, in 1975. Also among its styling features is the traditional Bristol way of housing the spare wheel in a concealed compartment in the front wing. The turbocharged version and the Beaufighter name were launched in 1980 and the superb car has been little changed since then.

Like the similarly-powered Brigand, it will reach 150mph and cover zero to 60mph in 5.9 seconds. The Beaufighter is the cheapest car in the Bristol range but with only a little change from £50,000 on the British market it is marginally more expensive than the cheapest Aston Martin or the newly intro-duced Bentley Eight—its most obvious esoteric British rivals. Price however is not the most important consideration at this end of the market and the Bristol appeal is unique. For such large, heavy and well-equipped machines they are surprisingly light in feel, easy to drive well and only a little harder to drive really quickly. What more could any sybaritic enthusiast ask?

BENTLEY MULSANNE

When the Bentley company was sold to Rolls-Royce in 1931 it was soon apparent that the old Bentley, the blood-and-guts fast sportscar, would be smoothed and softened into no more than a very nice but unremarkable open Rolls-Royce, and the days of real performance would be over. It took Rolls-Royce 51 years to introduce a Bentley that was more than a re-badged, re-radiatored Rolls-Royce. The Mulsanne model, named after the famous straight on the Le Mans racing circuit, the scene of the beginning of the old Bentley legend, is, at last, a really fast Bentley, one that W. O. Bentley himself would certainly not have disowned. W.O. always disliked and would have nothing to do with supercharged engines, feeling that if more power was required he could easily provide it with more capacity, while retaining all the flexibility and reliability that his cars were renowned for. In his day the supercharger was not for the ordinary motorist and was justifiably viewed with suspicion when fitted to an everyday car.

The Mulsanne has changed all that, for it is one of the very best of the current crop of boosted induction cars. Its 6.75-litre V8 engine produces an undisclosed amount of power, but sufficient to propel the heavy car (weighing 5,051lb) to speeds of over 130mph and from zero to 60mph in 7.4 seconds. It seats four people in great comfort and can transport them with a smoothness and speed that are uncanny. Handling is a little 'soft', with rather too much roll in cornering but a Bentley is not usually hustled around like a Ferrari and with normal Bentley-style driving it is a delight — albeit an expensive delight at £63,288 on its home market. Rolls-Royce-made automobiles have a justified reputation for retaining their resale value better than most other cars and it is almost certain that the Mulsanne will be one of the great collectors' cars of the not-too-distant future, fetching very high prices.

S P E C I F I C A T I O N	
MODEL/TYPE	BENTLEY MULSANNE
ENGINE	V8, 6,750CC, TURBO
HORSEPOWER	N/A
TRANSMISSION	3-SPEED AUTO
CHASSIS	STEEL MONOCOQUE
BRAKES	4-WHEEL DISC
TOP SPEED	135MPH
ACCELERATION 0–60MPH	7.4 SECS
PRODUCTION SPAN	1984 →

Ettore Bugatti once described the Bentleys which beat his own cars at Le Mans in the 1920s as *'les plus vites camions du monde'*—the fastest lorries in the world. No lorry however was ever as fast or as luxurious as the Bentley Mulsanne, named for the famous straight on the Le Mans circuit where Bentleys had their finest hour.

FORD

At the other end of the price and exclusivity spectrum are Ford's two fast cars in Great Britain, the XR4i and the Capri Special Injection. These two follow in the tradition of all Ford products in offering fine value-for-money vehicles, and in both cases they also have the bonus of being very fast!

FORD CAPRI 2.8i

The Capri was originally introduced in 1968 and like the Porsche 911 has so far refused to lie down and die, but now it looks as if 1985 will be positively the last year for the Capri as we know it and a replacement is already being developed to go into the dealers in the spring of 1986.

It is not difficult to understand why the Capri has lasted so long. It is a good looking car and it performs well — especially in the old 3-litre version and in the current 2.8-litre model. It is backed by one of the biggest service organizations in the world and parts and maintenance for it are not expensive. In short, it works and the customers love it!

The present ultimate Capri in Europe is the Injection Special, and for just under £10,000 in Britain the customer will get a stylish, hatchback coupé, that is well made and well finished, that will deliver 160bhp from its Bosch K-Jetronic injected engine, enough to hit 125mph in fourth gear at 5,700rpm. Acceleration from 0 to 60mph is also very brisk at 7.9 seconds.

Apart from sheer performance, what does the Injection Special offer the buyer over and above the 'ordinary' Capri? Well, for the extra money, the buyer gets Recaro seating, a leather-bound steering wheel, alloy road wheels and a limited slip differential. Fuel economy, which is most important in any Ford model, works out at an average of 25mpg, and that is very good in view of the car's performance.

Riding on 205/60 VR 13 Goodyear NCT tyres, the Capri is a marvellous car to drive fast on dry roads and its basic oversteer characteristics allow the competent driver to explore really fast cornering in great safety. In the wet, however, it is a different story and care has to be exercised, because as with any front-engined, nose-heavy car, the tail can move out too far if the driver is careless. Braking is initially good but from really high speeds there is a lack of real bite and stopping from speed can be ragged. Nevertheless, the Capri remains one of the best performance-for-money buys around today and Ford will have a very hard job replacing it

Both top-of-the-range cars use essentially the same V6 engine (with minor power output differences) and the same five-speed gearbox, but the utterly conventional Capri is still the cheaper of the two—and the better equipped. Although four-wheel-drive and turbocharged Sierras are also now available, it will probably be a long time before the new car's popularity reaches the peaks once enjoyed by the Capri.

S P E C I F I C A T I O N	
MODEL/TYPE	FORD CAPRI 2.8i
ENGINE	V6, 2,792CC
HORSEPOWER	160BHP @ 5,700RPM
TRANSMISSION	5-SPEED MANUAL
CHASSIS	STEEL MONOCOQUE
BRAKES	4-WHEEL DISC
TOP SPEED	130MPH
ACCELERATION 0–60MPH	7.9 SECS
PRODUCTION SPAN	1968 →

Power to the people! Ford may not build a true sportscar but the 2.8 injection version of the enormously popular Capri coupé offers exciting performance without breaking the bank— although not for much longer.

S P E C I F I C A T I O N	
MODEL/TYPE	FORD SIERRA XR4i
ENGINE	V6, 2,792CC
HORSEPOWER	150BHP @ 5,700RPM
TRANSMISSION	5-SPEED MANUAL
CHASSIS	STEEL MONOCOQUE
BRAKES	4-WHEEL DISC
TOP SPEED	130MPH
ACCELERATION 0–60MPH	8 SECS
PRODUCTION SPAN	1982 →

FORD SIERRA XR4i

The Sierra XR4i can perhaps best be thought of as a four-seater version of what the new Capri will offer in coupé form. As with the Capri, a front-mounted pushrod V6 engine is used to drive the rear wheels via a five-speed manual gearbox. The 2,792cc engine develops 150bhp at 5,700rpm. The Sierra's suspension, unlike the Capri's, is all-independent, and its brakes are ventilated front discs and rear drums, these just like the Capri. Because of the XR4i's more aerodynamic shape, it slips through the air much better than the older Capri and the lower horsepower actually produces both better acceleration, with 0–60mph in 8.4 seconds, and a higher top speed, at 130mph. Over long distances the XR4i's quieter mode of travel is considerably less tiring than the Capri. Lacking a limited slip differential, however, and on narrower 195/60 VR 14 Goodyear NCT tyres, the XR4i is not so pleasant to drive fast as the Capri, it feels 'looser', and the power-assisted steering is not so crisp and accurate in feel as that of the Capri. The Sierra's braking has a better feel than the Capri's stoppers, but the brakes tend to be noisy when used hard.

The XR4i really takes off where the Capri finishes, it is a very good car, capable of much development over the next few years and it seems likely that it will simply get better and better as time passes.

There has also been some debate over the Sierra's high-speed stability in strong crosswinds and this has added—probably more than the car deserves—to the worrying sales resistance caused initially by the controversial styling. Ford are certainly keeping faith with the Sierra however, both in Europe and in America, where the car is the basis of the turbo-engined Merkur, described later.

The Ford Sierra's styling is nothing if not controversial; variously loved or hated, it has been affectionately dubbed 'the jelly mould'. With typically accurate feel for what the people want, Ford gave the XR4-i its bi-plane spoiler and racier trim and created a totally different image which spoke of performance.

FORD (SA) XR8

In July 1984 Ford of South Africa announced a variation on the XR4i theme, the XR8. This is a limited edition of the Sierra model but with the Mustang V8 engine, rated at 200bhp, plus a five-speed close-ratio gearbox and with disc brakes fitted all round. If the specification sounds rather on the racy side, then it will come as no surprise to learn that the XR8 is intended as an homologation special so that Ford of South Africa can go production saloon car racing. The 5-litre engine will run the car up to more than 140mph and from 0 to 62mph in less than 8 seconds. The car has the five-door body shell and it will be offered only in white. Only 250 examples will be built and all of them are expected to be sold before the last car is finished, at a price which has not yet been announced but is likely to be substantial.

The South African-built Ford XR8 is a hybrid of the European Sierra body shell (*below left*) and American Ford V8 power — aimed unashamedly at putting Ford's South African cars in the forefront of production saloon racing.

S P E C I F I C A T I O N	
MODEL/TYPE	FORD (SA) XR8
ENGINE	V8, 5,000CC
HORSEPOWER	200BHP @ 4,800RPM
TRANSMISSION	5-SPEED MANUAL
CHASSIS	STEEL MONOCOQUE
BRAKES	4-WHEEL DISC
TOP SPEED	140MPH PLUS
ACCELERATION 0–60MPH	7.6 SECS
PRODUCTION SPAN	1984 →

FORD

Since the introduction of the XK-120, Jaguar have established themselves as the makers of some of the finest high speed cars in the world — at any price. Classic examples include the 150S, the C-type, D-type and E-type models, the fabulous, one-off XK-13, the XJ-S and the superb XJ-S HE. All but one of Jaguar's current cars will exceed 125mph and the XJ-S HE will reach 155mph!

JAGUAR XJ-6

I intend to look at two models, the XJ-S HE and the XJ-6 4.2-litre. The latter is powered by an in-line six-cylinder twin-cam engine, possibly the final flowering of the same engine that powered the XK-120 over 30 years ago. It now uses Bosch L-Jetronic fuel injection to produce 205bhp at 5,000rpm and this is enough to propel the car to a top speed of 130mph, and accelerate it from a standstill to 60mph in 9.8 seconds, in spite of a weight of 4,035lb.

As with all the XJ models, that is not the whole story. It is much more the manner of the Jaguar's performance that is important. On a value-for-money basis there is nothing to touch the way the Jaguar goes about its work. Smoothly, very quietly and with a silky quality that nothing else can match, the car from Brown's Lane, Coventry puts every other high-quality fast car into the shade.

Until the arrival of John Egan, as managing director, Jaguar suffered from a build quality problem, but under his direction this has changed dramatically; and there are even waiting lists. Buyers are snapping up all models of the car world-wide. This Jaguar revival is particularly apparent in North America and in Germany, where sales have taken off in the last two years to such an extent that in some places a premium has to be paid to get a new Jaguar!

S P E C I F I C A T I O N	
MODEL/TYPE	JAGUAR XJ-6
ENGINE	6-CYL, 4,235CC, DOHC
HORSEPOWER	205BHP @ 5,000RPM
TRANSMISSION	5-SP/3-SP AUTO
CHASSIS	STEEL MONOCOQUE
BRAKES	4-WHEEL DISC
TOP SPEED	130MPH
ACCELERATION 0–60MPH	9.8 SECS
PRODUCTION SPAN	1984 →

Unmistakably Jaguar: the simple lines of the XJ-6 are instantly recognizable as a product of Britain's best known maker of sportscars and luxury sporting saloons.

JAGUAR XJ-S HE

If it is a two seater or 2+2 Jaguar that is required then the XJ-S HE model is the one to go for. Equipped with a fuel-injected V12 engine that even Mercedes-Benz admit is the best mass-produced high performance engine made anywhere in the world, the big coupé has no real rival at its home market price of £23,385. The 5.3-litre overhead-cam engine uses Bosch digital electronic fuel injection and an electronic ignition system. Fuel economy works out at 22.5mpg at 75mph, which is quite remarkable for this large, very fast car which will reach 155mph and storm from zero to 60mph in 7.5 seconds.

Both these cars are beautifully made and finished and Jaguar cannot build enough to meet the current demand for either of them.

Jaguar purists may never have been quite sure about the XJ-S's controversial shape but this car, with its superb V12 engine, is quite simply one of the best cars in the world at any price.

S P E C I F I C A T I O N	
MODEL/TYPE	JAGUAR XJ-S HE
ENGINE	V12, 5,345CC, DOHC
HORSEPOWER	299BHP @ 5,500RPM
TRANSMISSION	3-SPEED AUTO
CHASSIS	STEEL MONOCOQUE
BRAKES	4-WHEEL DISC
TOP SPEED	155MPH
ACCELERATION 0–60MPH	7.5 SECS
PRODUCTION SPAN	1980 →

As with Jaguar, I have selected two cars from the Lotus range, the Excel and the Esprit Turbo, to demonstrate the special Lotus qualities. For 1985 Lotus have revised these models quite significantly, with new body styling, wheels and tyres, electrics, instruments, air conditioning, hard trim and soft trim. The new body is certainly better looking than the old, it is cleaner and more 'of a piece' than before. The chassis is still the familiar steel backbone with a five-year anti-corrision warranty. Thanks to the restyled body, the rear window is 25% bigger and access to the boot is much improved. New VDO instruments called Night Design have been relocated in the dash panel to better effect.

The engine is the 912-type 2.2-litre 16-valve double overhead cam four-cylinder unit, which produces 160bhp at 6,500rpm. A five-speed gearbox is used and rear-wheel drive. All-independent suspension displays all the features that Lotus are famous for, the very highest levels of roadholding with no sacrifice to ride or comfort. Power-assistance to the rack-and-pinion steering is optional. Ventilated disc brakes are used all round and the system is servo-assisted. Alloy road wheels of 14 × 7in carry 205/60 VR 14 Goodyear NCT tyres.

LOTUS EXCEL

The Excel has the performance to go with its good looks, with a top speed of 134mph and 0–100mph in 20 seconds, with a fuel consumption of 29.4mpg at 75mph. A colleague who loves Porsches recently reported that he had tried a new Excel and was astonished not only at how well it performed but also at the very high standards of build quality. There is no denying that for far too long Lotus have had a very poor reputation for quality in their cars but in the last two or three years they have made great efforts to overcome these problems and it would appear that they are having success, which, happily, is being reflected in increasing sales.

S P E C I F I C A T I O N	
MODEL/TYPE	LOTUS EXCEL
ENGINE	4-CYL, 2,174CC, SOHC
HORSEPOWER	160BHP @ 6,500RPM
TRANSMISSION	5-SPEED MANUAL
CHASSIS	STEEL BACKBONE
BRAKES	4-WHEEL DISC
TOP SPEED	134MPH
ACCELERATION 0–60MPH	7 SECS
PRODUCTION SPAN	1984 →

A subtle rounding out of the Lotus Excel's extremities has given looks to match the car's performance from the neat 16-valve four-cylinder engine *(opposite bottom)*. The four-seater Lotus is big but not heavy, quick but easily handled and exclusive but not unattainable.

LOTUS ESPRIT TURBO

The 1985 Esprit Turbo has a number of all-new features, in particular a new chassis and revised front suspension, as well as new brakes, electrics, tyres and body and trim details. The chassis now has an eight-year anti-corrosion warranty.

The heart of the Turbo is the mid-mounted 910 2.2-litre four-cylinder engine with four valves per cylinder. The turbo-charger blows through two Dellorto carburettors which are mounted as close as possible to the intake manifold so that turbo-lag is virtually eliminated. Power of 210bhp is delivered at 6,500rpm, giving the car a top speed of 152mph. Acceleration from zero to 100mph takes an astonishing 14.6 seconds. Remarkable fuel economy bears out the high efficiency of this engine, being quoted as 24.1mpg at a steady 75mph.

This extraordinary car is given one of the most dramatic shapes by the Italian stylist Giugiaro and like so many of his best designs for fast cars it looks to be travelling fast even when standing still. For two people (with only a small amount of luggage) it is one of the best ways of covering long distances at very high speeds in comfort and safety.

LOTUS

S P E C I F I C A T I O N	
MODEL/TYPE	LOTUS ESPRIT TURBO
ENGINE	4-CYL, 2,174CC, SOHC
HORSEPOWER	210BHP @ 6,500RPM
TRANSMISSION	5-SPEED MANUAL
CHASSIS	STEEL BACKBONE
BRAKES	4-WHEEL DISC
TOP SPEED	152MPH
ACCELERATION 0–60MPH	5.5 SECS
PRODUCTION SPAN	1980 →

The mid-engined Lotus Esprit Turbo amply demonstrates Lotus's late founder Colin Chapman's philosophy of 'no bloody compromise'. If you want this kind of performance you must travel light and if you don't want to hear the engine noise, buy a bike.

LOTUS ETNA

LOTUS

In October 1984 Lotus announced their new 'Concept' car, called the Etna. This could be, indeed should be, the Lotus standard-bearer to take them into the 1990s. Styled by Giugiaro at Ital Design, it has one of the cleanest, most dashing body shapes ever seen on a British car. Slightly larger than the current Esprit model, it is hoped that it will be very little heavier than that car in spite of having the exciting new Lotus V8 engine installed. It is expected that it will cost £35,000 in Britain when in production. The whole car promises to be state-of-the-art in super-fast car construction and performance and other fast car makers will have to watch out once this car gets into the showrooms.

The heart of the Etna will be the new V8 engine. This 4-litre unit develops 340bhp now, with much more to come if the care in development that Lotus is lavishing upon it is anything to go by. This engine will be the jewel in the crown of the remarkable new Lotus, but it looks as if it will be 1987 before the first production cars come off the Hethel production lines.

S P E C I F I C A T I O N	
MODEL/TYPE	LOTUS ETNA
ENGINE	V8, 4,000CC, DOHC
HORSEPOWER	340BHP @ 6,500RPM
TRANSMISSION	5-SPEED MANUAL
CHASSIS	STEEL BACKBONE
BRAKES	4-WHEEL DISC
TOP SPEED	182MPH
ACCELERATION 0–100MPH	10.6 SECS
PRODUCTION SPAN	1987 →

Lotus's next-generation supercar, the Giugiaro-styled V8-powered Etna, caused a sensation when it was unveiled in prototype form in 1984—and not surprisingly so. It is by far the most sophisticated Lotus to date and by far the quickest ever for the road.

JAPAN

Until recent years, the Japanese auto industry has concentrated mainly on producing transportation for millions of buyers world-wide who require no more than reliable, inexpensive cars. Their performance cars could be counted on the fingers of less than one hand but in the last four or five years that has begun to change and now there are several very worthy vehicles coming out of Japanese factories that, on their own merits, qualify for a place in this book.

A car that can probably make an honest claim to having been the first complete Japanese performance car must be the Datsun 240Z. The trouble with the 240Z is that the makers, Nissan, were so impressed by their success in the North American market that they fell into the trap of making regular changes to the car along the lines of giving it more comfort, more chromium plating, more styling features, more weight, more engine and more gadgets. All of that simply added more bulk to the whole car and gradually eroded the vehicle's initially impressive performance, making the last of the line, the 280ZX, into a caricature of the original (a pig's ear out of a near silk purse).

Japanese industry, however, whatever the product, has the flexibility and the long-range commercial vision to take heed of past mistakes and it also has the money to put them right, even if that means starting with a clean sheet of paper. There are now several Japanese cars that deserve close scrutiny.

S P E C I F I C A T I O N	
MODEL/TYPE	NISSAN 300ZX TURBO
ENGINE	V6, 2,960CC, OHC, TURBO
HORSEPOWER	228BHP @ 5,400RPM
TRANSMISSION	5-SPEED MANUAL
CHASSIS	STEEL MONOCOQUE
BRAKES	4-WHEEL DISC
TOP SPEED	141MPH
ACCELERATION 0–60MPH	7.2 SECS
PRODUCTION SPAN	1984 →

NISSAN 300ZX TURBO

As Nissan were the first mass producer of a fast Japanese car it is only right that they should start off this chapter with their latest 300ZX Turbo. The car's makers claim a top speed of 141mph and 0–60mph in 7.2 seconds, while the 300ZX Turbo also has a reasonable fuel consumption figure of 21.5mpg. Those are the bare facts but there is more to any car than just those, and it is interesting to see that the 300ZX shapes up pretty well on the road.

The car's clean shape is broken only by the necessary bonnet top bulge and a 'sameness' about its overall styling; aerodynamic considerations now play such a significant part in any car's appearance that they just have to be overlooked. The 2.96-litre V6 engine is boosted by a Garrett turbocharger to give 228bhp at 5,400rpm. Electronic fuel injection and ignition are fitted to aid the splendid flexibility which is one of the V6's best features.

On driving off in the 300ZX Turbo, the comfort and refinement are most noticeable. Noise insulation is good but not so good is the rather too soft ride, an obvious sop to a part of the American market that the car could well do without. At high speeds there is too much wind noise for real comfort.

Roadholding is uniformly good and the car has no particularly bad habits so long as its understeering tendency is kept in mind. Slow in and fast out is the watchword when driving the 300ZX Turbo fast through corners. Wet road behaviour is not so good, mainly because of the lack of real grip from the Japanese-made 205/55 VR 16 Dunlop tyres, which let go far too early for any driver's peace of mind. The dampers have a dash adjustable control which allows the driver to select either soft, normal or firm settings. Set on 'firm', the car becomes too nervous and could give a driver problems if driven too fast on twisty roads, so most people stay with the 'soft' setting, which suits the car's American nature much more. The brakes, discs all round, are well up to the task of stopping the 300ZX Turbo at

S P E C I F I C A T I O N	
MODEL/TYPE	NISSAN SILVIA TURBO
ENGINE	4-CYL, 1,809CC, TURBO
HORSEPOWER	135BHP @ 6,000RPM
TRANSMISSION	5-SP/3-SP AUTO
CHASSIS	STEEL MONOCOQUE
BRAKES	4-WHEEL DISC
TOP SPEED	126MPH
ACCELERATION 0–60MPH	8.9 SECS
PRODUCTION SPAN	1984 →

all the speeds that it is capable of.

At nearly twice the price of a Ford Capri 2.8 Injection Special the Nissan is not twice as good a car and on this basis, at least, does not represent good value for money.

NISSAN SILVIA TURBO

The smaller sister car to the 300ZX Turbo is much more in the cast of a European sports coupé. This is the Nissan Silvia Turbo ZX. It uses a turbocharged 1.8-litre overhead-cam engine, which delivers 135bhp and a claimed top speed of 126mph, plus the benefits of engine efficiency revealed by an excellent fuel economy figure of 44mpg at 65mph.

For lazy drivers, the Silvia can be ordered with a three-speed plus overdrive top automatic gearbox but the manual five-speed 'box is really too good to pass up. With all-round independent suspension, rack-and-pinion steering and four-wheel disc brakes, the chassis is well equipped to handle the engine's fine performance. The Silvia is better balanced than the 300ZX Turbo, and has an outstanding ability to cover the miles fast and safely. Its styling is perhaps just a little too bland, even anonymous, to be a head-turner, but it is clean and aerodynamically stable. The car is a pleasure to drive when carrying just two people and their luggage but as a 2+2 it has only limited use for four adults. The Silvia Turbo ZX then, can be summed up as an efficient, fast coupé but bland to the point of being characterless.

The Nissan 300ZX Turbo is the latest in a line which started with the 240Z—when Nissan still called its cars Datsuns—and it is the best in the series since the classic original. The Nissan Silvia Turbo is Nissan's alternative performance car.

COLT

COLT STARION

The Mitsubishi Colt Starion is another Japanese performance coupé which uses the assistance of a turbocharger to boost its power. This model has a 2-litre engine, rather smaller than the norm for this size of car, but the latest model utilizes all the latest turbo technology to extract an excellent 168bhp at 5,500rpm, giving the Starion a claimed top speed of 137mph. Acceleration from zero to 62mph is equally impressive, at just 7.6 seconds.

Spoilers front and rear aid aerodynamics and combat lift at speed but do not detract from the clean shape of the car, especially now that it has a clean bonnet top, without the previous power bulge. The Starion's steering is different from that of other Japanese fast cars (with the one exception of the Mazda RX-7) in being of recirculating-ball type. This in a Japanese application usually means a deadness in the straight ahead position and a certain looseness in feel. However, like BMW, Mitsubishi have produced a system using this method that is very close to being as good as a rack and pinion set-up. A five-speed manual gearbox is standard with ratios that complement the blown four-cylinder engine's power output extremely well.

The Starion also has a new door hinge design that is double jointed and allows a wider opening, making for easier entry and exit. The driving compartment is very fully equipped, with good seats, an equally good driving position with all controls to hand and vision out is as good as that in any other fast coupé, and better than some.

On the road the Starion is great fun, yet not tiring to drive for long distances. Wind noise is unusually low, complementing the easy nature of the car. At 100mph, with less than 4,000rpm on the tachometer, the car is uncanny, it is *so* quiet. With its 16.5-gallon fuel tank and an average consumption of around 25mpg, the Starion can really cover the miles between refuelling and at least 350 miles per tank is normal. Because of the size of the fuel tank, however, luggage space is rather more limited than in other coupés.

Handling is good, being firm and slightly choppy as the all-round MacPherson strut-type suspension is more biased to handling than to ride comfort and in my opinion that is justified by the competent manner of its going. The brakes are quite simply superb — they stopped the car from all speeds without any drama at all and are one of the best features of the car (although the interior is also a feature to be commented upon, as it is to a very high standard, in fit and finish and in its ergonomics which allow the driver and passenger to enjoy the car to the maximum).

Unlike many Japanese cars which I find rather bland, the Starion has real character, is enormous fun to use and is well enough made to represent a long term investment in a fast car.

S P E C I F I C A T I O N	
MODEL/TYPE	COLT STARION
ENGINE	4-CYL, 1,987CC, TURBO
HORSEPOWER	168BHP @ 5,500RPM
TRANSMISSION	5-SPEED MANUAL
CHASSIS	STEEL MONOCOQUE
BRAKES	4-WHEEL DISC
TOP SPEED	137MPH
ACCELERATION 0–62MPH	7.6 SECS
PRODUCTION SPAN	1983 →

Colt's considerable experience—and success—in production racing is evidenced by the company's reputation for building rapid and rugged cars for the road, from small turbo hatchbacks to this top-of-the-range Starion coupé.

S P E C I F I C A T I O N	
MODEL/TYPE	TOYOTA CELICA SUPRA
ENGINE	6-CYL, 2,759CC, SOHC
HORSEPOWER	168BHP @ 5,600RPM
TRANSMISSION	5-SPEED MANUAL
CHASSIS	STEEL MONOCOQUE
BRAKES	4-WHEEL DISC
TOP SPEED	136MPH
ACCELERATION 0–60MPH	8.3 SECS
PRODUCTION SPAN	1984 →

Toyota have made very great steps in the last three years to uprate their 'Old man' image. To this end they have been improving several of their cars and as recently as January 1985 they introduced two new fast models that should appeal to fast car fans world-wide.

TOYOTA CELICA SUPRA

The Celica Supra 2.8i has been updated, and is interesting in that in the suspension department it now displays the first results of the Toyota/Lotus partnership.

First, however, to the engine, which is a classic 2,759cc twin-cam straight-six driving the rear axle via a five-speed gearbox. It produces 168bhp at 5,600rpm using electronic fuel injection. Brakes are ventilated discs at both front and rear, with servo-assistance. Steering is by an excellent power-assisted rack-and-pinion system. These features, plus the use of 225/60VR 14 tyres and the Lotus-inspired changes to the chassis, make for a car that although lacking the power of its turbocharged rivals can happily stay with them during high speed cross-country travel.

The engine and transmission are a delight. Not having turbo-boost means not having any turbo-lag and the spread of engine power is such that the Supra is more relaxing to drive in all conditions of road, traffic and weather than most. Fit and finish are first-rate and although there is much evidence of plastic in the interior, it is very tastefully done and doesn't detract too much. With a top speed of 136mph and a time of 8.3 seconds for 0–60mph, the Supra is certainly no slouch and it is also very fine value for money.

The splendid mid-engined Toyota MR2 (top) is one of the most exciting new cars for many years for lovers of the fast car and with the more conventional but even faster Celica Supra (right), offers proof positive that the world's biggest motor manufacturer still believes in performance.

S P E C I F I C A T I O N	
MODEL/TYPE	TOYOTA MR2
ENGINE	4-CYL, 1,587CC, DOHC
HORSEPOWER	122BHP @ 6,600RPM
TRANSMISSION	5-SPEED MANUAL
CHASSIS	STEEL MONOCOQUE
BRAKES	4-WHEEL DISC
TOP SPEED	125MPH
ACCELERATION 0–60MPH	8.1 SECS
PRODUCTION SPAN	1985 →

TOYOTA MR2

The very latest in Toyota's fast car line-up is the long awaited MR2 sports coupé. This mid-engined device was announced to the British press in Portugal in January 1985, on a test route that was not in any way selected to pamper the cars but was capable of highlighting the smallest deficiency in their behaviour. After some time thrashing the MR2 around the mountains I was left with the impression, the firm impression, that with this car Toyota have a winner.

The car uses what must be the best mass-produced four-cylinder engine available in the world today, the twin-cam 4A-GE unit of 1,587cc capacity, which produces 122bhp at 6,600rpm and drives through a five-speed gearbox and transaxle arrangement. The MR2 will reach a top speed of 125mph and accelerate to 60mph from rest in 8.1 seconds. At a constant 75mph it has excellent 36.7mpg fuel economy. The electronic fuel-injection system gives instant starting, fast cold drive-away and superb response at all engine speeds, so good as to make the five-speed gearbox almost redundant!

I found just two small points of criticism to mention after driving the car. Firstly, the fuel tank is too small at only nine gallons, it really should be at least half as big again, and secondly the interior for someone of my (largish) size was just a little cramped. For two average-sized people wanting to cover long distances fast, however, with a reasonable luggage carrying capacity, the MR2 is superb. Steering, brakes, stability at speed, driving position, controls, finish, are all simply marvellous. In the vast quantities that Toyota are capable of making, the MR2 must be a distinct thorn in the side of many other fast coupé manufacturers the world over — and that is irrespective of any price considerations. It is certainly one of the best fast car bargains available today.

TOYOTA COROLLA GT

A very brief mention must be made here of the sister car to the MR2, the Corolla GT. Designed to compete with all the other fast hatchback models flooding onto today's market, the Corolla GT has the same superb 16-valve 1,587cc engine as the MR2 but front-mounted and driving the front wheels. Unlike the MR2 it is a genuine four-seater with all four sitting much higher off the ground. Disc brakes all round, rack-and-pinion steering, alloy wheels and 186/60HR 14 tyres and all-independent suspension with gas-filled dampers give the GT performance that enables it to challenge the mighty VW Golf GTi. Because of the higher seating position and the better visibility I actually prefer it to the MR2, and its low price, cheaper than a Volkswagen Golf GTi, makes it particularly competitive, a very fine car.

S P E C I F I C A T I O N	
MODEL/TYPE	TOYOTA COROLLA GT
ENGINE	4-CYL, 1,587CC, DOHC
HORSEPOWER	122BHP @ 6,600RPM
TRANSMISSION	5-SPEED MANUAL
CHASSIS	STEEL MONOCOQUE
BRAKES	4-WHEEL DISC
TOP SPEED	125MPH
ACCELERATION 0–60MPH	8.7 SECS
PRODUCTION SPAN	1984 →

Sharing the same basic powertrain as the new mid-engined MR2, the 125mph Corolla GT finally lays to rest Toyota's formerly well-deserved image as a maker of very ordinary motorcars.

MAZDA/ELFORD 929C-TURBO

The Elford Engineering Company in Great Britain have turned their hand to the rather gutless Mazda 929 coupé, which shares the Wankel engine, giving it turbo-power and turning it into one of the best value-for-money four-seater cars in Europe. I have driven the first example of the converted car, trying it both with and without the turbo operating. The difference is astonishing. Without the turbo the car has a real struggle to get to 98mph, with the meagre 90bhp that is available from the four-cylinder single overhead cam engine. The Elford-Garrett T3 turbo changes all that to 135bhp at 5,800rpm. In making the car faster the extra power changes the function of the gearbox from a four-speed plus overdrive fifth, to something that feels much more like a close-ratio sports 'box. In top gear the car really benefits from the added engine power instead of struggling to maintain a fast cruising speed and will accelerate happily and rapidly up to its 127mph top speed with ease and hold it in the face of most gradients.

The turbo installation is neat and tidy, looking for all the world like a factory fitment. The rest of the car is equally good, a very comfortable four-seater with all the controls and instruments that any driver could wish for. Power-assisted steering and four-wheel disc brakes allow the car's performance to be exploited to the full. The car looks good and unlike so many other Japanese models it is both competent and full of character.

The cars that have featured in this chapter represent the cutting edge of a new wave of performance cars that will be coming out of Japan from now on. With their dedication, mass production backing and very keen appreciation of what the market wants, plus their policy of very competitive pricing, Japanese car makers are likely to become increasingly prominent in this once solely European field.

Turbo power by courtesy of Elford, turns Mazda's rather dowdy 929 coupé into something altogether more interesting and individual—a Q-car in the finest tradition.

SPECIFICATION	
MODEL/TYPE	MAZDA/Elford 929C TURBO
ENGINE	ROTARY-TURBO
HORSEPOWER	135BHP @ 5,800RPM
TRANSMISSION	5-SPEED MANUAL
CHASSIS	STEEL MONOCOQUE
BRAKES	4-WHEEL DISC
TOP SPEED	127MPH
ACCELERATION 0–60MPH	N/A
PRODUCTION SPAN	1984 →

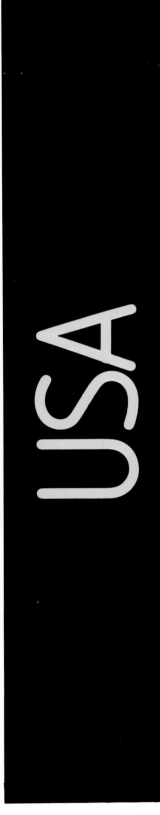

CHEVROLET CORVETTE

Although it is no longer the fastest American car (that honour nowadays rests with the Chevrolet Camaro IROC-Z machine which is two or three mph faster) the Chevrolet Corvette is the longest-running sporty car still being produced in the USA. Real performance is again beginning to tempt American buyers and manufacturers and many very quick cars are likely to be announced in the USA in coming months.

The 'Vette was given a whole new suit of clothes two years ago but until the 1985 model appeared, it flattered only to deceive with production examples not living up to the pre-production demonstrator cars. Chevrolet took a tremendous battering from customers and other critics about the car and buckled down to putting all the points raised to rights. The 1985 Corvette, it is good to report, is all that the car should have been in the first place. The engine is the traditional pushrod 5,733cc V8, which, with fuel injection makes a lowly 230bhp at 4,000rpm, but torque is an excellent 330lb ft at 3,200rpm.

The new body shape has lost all the odd bumps and lumps that marred the previous model and now looks modern and up to date. The interior features a digital instrument layout (which is not as good as the old analogue), proper adjustable seats, with leather as an optional covering, and a Delco-GM/Bose sound system that gives concert hall quality.

On the road the new 'Vette is tight and solid, whereas the 1984 model was a mass of squeaks and rattles. It goes very well and a top speed of over 150mph, with 0–60mph in 6 seconds is not hanging about by any standards. Roadholding is equally good but the brakes, while good in most circumstances, lack conviction at the limit. The Corvette will deliver an average of 16 miles from a US gallon of leadless gasoline. It may not have the very long term integrity of, say, a Porsche 928S, but it is excellent value for money.

S P E C I F I C A T I O N	
MODEL/TYPE	CHEVROLET CORVETTE
ENGINE	V8, 5,733CC
HORSEPOWER	230BHP @ 4,000RPM
TRANSMISSION	4-SPEED AUTO
CHASSIS	STEEL FRAME/GRP BODY
BRAKES	4-WHEEL DISC
TOP SPEED	150MPH
ACCELERATION 0–100MPH	16.5 SECS
PRODUCTION SPAN	1985 →

American fast cars come and go but the Chevrolet Corvette goes on forever. The latest model of America's favourite sportscar continues an unbroken line going back to 1953, when General Motors took the plunge with a European-style roadster. Today's Corvette is a far cry from the original but the name still evokes magic.

215

FORD MERKUR XR4T-i

The Merkur is a Sierra-based coupé, a three-door hatchback with the 'biplane' rear spoiler. Its engine is a 2.3-litre, four-cylinder single overhead cam unit with a Garrett TO3B turbocharger and it gives 170bhp at 5,200rpm in manual gearbox form. It is front mounted and drives the rear wheels via a five-speed manual or Ford C3 automatic 'box. Suspension is fully independent and brakes are discs at the front and drums at the rear. Steering is by power-assisted rack-and-pinion. Alloy wheels carry 195/60HR 14 Pirelli P6 tyres. With the possible exception of the brakes (rear drums do not indicate a full commitment to high speed use), the whole design of the Merkur XR4Ti suggests the intention of the makers to provide the customer with a proper fast car. It will reach 125mph easily but no acceleration times are published.

FORD

S P E C I F I C A T I O N	
MODEL/TYPE	FORD MERKUR XR4T-i
ENGINE	4-CYL, 2,298CC TURBO
HORSEPOWER	170BHP @ 5,200RPM
TRANSMISSION	5-SP/3-SP AUTO
CHASSIS	STEEL MONOCOQUE
BRAKES	DISC FRONT, DRUM REAR
TOP SPEED	125MPH PLUS
ACCELERATION	N/A
PRODUCTION SPAN	1985 →

With the coming of the 'world car', Europe and America have shared more ideas than ever before. The Ford Merkur XR4Ti is the American incarnation of the Sierra, with a turbo for good measure.

FORD MUSTANG GT

The Ford Mustang has always had a reputation as a fast car even if that reputation has not always been justified. Now, after some years in the doldrums, two new Mustangs have been offered to American buyers and these Mustangs really do have a claim as performance cars. The Mustang GT and the SVO models are significantly different in the way they go about being fast cars but in the end that is what they both prove to be. The GT model has a 5-litre pushrod V8 engine that develops a very unstressed 210bhp. It drives through a five-speed gearbox that seems just a touch heavy in operation, to a solid rear axle which is located by coil springs and 'Quadra-Shock' suspension.

The Mustang GT rides on handsome alloy wheels of 15-in diameter and which carry P225/60VR 15 Goodyear Eagle tyres. These fine tyres contribute a great deal to the Mustang's handling and stable ride. The whole car is very solidly built, the interior is well trimmed and only the masking of some of the instrument faces spoils the overall good impression.

Brakes are again a disappointing mixture of disc front and drum rear but in today's American driving environment they prove to be adequate rather than inspiring. Power-assisted rack-and-pinion steering is used, and I found this to be excellent.

From a performance point of view the GT is really good. It has bags of acceleration and Ford claim it will exceed 130mph, which I have no reason to doubt, having driven it. The GT version of the Mustang theme represents the ultimate expression of the traditional big American V8 in a small, or at least compact, body, this time with decent brakes and good roadholding as well. The Ford GT is also available in convertible form and, unusually for an American car, it cannot be ordered with an automatic gearbox!

S P E C I F I C A T I O N	
MODEL/TYPE	FORD MUSTANG GT
ENGINE	V8, 5,000CC
HORSEPOWER	210BHP @ 4,400RPM
TRANSMISSION	5-SPEED MANUAL
CHASSIS	STEEL MONOCOQUE
BRAKES	DISC FRONT, DRUM REAR
TOP SPEED	125MPH
ACCELERATION 0–60MPH	N/A
PRODUCTION SPAN	1984 →

FORD

The original Mustang was one of Ford's major triumphs but the name was later used on some very ordinary cars. The latest Mustang GT goes some way to restoring some of the name's former reputation.

FORD

FORD MUSTANG SVO

The Ford SVO (Special Vehicles Operation) is the next step in the direction that American Fords are taking. It represents the hi-tech way of doing things, no more brute muscle as in the GT, but more of the subtler European-type approach, that is using turbochargers allied to relatively small engines, with digital electronic fuel-injection and ignition systems to produce the horsepower. In the case of the SVO, a 2.3-litre four-cylinder overhead cam engine and Garrett turbocharger produce 175bhp at 4,400rpm. The EEC-IV computer-controlled blower allows an infinitely variable boost up to an unusually high 14psi.

The SVO's suspension has the excellent Koni dampers installed. Power-assisted rack-and-pinion steering is fitted and 16 × 7in cast alloy wheels carry P225/50VR 16 Goodyear tyres. This complete package gives the car very good handling and ride qualities. I have driven the car for considerable distances on freeways and minor roads of a very twisty nature and at all speeds the SVO stuck to the road as though it was glued there! The handling in corners, fast and slow, was excellent, supplemented by the fine steering. The brakes, unlike those on the GT are ventilated discs at the front and rear, and power-assisted, of course.

A 200% Porsche fan who I have known for some years surprised me with his enthusiasm for the SVO. He likes the car so much that he has sold his current Porsche and ordered one of these very special Fords. He calls it the best all-round, value car in America today, and he cannot wait to take delivery of it!

Now that US manufacturers have rediscovered performance and found that it still sells, it seems that the next few months will produce a great many really quick, interesting cars from the USA; in particular, you might watch out for the results of the Ford Saturn project. It will be spectacular!

S P E C I F I C A T I O N	
MODEL/TYPE	FORD MUSTANG SVO
ENGINE	4-CYL, 2,300CC, TURBO
HORSEPOWER	175BHP @ 4,400RPM
TRANSMISSION	5-SPEED MANUAL
CHASSIS	STEEL MONOCOQUE
BRAKES	4-WHEEL DISC
TOP SPEED	OVER 125MPH
ACCELERATION 0–60MPH	7.76 SECS
PRODUCTION SPAN	1984 →

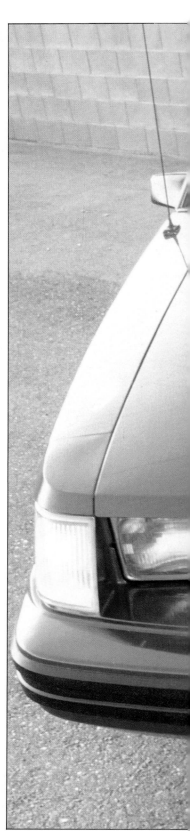

The cockpit *(above)* of the Ford Mustang SVO *(left)* shows America's growing acceptance of the more restrained interior styling of European cars— especially sporting models.

FRANCE & SWEDEN

CITROEN CX25 GTi-TURBO

The French have been making fast cars for as long as anyone else but for some time now they haven't had more than one or two really quick, specialist-built cars, such as the Facel Vega or the short-lived Monica. Now they have two excellent fast machines, one a normal production car, the Citroën GTi Turbo and the other a homologation special, the Peugeot 205 Turbo-16, both of which are genuine over-125mph cars.

Citroën claim that their CX GTi Turbo can reach 136mph and I for one am certainly not inclined to disbelieve them, in fact I suspect that if anything they are being rather conservative in this assertion. It has been reported that the CX's turbo installation is one of the very best available today. It gives the venerable 2.5-litre four-cylinder engine a whole new lease of life.

A new rear spoiler serves to maintain a decent drag figure of 0.36 and this plus the increased urge of the engine, up from 138bhp to 168bhp with the Garrett turbo and Bosch fuel injection, give the car its new high speed image. Acceleration too is good for such a big car, at only 8.6 seconds for zero to 60mph.

All the usual CX advantages are still present, including a long-legged ability to eat up the motorway miles, the excellent, but just a little too sensitive, all-round disc braking system, which makes light of stopping the 3,053lb car from any speed, the very comfortable interior and the slightly 'odd-ball' instrumentation and controls. Like all previous Citroëns it is not really a car to jump into and drive off without thinking. A Citroën rewards its driver if he or she takes the time to get to know the car and, once acquired, the Citroën addiction is very hard to get rid of.

S P E C I F I C A T I O N	
MODEL/TYPE	CITROEN CX25 GTi-TURBO
ENGINE	4-CYL, 2,500CC TURBO
HORSEPOWER	168BHP @ 5,000RPM
TRANSMISSION	5-SPEED MANUAL
CHASSIS	STEEL MONOCOQUE
BRAKES	4-WHEEL DISC
TOP SPEED	136MPH
ACCELERATION 0–60MPH	8.6 SECS
PRODUCTION SPAN	1984 →

It may not be the most obvious of sporting cars but the front-wheel-drive Citroën CX25GTi Turbo shows that the makers of the 2CV have not forgotten the opposite end of the market. The Turbo's top speed is almost exactly double that of the much loved *deux-chevaux!*

S P E C I F I C A T I O N	
MODEL/TYPE	PEUGEOT 205 TURBO 16
ENGINE	4-CYL, 1,775CC, TURBO
HORSEPOWER	200BHP @ 7,250RPM
TRANSMISSION	5-SPEED MANUAL
CHASSIS	MONOCOQUE/TUBULAR
BRAKES	4-WHEEL DISC
TOP SPEED	130MPH PLUS
ACCELERATION 0–60MPH	5.8 SECS
PRODUCTION SPAN	1984 →

PEUGEOT 205 TURBO 16

When the Peugeot 205 model range was announced, early in 1983, it created a sensation. The 205 had up-to-date styling, fine performance, very good ride and handling and it had what no other Peugeot had had before, it had chic — a charm that drew the customers into Peugeot dealerships in their thousands. The company has had to increase production rates of the car several times over in the two years since then to meet the demand. With their super GTi model the demand shot up again with the 205, Peugeot could do no wrong.

The company also went rallying, but with a car that was even more outstanding: the 205 turbocharged 16-valve-engined, four-wheel-drive machine. They won rallies, including the 1985 Monte Carlo, in which they took first, third and fifth places overall. To be able to enter this extraordinary car in international competition Peugeot had to build at least 200 customer examples, which they have done, and they have sold every available car.

On seeing the car for the first time it is obvious even to the uninitiated that this is a racer. It could be nothing else, with its big wheels, the air intake for the mid-mounted engine, the spoilers — they all go to state that this is not a normal drive-to-the-station commuter car. The 1,775cc engine uses four valves per cylinder and is blown by an intercooled German-made KKK turbocharger. It churns out 200bhp at 7,250rpm and there is little real power under 3,000rpm but once the tachometer needle hits 4,000rpm things really start to happen. If it were not for the four-wheel-drive arrangement the car would be difficult to control.

Driving this competition-inspired vehicle calls for firm and positive action on the part of the driver, the Peugeot has to be made to obey directions and this is no car to pussyfoot around, it has to be dominated. There is little, if any, luggage room in the car, it is noisy and can be tiring to drive far, but the *fun* factor is sky-high.

The Peugeot 205 Turbo 16 in
works competition guise ended
the Audi Quattro's near monopoly
of rally wins in 1984 and the
model is also now available as a
rather special road car.

S P E C I F I C A T I O N	
MODEL/TYPE	SAAB 9000T
ENGINE	4-CYL, 1,985CC, DOHC
HORSEPOWER	175BHP @ 5,500RPM
TRANSMISSION	5-SPEED MANUAL
CHASSIS	STEEL MONOCOQUE
BRAKES	4-WHEEL DISC
TOP SPEED	130MPH
ACCELERATION 0–60MPH	8.2 SECS
PRODUCTION SPAN	1985

SAAB 9000T

Apart from their rally cars, Saab have never had a reputation for building wild, fast, ultra-exciting vehicles. Sensible — yes; functional — yes; very well made — yes; but *not* cars that get the blood boiling, more cars of the head than of the heart. With Saab's new 900 16S and 9000 models however, there could well be a change in the wind.

The 9000's styling has none of that 'Look at Me, I'm a Super Car' gimmickry that others go for. It is a sober, functional shape, with enormous interior space, a well laid out set of instruments and controls to aid the driver at his task and, under the bonnet, all the latest sophistication to be expected of a fourth generation turbo-car.

It undoubtedly goes; a factory claim of over 135mph has been confirmed in many road-tests. It has stability at speed, it has excellent roadholding and ride qualities, it shows all the effort put into it after ten years of painstaking research and development. The 1,985cc four-cylinder engine has four valves per cylinder and double overhead cams. The inter-cooled turbo unit produces a full 175bhp but there is a problem, or rather two problems with the 9000. Its steering is lacking in feel, which doesn't help the strong understeering nature of the chassis, and there is a disconcerting 'On-Off' character in the engine's power delivery. Both of these items can make it difficult to drive the 9000 fast in the dry and very difficult in the wet. Power delivery goes from almost nothing to full blast in a spread of only 500rpm. At 2,500rpm there is little in the way of real power but by 3,000rpm the turbo is well into its work.

Maybe the answer to the steering response lies in the tyre size, because they do appear to be on the narrow side, and compared to, say, an Audi 2005T, the Saab 9000 is a little deficient in the way it puts its 175bhp down on the road. By the time it is in the dealers' showrooms these small deficiencies will undoubtedly be sorted out.

The attractive Saab 9000 saloon features the first all-new bodyshape from the Swedish manufacturer for several years and much new engineering under the skin further enhances Saab's considerable reputation for solid sporting performance.

HISPANO-SUIZA

Glamorous
Automobiles

The very glamorous cars

Staking a real claim to be 'The Most Glamorous Car' must be the Rolls-Royce Phantom II that belonged to the Hollywood socialite, the Countess DiFrasso. Determined to outshine her close friend, and deadly social rival, film star Constance Bennett, the Countess commissioned the Paris-based designer and stylist, Dutch Darrin, to produce the most stunning body for her Rolls-Royce, one that would really top anything ever seen in the Hollywood of the mid-1930s.

Darrin, as they say in Las Vegas 'came up trumps!' His coachwork on the Phantom II remains to this day the most beautiful body ever put on a Rolls-Royce. It would not have been unreasonable to have expected the result to be outlandish and vulgar, but Dutch Darrin was too much an artist to fall into that trap and the Countess had too much taste to allow such a thing to happen. The result is simply gorgeous. Their first meeting, in 1936, was at the home of Clark Gable, a mutual friend, and the Countess immediately commissioned from Darrin the re-bodying of her 1933 Rolls-Royce.

It took Darrin two years to complete the work, which was done in his Sunset Strip establishment in Los Angeles. The body is especially notable for the fact that it does not contain a single weld in its aluminium shell. Rudy Stoessel and Paul Erdos carefully gave shape to the detailed Darrin drawings which incorporated several items from the current American automobiles. The car has Buick front and rear bumpers, the door handles and the headlights are from the Packard partsbin, the steering wheel comes from a Lincoln and the rear tail-lights originated from Fords.

After completion, Dutch Darrin was quoted as saying, 'This was the only car I ever designed that came out better in real life than it looked in the rendering.'

There is no record of the Countess DiFrasso's reaction on taking delivery of the Rolls-Royce, but it would appear that she had no cause ever to be upstaged by her friend and rival, Constance Bennett, in regard to their transport!

It is interesting to note that someone, still very involved with the DiFrasso car, once owned it and devoted so much time to it that his wife demanded that he had to choose between it and her. Shortly afterwards they were divorced! That gives just a little idea of the beauty and attraction that the 1933 Rolls-Royce still exerts today.

The 1930 Cadillac V16 is one of the most impressive looking cars ever built. It was designed by the famous Harley Earl who decided to name it the 'Madame X' after a character in a popular play of 1929. Harley J. Earl was an extraordinary character. He began his working life with a Los Angeles Cadillac dealer, Don Lee, who catered to the exotic automotive tastes of the celebrities of the booming Hollywood movie industry. Earl had been recruited into the General Motors Corporation Fisher division (they made all the G.M. bodies) by the acknowledged genius of the American car business, Alfred P. Sloan. Sloan had decided that it was cheaper to restyle the G.M. cars annually with panel

LEFT: The Countess DiFrasso Rolls-Royce is accepted by many experts as the most beautiful body ever to grace a Rolls-Royce chassis. It is perfectly styled and finished as befits the car of a leading Hollywood socialite of the 1930s.

ABOVE: Wire-spoked wheels normally associated with sports cars rather than limousines, nevertheless work perfectly, the delicacy of the wheel design complementing the whole car.

Like Rolls-Royce, Cadillac used a female figure as its radiator mascot. It may not be as elegant as the Flying lady, but its design suits the car well.

and colour changes, than to undertake very expensive engineering improvements, and Harley J. Earl was just the man to carry out that policy.

Earl soon became the man who introduced 'Hollywood Styling' to Detroit. His own definition of his contribution to the American auto industry is even more revealing; he called it 'dynamic obsolescence'!!

But there was nothing obsolescent or cynical about his work on the 'Madame X' car. It is sober, timeless in its appeal, a stately vehicle in the best possible taste. It is no wonder Harley J. Earl had a long career with G.M., a charlatan could not and would not have lasted for very long in the Corporation with its reputation for high quality.

High quality is what you get from the products of the Daimler-Benz company. The Mercedes-Benz has been voted as the top quality car in North America every year since they were first exported to that continent in any quantity. A car from the Unterturkheim/Singelfingen plants has the highest secondhand value of any mass-produced car made today.

For some people even this fact is not enough to make them

The hand-built Cadillac V-16 town car known as the Madame X, displays all the features necessary to justify the company's slogan 'Standard of the World'

1931 V16 CADILLAC
MADAME X LIMOUSINE
ONLY 2 OF THIS RARE
BODY STYLE WERE BUILT
BY FLEETWOOD

buy and use a standard Mercedes-Benz. They still insist on having one, but it must be an even better car than that delivered by their Mercedes dealer. One of the few places they can go to for this better Mercedes is Liege in Belgium. In this old industrial city the Duchatelet coachbuilding firm will take your brand-new car, and for a great deal of money turn it into an even better S-class Mercedes-Benz.

The company was formed by Frederic Duchatelet in 1977 with its headquarters located beside the river Meuse close to the city centre. The author met Frederic Duchatelet in March 1984 when preparing this book and the immediate impression was of a man obsessed with attaining perfection in his work. He insists that his workers, some of the very best in Europe, give 101% effort at maintaining and extending the reputation for the very best in craftsmanship that Duchatelet has won. The company can perform every single skill in the production of a finished car, and woe betide any worker who gives less than the best. In respect of his temperament, Frederic Duchatelet is similar to those two other giants of European high quality, high performance motoring, Enzo Ferrari, and Ettore Bugatti. Like them he is a benevolent dictator although sparing with his praise, but with a terrible temper when he finds work done that does not come up to the company's standard of excellence.

During the author's visit the Carat Cullinan, the Duchatelet version of the 500SEL four-door sedan, and the D. Arrow, based on the 500SEC coupe were sampled. Both cars were equipped with just about every accessory that the wealthy owner would want. The re-upholstered seats featured electrical adjustment in every direction and were supremely comfortable and beautifully constructed like every other feature of the car, care of Duchatelet. On the road the car behaved exactly as a standard S-class Mercedes-Benz. The D. Arrow model was taken to nearby Spa-Francorchamps Grand Prix race track, and in the hands of the company's test driver was put through its paces hard. Apart from the Duchatelet bodywork and interior changes this car had a set of BBS alloy wheels and some Goodyear NCT tyres fitted. On the wet race track it stuck to the tarmac as if it were glued, allowing the unmodified engine to deliver all its power in spite of the slippery road surface and the tricky nature of the famous track.

During two very interesting days at Liege, hints were given that the future may well see the development of more power from the magnificent German engines, very probably by using a turbocharging system which is presently undergoing final testing.

The Duchatelet range of Mercedes-Benz cars must represent some of the most desirable vehicles available today. The coupling of the best of German engineering, and the care and attention to detail of the Duchatelet company make for unbeatable value, even though a Duchatelet Mercedes can cost over twice as much as the standard one.

An English company also produces a car that has more than close connections with the mighty giant of Stuttgart.

The interior of the original Mercedes is scrapped, and replaced with top quality fittings from the seats, trimmed in the best Connolly leather, to the top quality Wilton carpet.

The Duchatelet 500 is one of the very best of today's customized, high-quality cars. Hundreds of hours of work by Belgian craftsmen result in a driving machine that combines the highest quality of finish with a performance to match.

ABOVE: No naked lady or leaping cat mascot—the 1928 Mercedes-Benz SS is graced by the simple, and now familiar, three-pointed star.

LEFT: Considered to be one of the few great sports cars of all time, the Mercedes-Benz 38/250 SS would compare favourably with more modern cars.

Greenchurch Engineering live deep in the Dorset countryside and led by Paul Weldon they make, to special order, a superb recreation of the 1928 Mercedes-Benz SS/38/259 sportscar. This car came about as a result of a collaboration between Paul and a Japanese company. Their president had always wanted to own a Mercedes-Benz 38/250 sportscar, and commissioned Paul to find him one, restore it and ship it to Japan. Then Paul was asked if it would be possible to manufacture a replica of the Merc. using modern engine/transmission units, but to make the rest of the car as close to the original as possible.

Paul commissioned Len Terry, the ex-Lotus designer to redesign the chassis, keeping the basic layout, but using up-to-date springs, shock absorbers, and location points. The result looked remarkably similar to the 1928 car, but handled and rode so much better. The overall dimensions were the same as the original car and only the engine and transmission were modern—in the case of the car in the photographs, these items came from a 280S model Mercedes-Benz.

The whole car is very well constructed, looks superb and goes even better. It is very easy to drive well and easy to drive very fast as the seating position and all-round view from the high

mounted seat allow the car to be positioned on the road to the inch. From the driving compartment the long white bonnet stretches ahead, and the separate front wings enable the fullest advantage to be taken of the road width. The apparently crude suspension works very well with the long wheelbase and gives the car a fine ride with excellent roadholding characteristics. Of course, the Mercedes-Benz engine delivers more than enough power for the lightweight car, and only the lack of aerodynamic efficiency limits the car's top speed to about 118mph.

Paul has named his car the *Gozzy*, and has been paid the highest compliment by Mercedes-Benz who allow him to use a very close facsimile of their famous laurel leaf radiator badge to adorn the Gozzy, which can also be found on the steering wheel centre. Costing over £35,000, the Gozzy is not cheap, but of all the many excellent recreations of famous cars that have been seen in the last five years it must rank with the Favre/Ferrari GTO (which is very much more expensive), and the Red Stallion Cobra as the most usable cars' of their type that are available today.

In 1936 Mercedes-Benz converted their excellent sportscar, the 500K into the 540K, and the result was an instant classic. With an engine capacity of 5401cc the supercharged car had a maximum

ABOVE: Using modern Mercedes-Benz mechanicals, the British-built Gozzy succeeds in its attempt to recreate the original 1920s Mercedes-Benz.

power output of no less than 180bhp, and the car fully justifies the claim to be the ultimate Mercedes-Benz sportscar of the 1930s. Over 700 500Ks and 540Ks were built between 1934 and 1939. In that latter year even the wonderful 540K would have been eclipsed by its planned successor the 580K if war had not brought its production plans to a halt.

As it was the 540K was a very genuine high performance car with a guaranteed top speed of over 110mph. Its supercharger arrangement followed the usual Mercedes-Benz pattern of being engaged by flooring the accelerator pedal, and was only to be used for very short bursts of full power.

Apart from the outstanding performance, the 540K's greatest attraction lay in the stunning bodies that were commissioned for its chassis, which lent itself well for stylish coachwork to be built and fitted easily. Many of the great European coachbuilding houses, as well as Daimler-Benz themselves, constructed elegant and tasteful bodies for the great sportcar.

This combination of power and beauty attracted the attention of the filmstar Barbara Hutton who commissioned one for her new husband, the Georgian Prince Mdivani. The Mdivani 540K is a valued item in the Blackhawk collection at the moment. It is in pristine condition and fully justifies the claim that it is one of the most beautiful sportscars ever built. As it also goes as well as it looks it would appear that this claim is accurate.

The coachwork by Erdmann and Rossi, Berlin is unblemished, the red finish being particularly suited to the body style, and highlighted by the excellent, and discreetly understated chromium plating. It has been said that the Mdivani 540K's lines are rather exaggerated, but in the late 1930s in the social whirl of the Hollywood elite, the car's looks were just perfect. It is one of the most exciting sportscars ever seen. Tucked away in the back of the Blackhawk holding building awaiting cleaning and some slight restoration in 1984, the sheer elegance of the car shone out quite clearly in the gloom.

From the time Chrysler was first formed, the company had a fine reputation for good engineering. Enormous stress was placed upon the quality of their engineers' training, and as a compliment their brightest people were constantly being lured away by Ford and General Motors. In the early 1930s it was felt that they should move into the quality car market. As a result of this decision the excellent Imperial model was born. In 1932 only three models of the CL convertible sedan were built, with two being sold in the New York area and one in Los Angeles. The California car fell into a bad state of repair before it was rescued and restored, and now resides in the Nethercutt collection.

One of the New York cars somehow found its way to the West Coast. Nobody knows just when, but it was discovered in a barn in a state that its present owner describes as, 'Unrecognizable as an automobile!' Gerry Jensen was not a classic car expert when he first saw this pile of junk nearly ten years ago, but he was sufficiently alert to feel that it just might be something special and persuaded the farmer to sell him the wreckage. Gerry is not a rich

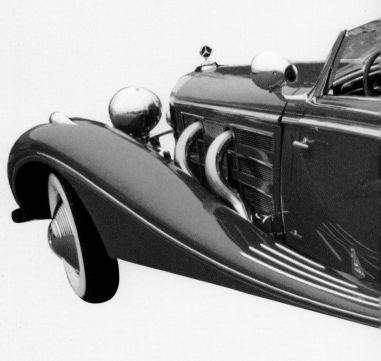

This Mercedes-Benz 540K was specially commissioned from the Berlin coachbuilders Erdmann and Rossi, by Barbara Hutton, the heiress of the Woolworth chainstore fortune.

The high build quality of the Imperial is reflected in the mascot and radiator design—the ultimate in good taste and discretion.

man; he works in an auto parts dealership in northern California, lives in a small house with his family, and shares with most Californians a love of the car. Over the next three or four years he saved the necessary money to have the ruins of what he now knew was one of the three 1932 Chrysler CL models restored.

On completion he was persuaded to enter the car into the world's most prestigious concours d'elegance event, at Pebble Beach.

'It was like a fairy story', was Gerry's reaction to that competition, because he not only did well, he won THE award, the Blue Ribbon class of the whole meeting for the Best of Show! For those of a mercenary nature it might be of interest to know that just before the judging started Gerry had been approached by a collector who offered him $200,000 for the car. Three hours later, having just won the top award, the same man increased his offer to $400,000!

At the time of photographing the Chrysler, Gerry had driven the car only 11 miles in three years, out of his garage on to his trailer and off the trailer on to the show stand, with the reverse taking place after the show was finished. In that manner few miles have been totted up, but unlike many other owners of classic cars (for whom this kind of mileage is the norm) Gerry wants to use his car on the road, not as everyday transport, but at the weekend for pleasure driving. Gerry's total expenditure on his lovely Chrysler is relatively low, and he intends exploiting his investment by having some fun with the car in the manner in which it was intended when it was built in Detroit all those years ago.

Italy's entry for the 'Best Car in the World' competition can be claimed by the Isotta-Fraschini concern from Milan. In the 1930s they produced some of the nicest cars for the luxury market, several of which, by virture of their bodywork, turned out to be exceptional cars—for example, the Nethercutt collection model 8A with Castagna coachwork.

This car was in as bad a state as the previous Chrysler Imperial.

The four headlamp system on the 1932 Chrysler Imperial incorporated features ahead of its time—the lower pair of lights move with the steering (à la Citroen) for improved lighting on bends.

RIGHT: Much more than just a static museum piece, this superb Isotta-Fraschini from the Nethercutt collection, is fully roadworthy.

FAR RIGHT: The radiator mascot of the Isotta-Fraschini is one of the very best examples of Italian decorative design.

In fact, to listen to the Nethercutt restoration staff it must have been in as bad a state as any car could be, and only just qualified as a rebuild project. Everything on the car, from the mechanicals to the bodywork, trim, paint and plating required attention, but the finished result is magnificent. So good in fact, that the Isotta-Fraschini has taken many prizes in concours events all over the USA and, in particular it has been runner-up twice for the Pebble Beach Best of Show Award.

Emil Delahaye died in 1905, but he left his name to go on a series of very fine French luxury and sporting cars that achieved success both on Europe's race tracks and on the boulevards and fast roads of the Continent. In particular, Delahaye have the distinction of winning the French Grand Prix in 1935 and 1938 in virtually the same car, the first race driven by Phillipe Etancelin, famous for his insistence on wearing his cloth cycling cap, reversed, instead of a racing helmet. The second race was won by the great René Dreyfus in '38. René, now well into his late 70s intends returning to the sport in 1985 when he hopes, health permitting, to drive in the second running of the One Lap of America race. Even that event's 9,000 miles of every kind of difficult driving condition is not enough to put him off.

Of all the Delahayes the most spectacular car must have been the *145MS* model, an example of which is shown here. This particular car is on display in the Los Angeles Museum of Contemporary Art. A remark, 'What a campy car!' was overheard when a spectator saw the Delahaye for the first time. Reference was obviously being made to the driving compartment with its transparent plastic steering wheel and lurid colour scheme, but there is general acceptance that the Delahaye was a fine car from a factory with a long and distinguished history of automobile manufacture. When the Paris factory closed in 1954 another car from the world list of worthy vehicles was lost.

The very name of the Bugatti type 41—the Royale—really says it all. In a letter to a friend in 1913, Ettore Bugatti said that he intended to build a bigger, better, more expensive car than either

The huge brass headlights sport unique twin lenses.

a Rolls-Royce or a Hispano-Suiza. Fourteen years later he had done just that with the type 41. It certainly was bigger; the engine, a straight-8 had a capacity of 12,763cc, the wheelbase was 170 inches and the huge wheels were waist-high. Travelling at 125mph, the vast engine was only turning over at 1680rpm, at which time it was developing over 200bhp.

Only six Royales, plus a prototype, were ever built, as it was hoped that sales could be restricted to the use of the royal families of Europe of the time, or at least heads of state. But, apart from an enquiry from King Carol of Rumania, nobody else seemed interested in the car. Whatever happened to the prototype is not known, but the six customer cars were disposed of as follows; one each to an English, German, and French client of Bugatti's, and the remaining three cars were given to various members of the Bugatti family.

One of the ex-Harrah Collection cars (Bill Harrah had owned 2!) on display in the L.A. Museum of Contemporary Art, and some details from the car were photographed in the Cunningham Museum. At the Cunningham Museum, John Burgess pointed out that the type 41 had the most perfectly arranged steering system ever put on a large car. He said that it made no compromises in catering to the driver who wanted to be isolated from road shocks. It is even more direct and free from deficiencies than a modern Grand Prix car, yet could be easily used by a woman driver, as was the Cunningham car which had been owned by Ettore's daughter, L'Ebé. He went on to say that at all the speeds the car was capable of, the steering remained light, with full feel and very responsive, a remarkable achievement for such a gigantic machine.

In 1927 a type 41 cost $25,000, and a body would require another $10,000 to be spent. The Cunningham Royale was hidden from the Germans in 1940 by being bricked up between two walls for the duration of the War, and in 1950 Briggs

This near-perfect example is one of only four Isotta-Fraschini Tipo KM racing cars ever built.

An example of extravagant French automotive design? This Delahaye 145 sports the most exotic body styling available on the car.

The lattice-work radiator grille design is said to have been influenced by the face guard of an Olympic fencer.

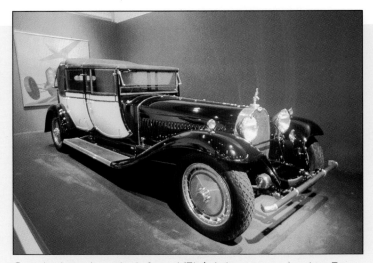

The massive Bugatti Royale Type 41 was not a sales success. It failed to find favour with royalty and heads of state for whom it was intended, and of the six offered for sale, the Bugatti family ended up with four.

Cunningham bought it from L'Ebé. It is no wonder that Ettore chose an elephant for the radiator mascot for this very large, splendid automobile.

The Napier car company had a short but hectic history of only 24 years, ending in 1924. The name is always linked to the name of S. F. Edge, the company's managing director. Edge firmly believed that racing, and more importantly, the publicity gained from that activity, sold cars. The Napier company had already a very fine reputation for precision engineering long before they became involved with the automobile, and this tradition carried over into their cars.

In 1902 Napier won the prestigious Gordon Bennett Trophy, and also gave Napier green to future British racing teams as the official British racing colour. At the then new Brooklands Racing Track in 1907 S. F. Edge averaged 65.9mph in a Napier 60hp model, a track record which stood for 18 years. In fact, THE record for the Brooklands Track is held by a Napier-Railton at 143.44mph, set by John Cobb in late 1939. As the Track was never opened for motor-racing after 1939, this remains its ultimate speed record. After Napier stopped making cars in 1925 they put all their efforts into aero-engines, and were world renowned for their work in this field. But in 1931 they were nearly tempted back into the car market in a tie-up with W. O. Bentley of Bentley Motors fame. The Bentley company had gone into liquidation earlier that year, and W.O., as he was known to everybody, had been approached by Napier to design an expensive, high performance sportscar for them, to be known as the Napier-Bentley. Napier would bid for the assets of the old Bentley company, pay off all that company's debts, and then go into production of the new car. There was even a new aero-engine contract for W.O. to be involved with in the new deal, so all was looking rosy for both companies when the Bentley receiver came to apply to the court for approval of the Napier contract in late 1931. Terms had been agreed, everything seemed to be tied up, and the court was simply expected to go through the motions of the hearing to finalize the deal. At this point a representative of Rolls-Royce stood up in court and offered

Ettore Bugatti chose the elephant mascot for the Royale because he felt it typified the size and engineering of the car.

slightly more than Napier for the assets and goodwill of the Bentley company. Napier upped their offer and were again topped by the R–R agent! Finally Napier gave up in disgust, not expecting or wanting to be involved in a public auction for the defunct Bentley company. The new Napier car never came to anything, W.O. finally joined Rolls-Royce to work on the 'Rolls-Bentley', and Napier as a car-maker was lost in the whole sordid mess. They went on with their aero-engine work and prospered, but for the car enthusiast it is still sad to drive through Acton in west London, past the D. Napier & Sons factory, and think what might have come out of the collaboration between Bentley and Napier.

The Auburn 852 Speedster with the boat-tail bodywork could be described as the epitome of the Hollywood special, the sort of car that the filmstars of the 1930s would be photographed in against a background of palm trees and white painted, Spanish style houses, under a bright Californian sun.

Unsurprisingly, that is where many 852s did finish up, being owned by film stars.

The 852 Speedster was a very large two seater roadster with sweeping lines and good proportions, which gave the car a very

SELWYN FRANCIS EDGE

Selwyn Francis Edge (1868-1940), was born in
Sydney, Australia and came to England where he
achieved success as a racing cyclist. He joined the
Napier company and proceeded to race and promote the British luxury car at every opportunity.
His brashness and peculiar brand of Australian
enthusiasm rather shocked the staid British auto
industry but he was nevertheless an able
promoter of Napier's products.

muscular, virile appearance. In profile it is particularly pleasing,
but from the front some consider that it has a rather too narrow
look, emphasized by the high build of the car. The coachwork is
the result of a collaboration between Gordon Buehrig, a superb
stylist and August Duesenberg, chief engineer of the Duesenberg
company, a collaboration of the happiest kind of two eminent
practitioners of their respective art forms.

August Duesenberg produced an efficient and reliable
supercharger for the straight-8 Lycoming engine which boosted
the power from 115hp at 3500rpm to 150hp at 4000rpm. Every
852 carried a plate mounted on the dash panel guaranteeing the
top speed, which was always on the high side of 100mph, and
the car sold for a very modest $2245 when new.

About 200 model 852s were built and every one cost the
Duesenberg company hundreds of dollars, because in the years
of the Depression the days of such exotic automobiles were
numbered, so each and every 852 had to be sold at a loss.

The loss of money on the 852 was one of the several major
factors in the demise of the Auburn-Cord-Duesenberg company.
In the harsh climate of the American depression, any car that

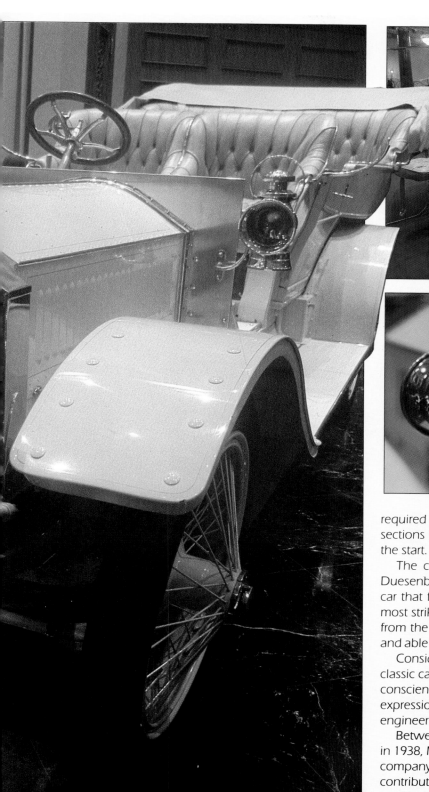

FAR LEFT: The Napier touring car is typical of the type of high quality vehicle favoured by the rich before WW1.

ABOVE: The interior of the Napier exudes class—all the seats are trimmed in the finest quality British leather.

LEFT: The brass acetylene lamps, although complementing the car's styling, did little to light the way ahead.

required as much hand work as the Auburn body, with 22 sections needing hand fitting and finishing, was doomed from the start.

The combination of the superb Buehrig body styling, and Duesenberg mechanical design and excecution has resulted in a car that from its very beginning was destined to be one of the most striking looking cars of all time. Not only is the 852 Auburn from the Blackhawk Collection a 'looker', it is also still a fast car and able to dash to 100mph when the opportunity presents itself.

Considered by many experts to represent the ultimate in classic cars', the Hispano-Suiza J12 did not burst upon the public conscience out of the blue. It came into being as the fullest expression of the genius of Marc Birkigt, the Swiss-born chief engineer of the Hispano company.

Between 1904 and the demise of the Hispano-Suiza company in 1938, Marc Birkigt penned the design of every engine that the company built for their cars, and made a very considerable contribution to the war effort against Germany in the 1914-1918 conflict by designing the V8 water-cooled engine that powered so many of the fighter and bomber aircraft in the allies' air fleets.

The choice of the rich, the film star and the sportsman, this 1930s Auburn 852 sportscar combined sweeping lines with a 100mph plus performance.

Despite its flamboyant styling, the Auburn's mascot was a distinctly plain affair.

A high-performance car, with power braking to match, the Hispano-Suiza rivalled and often beat the Rolls-Royces and Cadillacs of the day.

By 1918, 49,893 models of his aero-engine had been built by 21 different engineering firms in America, France, and Great Britain. Marc Birkigt received his technical education in Barcelona, where he was living with his grandmother, qualifying with the highest honours in Mechanical Engineering. Between 1904 and 1920 he is credited with designing no fewer than 35 different vehicles! He stayed with the Hispano-Suiza company for 34 years, in one of the most productive partnerships in automotive history.

He was brutally honest about his abilities, as he viewed them, and in one of his rare speeches he said, 'I am only an engine designer', which must be one of the great understatements of all time. One has only to consider his work on power assisted braking, which was fitted to all his cars from the early 1920s. Braking performance was the Achilles' Heel of many automobiles of the period, some cars being equipped only with rear wheel brakes, most of the rest having only mechanically operated means of stopping. The Hispano-Suiza patented friction motor powered braking system was so good that even those arch-conservatives in the Rolls-Royce company negotiated to use the system, built under licence, in their own cars, as did many other European car makers.

Birkigt was a perfectionist in every sense and his car reflected his care and appreciation of just how cars should be made with no concessions, half measures or compromises at any stage in their construction. He repeated his aero-engine success 21 years later with his 20mm automatic cannon design, just to display that

Simple but elegant—the subtlety of the car's styling extends even to the cockpit of the Hispano-Suiza J12.

34 years of designing cars had not blunted his ordinance-trained abilities—the cannon was used in aircraft in World War II.

The J12 was, at one and the same time, a town carriage par excellence, a high performance machine capable of covering hundreds of miles a day across continents in great comfort and a superbly good looking vehicle. Figures can give only some idea of the J12's ability when it was tested at the famous Brooklands track—it lapped at over 95mph in 1933. 0-60mph in 12 seconds, over 108mph top speed and an amazing braking performance of 30mph-0mph in 26 feet were all amazing for a two ton vehicle then and are still very respectable now. The car's fuel consumption, at an average of 11mpg, was more than good bearing in mind the weight and performance. Suspension could be adjusted by using the driving compartment located shock absorber control to compensate for varying loads and speeds.

Between 1931 and the closure of the factory at Bois Colombes in 1938, 120 J12s were constructed at a chassis price of £2750. Any of the many high-class coachbuilders would equip the chassis with the customer's choice of body for £750-£900 in those days. The quality of the J12 can be appreciated by the knowledge that over a quarter of the 120 J12s built are still in use. During its lifetime the J12 faced stiff competition from the Rolls-Royce Phantoms II & III, the Cadillac V16, and the Packard V12, all marvellous cars, and it matched them in all respects, even bettering them in the engine department by an appreciable margin. With the J12 Hispano-Suiza, Marc Birkigt has earned a place in the hearts of lovers of great cars the world over.

The Duesenberg

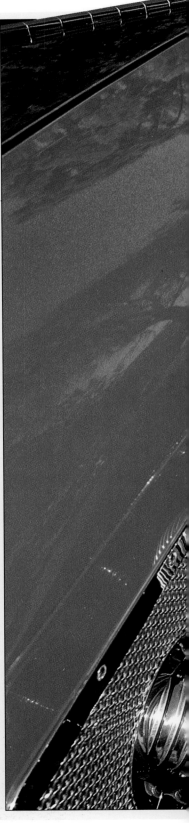

The Duesenberg holds a special place in American automotive
history, even though production stopped nearly 50 years ago.
The Duesenberg is one of the most collectable of all cars in the
USA and no real car enthusiast can fail to be impressed at seeing
one of the Indianapolis-built cars for the first time—its massive
construction in all respects promises both high performance and
great durability. It also reminds the modern day motorist of the
features that his counterpart looked for in the 1920s and 1930s:
glamour, style, power and more than a hint of the fabled days of
the Hollywood of the pre-World War Two period. Many of the
great stars of that time owned and used Duesenbergs; Gary
Cooper, Clark Gable, Carol Lombard and Tyrone Power to
mention just a few.

Fred and August Duesenberg were automotive engineers in
the true American pattern of the early part of this century, trained
by a combination of theory and very practical experience,
interested only in producing the best possible product that
carried their name. They were more engineers than
businessmen, a combination that did not, sadly, stand them in
good stead during the years of the Depression.

In one respect they, in their small way, anticipated a trend of
automobile production still current today. They were assemblers
rather than makers; a modern-day parallel would be to compare
them to the Lotus Car company of 15 or 20 years ago. The
Duesenberg brothers subcontracted out their engine and
transmission work to specialists such as the Lycoming engine
company who made all their production motors. Bodies were
handled by many of the excellent American coachbuilders like
Murphy, Le Baron, La Grand, Darrin, Fleetwood and Rollston. In
the factory the various components were brought together and
assembled into the finished vehicle. Engines were checked by
Fred Duesenberg, adjusted where necessary, then road-tested
for hundreds of miles before going to the customer. An
interesting fact emerged when researching this book: John
Burgess, the director of the marvellous Briggs Cunningham Auto
Museum in Costa Mesa, California, told the author that the

ABOVE: Comprehensive instrumentation, and a simple cockpit layout gave the Duesenberg SJ the purposeful air of a high-speed travelling machine.

Duesenbergs would give the Lycoming factory a brief of what kind of engine they wanted, and leave it to Lycomings to build, produce and deliver the finished engines to the Duesenberg plant. This meant that the engines did not always conform to design tolerances, hence the post-production work by Fred Duesenberg. In this he was not always successful—so many of the Lycoming-built engines were down on power when delivered to the customer, many of whom never knew or experienced this fact. Recently the Cunningham restoration shop undertook to 'blueprint' an unsupercharged engine out of a J-model car; this is the lower powered version of the basic two model Duesenberg range, the SJ carrying the blown engine with much more horsepower. After very carefully reworking the engine to bring it up to the original design tolerances it was found to be capable of outperforming the SJ model by an appreciable margin!

The Duesenberg engine is a massive affair, looking more suitable for service in a large ocean-going yacht than a mere automobile. Luckily, there is an exhibition engine, available for photography, mounted on a stand in the J. B. Nethercutt Collection and a very good idea of the size and proportions of this huge straight-8 powerplant can be gained by looking at it with the knowledge that the engine alone weighed over 1200lbs. The 420 cubic inch engine was equipped with double overhead camshafts which operated four valves per cylinder and produced a claimed 265bhp. The SJ blown model with its twin carburettors and special supercharger was supposed to develop 397bhp at 5000rpm. Both of these engines were fitted with three-speed gearboxes, but their torque ensured that in most circumstances the second and top gears alone were quite adequate for normal driving conditions.

All Duesenberg cars carry quite beautifully designed bodies, most carefully constructed and finished. The very best of some of the most famous Duesenbergs are illustrated in the accompanying photographs in this chapter.

1932 saw two great Duesenberg cars appear on the automotive world scene, the 'Twenty Grand' Chicago World Fair car, and the model that has been known as either 'The French Speedster' or simply 'The Figoni'. A J model, it was given a boat-tail body by the Paris-based company Figoni, a body of great beauty and style which carried all the glamour and excitement of the marque Duesenberg. In the hands of its early owners the car won many honours in concours d'elegance competitions in Monte Carlo and Cannes. It was raced and rallied, although it did not enjoy great success in these events. However, the rallies were not as they are today, being more like reliability runs, but even so the Duesenberg must have been out of its element, far too valuable to throw around for the sake of a silver cup or two. At one time it was owned by a Peruvian playboy, Antonio Chopitea. Looking at the 'French Speedster' today, it is so very easy to imagine it being driven, fast, from the Negresco Hotel in Nice along the coast road to Monte Carlo on a warm summer's

Built to grace the Chicago World Fair of 1933, the Duesenberg 'Twenty Grand' is unique. Superb workmanship and materials combine to make the 'Twenty Grand' a fabulous car.

1933 DUESENBERG
TORPEDO SEDAN · '20 GRAND'
MODEL SJ
8 CYLINDERS
320 H.P.
BODY BY ROLLSTON   MFG'D INDIANAPOLIS, IND.

CALIFORNIA
20 GRAND

The Murphy coachbuilding firm from California designed and made 125 bodies for Duesenberg cars—most striking of all is this 1929 model J.

Attention to detail has resulted in a superb finish—the interior of the Murphy-bodied Duesenberg J after restoration.

evening for dinner, followed by a night's gambling at the tables of the famous casino. Today this car is a treasured exhibit in the marvellous Blackhawk Collection in northern California where it shares garage space with other rare and beautiful automobiles.

To the north of the city of Los Angeles at the top end of the San Fernando valley lies the sprawling town of Sylmar. It is typical of many of the small townships around L.A., the houses arranged in square blocks of single-storeyed timber-framed structures. At first it would appear that Sylmar has nothing to commend it to the visitor, but for those in the know it has within its boundaries one of the greatest, and certainly THE best displayed collections of desirable automobiles in the world. The Merle Norman Cosmetic Company is fortunate in having as its President Jack Nethercutt, who together with his wife Mary, have assembled inside a purpose-built building a unique collection of functional art. Furniture, musical instruments and automobiles are gathered together in the Tower of Beauty right next door to the main cosmetic factory and administration block. The second floor, known as the Grand Salon, is the setting for a display of cars that we once described as an 'automotive Aladdin's cave'. The room is nearly as big as three tennis courts, with the ceiling over 50 feet high. Bavarian crystal chandeliers illuminate the vast room, assisted by other supplementary lights and a giant mirror covering half of the back wall from floor to ceiling. The floor is marble, as are the pillars that support the painted ceiling. At one end there is a splendid curved stairway with a grand piano sitting on a level halfway up. The whole setting exudes style and good taste and is the most perfect place to display the 24 cars that occupy the floorspace.

The collection's most recent acquisition, or rather, re-acquisition is the SJN Duesenberg that sits on the green marble floor in front of the mirror; it was previously owned by Jack Nethercutt between 1956 and 1961. Jack had bought the SJN in 1956 for $5000, (the transaction taking place on 6 October at exactly 2.13pm!) Bill Harrah had purchased it from the Nethercutt Collection five years later for the same amount of money. This

Equal care and attention have been lavished on the engine and engine compartment of this Duesenberg JN, once owned by Clark Gable.

year it returned to the Tower of Beauty for a rather larger sum of money, exactly $800,000, an inflation factor of 1600%!! It goes without saying that the SJN Duesenberg is in as new condition, its Rollston-built body with black paintwork flawless, and the interior featuring butter-coloured leather upholstery looks as though it has never been sat in. If ever an automobile looked to be worth its price tag this one most certainly does.

While all Duesenbergs were extraordinary, one of the most glamorous was a J model 1929, Murphy-bodied example. This car is displayed in the current showroom of the Blackhawk Collection in San Ramon, California. (In 1985 the Blackhawk Museum building will be finished, and a selection of cars from the Collection will be exhibited in it.)

The J cost $13,000 in 1929, a very large sum of money to spend on an automobile, when a model A Ford cost less than $600. The car featured the straight-8, DOHC, 4 valves per cylinder engine, which delivered a claimed 265bhp at 4200rpm. Mercury vibration dampers, consisting of 2 cartridges containing 16 ounces of mercury were mounted on the webs of the crankshaft. As mercury finds its own level quicker than any other element, dampers effectively suppressed any periodic vibration that the crankshaft might suffer while the engine was running.

The carburettor was manufactured by Schedler and it drew fuel from a 26-gallon fuel tank. When tuned by Fred Duesenberg a J model would reach 89mph in second gear, with 116mph available in top. Not only could the J cover the ground fast, but it could stop, its hydraulic drum brakes 375 mm (15 in) in diameter and 75 mm (3 in) wide saw to that, and the handbrake drum on the propshaft of 200-mm (8-in) diameter and 75-mm (3-in) width.

Walter M. Murphy of Pasadena, California built 125 bodies for Duesenberg cars, and this distinction gained them the reputation of being 'Young, new coachbuilders', as E. L. Cord, who by the mid-1930s had gained control of the Duesenberg company, described them.

In all, 481 Duesenberg J and SJ cars were built in Indianapolis. 175 different body styles were listed in the company records (the

DUESENBERG

Frederick and August Duesenberg came to car production late in their working lives in 1930. They had already established themselves in 1913 designing and building aero-engines and formed the Duesenberg Motor company — Frederick had pencilled his first car as early as 1904. It was not until the extraordinary E. L. Cord took over their company in 1927 that they had the money, and the support, to realize and build the marvellous luxury J and SJ models. E. L. Cord had enough good sense to leave them out to get on with the job making one of the all-time great cars. One has only to examine any Duesenberg to appreciate a product of superb engineering.

Fred and Augie were racing enthusiasts too. Their various Indianapolis 500 cars are, of course, essentially competition machines. Although they combined all the latest racing technology they were nevertheless so well made as to be displayed as works of art.

Fred died, tragically, in a car crash in 1937, and the car world lost a great car man.

N suffix was attached to both SJ and J cars to denote the fact that they were built during the last two years of production up to 1937.

Possibly the most famous and glamorous Duesenberg JN model car was once owned by Clark Cable. He commissioned the Rollston coachbuilders to build a body of elegant proportions and balance, although it now looks rather extravagant for a mere two-seater, in its day it was exactly the RIGHT car for the most famous filmstar to be seen driving. After his marriage to Carol Lombard, Gable gave her the car as a wedding present, and she used it extensively until her tragic death in an air crash in 1942. After this, the Duesenberg was stored never to be driven again by Clark Gable. It is in quite splendid condition in the Blackhawk Collection waiting to go into their new museum in 1985.

One of the most extravagant Duesenbergs must be the 1932 Chicago World's Fair 'Twenty Grand' model. Attracting as it did the attention of the rest of the world, the 1932 World's Fair provided a splendid platform for displaying the quality of the Duesenberg company. At that time the Twenty Grand must have ranked as one of the world's most, if not the most, expensive vehicles: $20,000 was an enormous sum of money to spend on a car at that time. The Twenty Grand is massive, beautifully built and finished, and could only have come from a confident American manufacturer such as the Duesenberg company in those days. Today the car resides in the Nethercutt Collection.

Of all the many excellent American luxury cars made up to the 1940s the Duesenberg is the most widely known to the general public. It was massively built, it usually carried spectacular looking bodies painted in equally spectacular colours, and the engines promised vast amounts of real horsepower. Their appeal for today's spectators must lie in their direct association with the glamorous personalities and times of the dizzy Twenties and Thirties—a motoring era that will never be repeated.

FAR LEFT: the Cord was the car responsible for the collapse of E. L. Cord's business combine. It came too late, and failed to live up to the buyer's expectations. Its failure contributed to the demise of Duesenberg and Auburn.

LEFT: Formerly owned by the filmstar Clark Gable, this Duesenberg JN has been lavishly restored.

Sporting Coupés

OVERLEAF: Mythological overtones in the mascot hint at the grace and power of the Spanish-built Pegaso sports car. This bounding horse badge adorns a Z102-B model, a world record holder in its day.

BELOW: A formidable car in standard form, the Mazda RX-7 becomes a truly exhilarating sportscar in its turbocharged form. The additional aerodynamic aids have both practical and cosmetic value.

No longer the black sheep of the motor industry, the rotary engine in this RX-7 is fitted with an Elford Engineering turbo conversion.

When the Japanese company Toyo Kogyo (Mazda to the man on the street), introduced the RX-7 model in 1978 they, maybe unwittingly, produced an instant classic in the sporting coupé market.

The RX-7 had a beautiful shape, was very well made, trimmed and finished, and had a rotary Wankel engine. The rotary engine had five years earlier very nearly brought the company to its knees. To be strictly accurate, the rotary engine came along at a time of worldwide gasoline shortage and rotaries are inherently quite thirsty, although solutions to this problem are now being found. These two factors, the fuel crisis, and the natural thirst of the new Mazda engine, drove customers out of Mazda showrooms across the world, and left the company with thousands of unsold cars stocked in fields and storage areas in their Western export markets.

But Mazda was not allowed to die; they effected a rescue act that very nearly duplicated the BMW resurrection some years before. Not only did they come back from the dead, but they persevered with the rotary engine and made it considerably more economical while retaining the smoothness and power that characterizes this type of power unit. They designed the hugely successful RX-7 body around the rotary engine, and within two years had a smash-hit seller on their hands. The story of the financial and technical difficulties Mazda faced and defeated would fill a book. In short they succeeded by 'keeping the faith', they knew that they were right in staying with the Wankel engine, and with very hard work, technical brilliance, and the leadership of one of today's great automobile engineers, Kenichi Yamamoto they won through.

A two-seater coupé of good aerodynamic shape, fine driving habits, and a very smooth, powerful engine was exactly what the

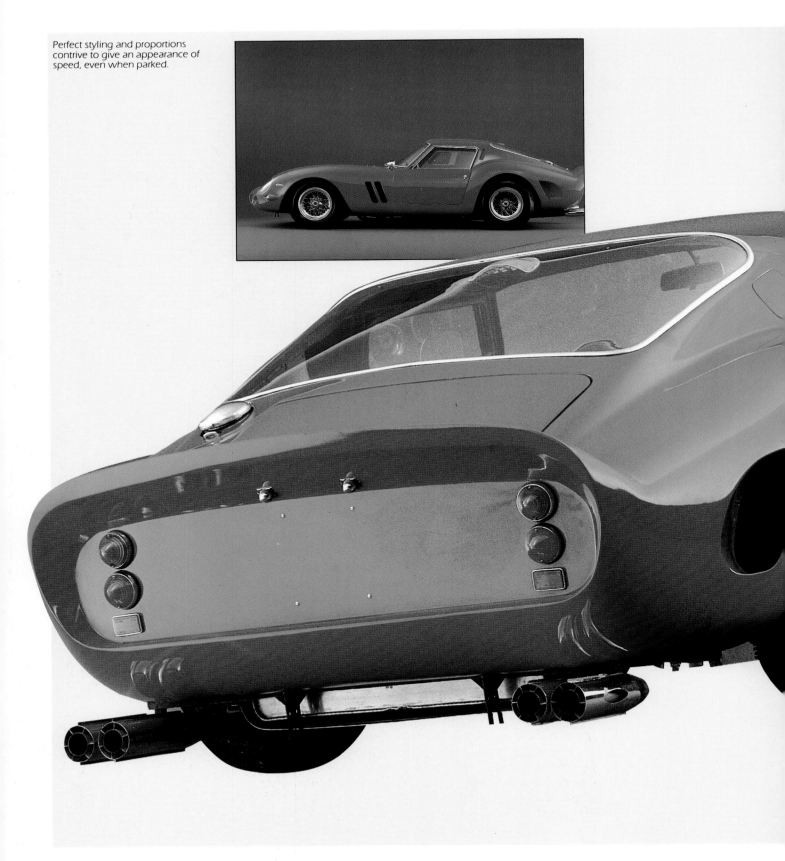

Perfect styling and proportions contrive to give an appearance of speed, even when parked.

KENICHI YAMAMOTO

When in 1961 the Toyo Kogyo car manufacturing company took out their licence to carry out research and development on the Wankel rotary engine it brought to light the talents of a young, virtually unknown, engineer Kenichi Yamamoto. He had previously completed his education at Tokyo University and first worked on the T.K. assembly line making their three-wheeled truck. Yamamoto rose rapidly through the company ranks and was a natural choice to head the small team on the Wankel project. He was to take on, with the chairman of T.K., Tsuneji Matsuda, the seemingly impossible task of making this new type of engine work, not only work in laboratory conditions, but installed in a car, to be sold to the general public, the hardest test for any mechanical device! The success of the rotary engine after 24 years' work, as a very durable, reliable automotive power unit, has contributed largely to the popularity of the Mazda RX-7.

public wanted. In Great Britain the Mazda importers decided that the RX-7 was so special that it would be sold as a direct challenger to the Porsche 924 model and the RX-7 was priced just below the Porsche. As it was able to match the Stuttgart machine in just about every possible way, and soundly beat it on price, the RX-7 became a desirable automobile to own. Specialist builders have modified the engine and bodywork of the car and the RX-7 is impressive all round—the only reservation being that the factory cars lack power when compared with several of the good after-sales turbocharged versions that are available. One of the very finest turbocharger installations comes from the British Mazda dealer, Elfords Ltd., of Tuckton, near Bournemouth in Dorset. Under the guidance of their technical director, Ted Marchant, the Elford turbo installation is so good that Mazda retain the guarantee warranty on the converted car, an almost unheard of arrangement. The Elford turbocharged RX-7 is very reliable and almost totally untemperamental. The car revels in the extra power, performing even better than the standard version, and the fuel consumption difference is so small as to be of no consequence.

Recreating one of the greatest sports cars ever built, the Favre GTO duplicates the 1963 Ferrari original in every detail except that the engine is even more powerful.

A Ferrari with a custom-built body, this Super America model features bodywork by Italian coachbuilders Boano.

The RX-7 has progressively been improved by the factory—each new model has been significantly better than the one before, but after nearly seven years the time has come for an all-new Mazda coupé. Nobody knows exactly what it will be like but it is one of the most eagerly awaited new cars for some years. Private rally drivers have experimented with turbocharged four-wheel drive RX-7s, so it seems likely that the next version will make use of some of this experience. Whatever happens to the RX-7, it will always remain one of the only genuine classic Japanese automobiles, a magic car.

Another magic, or glamour, car but from the recent past must be the Ferrari GTO model. It combined good looks with outstanding performance and only 39 examples of the original Ferrari GTO were ever built.

A young Frenchman, William Favre two years ago took the decision to recreate the Ferrari GTO, not to make a replica, but to re-make the 1963 GTO in the finest detail, using Ferrari chassis, engine, transmission, steering, and braking components taken from very similar Ferrari models and reclothing the finished mechanicals with a brand-new body, identical to the original, made by ex-Ferrari craftsmen in a factory near Turin.

William is a Geneva-based lawyer, and because of his training in the law, he did not go into this project with his eyes closed; he planned minutely before starting up. He invested a huge amount of his own money and already has his factory working on producing 27 new Favre/Ferrari GTOs. The cars look like perfectly restored genuine GTOs, just as they must have over twenty years ago when they came out of the Ferrari body shop. The Favre GTO will not be cheap, but at $130,000 it will be much cheaper than buying one of the original 39 GTOs and then having to pay the bills to bring it up to as-new condition. William has gone to great lengths to ensure that in all the important respects his car is exactly like the original. He discovered that the one item that really was in short supply was the four-speed gearbox. Everything else, V12 engines, chassis, brakes and steering components were available, albeit at a price, but the gearboxes were like hen's teeth, very, very scarce. So he took the expensive

The distinctive Boano badging on the rear quarter panel and wings.

but very necessary step, of remaking them in his new factory exactly as the originals.

The original Ferrari GTO came out of the factory in Maranello with 290bhp from its V12 3 litre engine. The Favre GTO 3 litre engine is blueprinted i.e. it is built to exact blue-print specifications of the original engine design using the latest engine assembly technology, and as a result delivers 325bhp!

The owners of each of the 27 Favre/Ferrari GTOs will get a car that has glamour in the true sense of the word.

The Blackhawk Collection contains two rather special Ferraris, both are 410 SuperAmerica models, one a coupé, and the other a convertible. Designed by the Pininfarina company and built by the coachbuilding concern of Piero Boano they are two of the most beautiful Ferraris ever built.

In 1956, the coupé model first saw the light of day and was the hit of the Brussels Auto Show in that year. It differed from the previous 410SA Ferrari in several respects: the front leaf spring was replaced by coil springs and the V12 single overhead camshaft engine had a compression ratio of 8.5:1; breathing through 3 twin-choke Weber 42DCF carburettors the 88mm × 68mm, 4963cc (310 cu in.) powerplant produced an easy 320hp at 6000rpm. With an all-up weight of 3080lbs the coupé had performance well in keeping with its attractive lines and proportions. A top speed of over 160mph made sure that the car went as well as it looked. With its 25-gallon fuel tank the 410SA coupé could also cover 450 miles between stops to refuel.

The Shah of Iran bought the actual Brussels Show car, and many personalities in the worlds of showbusiness, banking, property development, socialites, and simply lovers of the big-engined Ferraris bought similar models.

The cabriolet version went into production the following year, 1957, and with the 410SA coupé, continued to be turned out in small quantities at Boano's until the end of 1958.

The car in the Blackhawk Collection is simply superb in its appearance—the engine compartment looks almost too good, more like a piece of perfectly finished metal sculpture than simply motive power for an automobile. The alloy engine parts are stove enamelled grey, the valve covers are the familiar Ferrari crackle black, and the six-a-side exhaust manifolds are chromium plated. The whole compartment for this magnificent engine is spotless, every nut and bolt is plated, and look as though they have never seen or felt a spanner in their life.

Likewise the interior, which has been so carefully maintained that the evidence of light usage only increases one's regard for the car and its previous owner. The exterior of the Ferrari is a combination of tasteful, ageless lines, and a hint of the future in the elegant, rear fin arrangement that was taken to such excess in many American cars of that period. On the Boano Ferrari, Pininfarina has managed to combine these fins with the rest of the car most successfully, from their beginnings at the point in front of the door openings, across the door gradually, then swelling into the full fin shape past the bottom edge of the rear screen and becoming the complete fin at the back of the body shape. To some people it looks too American, even flashy, but to see it in the metal is to observe just how well the theme has been handled by designer and builder. The 410SA has a most distinguished appearance. Add the perfect Ferrari red paint finish, and the excellent chromium plating and it fully justifies its inclusion in any list of glamorous cars.

In 1950 the Spanish Empresa Nacional de Autocamiones, builders of some of Europe's best heavy commercial vehicles, decided to venture into the field of high quality, high priced, sportscar production. They engaged the services of Wilfredo Ricart, a designer with many years of experience at Alfa Romeo, gained while working on their Grand Prix and sportscar competition programmes.

Wilfredo Ricart drew up a design for a car that, on paper, had all the elements for performance and striking good looks and was equal to any car that had gone before. When it was introduced to the World in 1954 it had the necessary qualities to put it on an equal footing with the very few other contenders for the title of 'Best Sportscar', cars such as the Mercedes-Benz 300SL, the Jaguar XK120, and the Ferrari 250 Europa.

LEFT: Despite its world-beating performance, the Pegaso Z102-B failed on economic grounds—there was more profit in making trucks than supercars.

ABOVE: Huge finned drum brakes on the Pegaso require a good airflow for cooling. The air ducting intake for the rear brakes is cleverly blended in with the door lock.

OVERLEAF CENTRE: With its Chrysler V8 engine, in Michelotti-designed bodywork, the Briggs Cunningham C-3 was a road going version of the Le Mans racing car.

OVERLEAF RIGHT: Showing its racing heritage, the interior of the C-3 has a functional air. All the controls fall easily to hand, and the comprehensive instrumentation gives the driver all the information he needs.

Just consider for a moment the technical specification of the Pegaso, as it was to be called. There were not many full competition cars around in those days that could match it. It had a 2.8 litre V8 double overhead camshaft engine that could be ordered with any one of nine different compression ratios, three induction arrangements of either single carburettor, quadruple carburettor, or supercharger, with horsepower ranging from 140bhp to over 200bhp (at the end of 1954 a larger 3.2 litre engine was introduced, and with the single carburettor this unit produced 225bhp!) depending on which induction system was used. The 5-speed gearbox was built in units with the differential and located at the rear of the car for better balance. It is of considerable interest to note that this superb gearbox had no syncromesh installed, yet was so easy in use that it was possible to change gears without recourse to the clutch pedal. Suspension was all-independent front and rear based on torsion bars, the rear arrangement following the classic DeDion principle, a method that ensured that the rear wheels remained vertical during suspension movement retaining a full, and consistent tyre contact with the ground. The Pegaso's brakes were massive finned, ventilated, drum-type components, as powerful as any fitted to the Grand Prix cars of the day. Steering was ultra-fast with no more than 1.7 turns of the steering wheel from lock to lock. All of these features were mounted on a chassis that did not dampen these components' individual qualities, and which carried one of two body styles that were stunning in their beauty, a coupé and a convertible.

The Blackhawk Collection has the coupé version and even today thirty years after it first appeared stands out from the crowd by virtue of its good looks and performance potential. Every line and curve of the Pegaso speaks of exciting, fast travel. Road tests of the day shower praise on its high levels of roadholding, braking, and safety performance, with every control being light and efficient. The Pegaso looked to be at least a match for the few other high performers that were available to the fast car customer.

To prove that it was a car that had to be taken seriously as a truly fast machine Pegaso took a Z102-B to the famous Jabbeke stretch of autoroute in Belgium in September 1953 and established world records in the flying mile and kilometre classifications, with speeds of 234km/h (146mph) and 244km/h (153mph) respectively. The car also attained an outright speed of 250km/h (156mph).

In 1957, only six years after beginning production, the factory closed down its sportscar programme and reverted to building the trucks that still dominate Spain's highways. The reasons given for this move were that it was not perceived that the high performance, high priced market could support another very expensive car. The costs involved in establishing a proper dealer network were too much for the factory to bear, and the factory in any case had enough to do in building trucks. The car production was seen as a hindrance to the profitable running of the

Barcelona factory, and in the commercial climate of the 1950s that was really all that was needed to stop Pegaso production once and for all.

Like its closest rival, the Mercedes-Benz 300SL, the Pegaso Z102-0 has become a much desired automobile by collectors the world over. To see one in a collection such as the Blackhawk is still a thrill but to see one being used would be even better.

That great American sportsman, Briggs Cunningham, during the five years of building sports/racing cars to win the Le Mans 24 hours race, also established a very small production line of powerful, large road-going coupé versions of his racers. He called them the C-3 coupés and adapted the best of American and European automobile techniques and parts, namely the splendid Chrysler V8 Hemi engine and Torqueflite transmission housed in a European-styled, and roadworthy chassis/body unit. Using the skills of Michelotti to design the body, and Vignale to build it resulted in a magnificent road car with a very high price tab. This model was featured in the motor-racing film 'Such men are Dangerous' starring Kirk Douglas.

The few C-3 Cunninghams are still regarded as splendid sporting coupés by their fortunate owners and reminders of the great days at the Sarthe circuit in north west France when the big Cunningham R-type racers thundered around the track from 4pm on Saturday until the same time on the Sunday, in front of 300,000 spectators.

Modern glamorous cars

The driver of a modern Stutz Blackhawk enjoys a power hood, good seats and full instrumentation.

The dictionary defines 'Glamorous' as a charm on the eyes, making them see things as fairer than they really are: witchery: deceptive or alluring charm!

If that is accurate then the cars in this chapter fall very neatly into that category. Consider the first car, the 'modern' Stutz Blackhawk. A rebodied Pontiac that has pretentions to be more than that. To say that it is an example of attempting to make a silk purse out of a sow's ear, in automotive terms of course, may be an exaggeration because the base Pontiac is by no stretch of the imagination 'a sow's ear' But that phrase, used as a simple analogy, will serve its purpose for the moment.

In 1970 the Stutz Motor Company of America was formed to produce a luxury car based on an American chassis, engine and transmission unit. They engaged Virgil Exner to style the car which was to be called the Blackhawk. The name Stutz was used because it was thought that it epitomized the best—as defined by the Stutz Company of course—that money could buy.

In 1949 Virgil Exner had left the Studebaker company to join Chrysler as chief stylist. The Chrysler corporation was engaged in an intensive sales fight with G.M. and the Ford Motor Company, and their new president, Lester 'Tex' Colbert had decreed that styling would spearhead their efforts. He gave his full blessing to Virgil Exner to develop the 'forward look' in their corporate styling programme. This was no more than a cynical, inexpensive method, and a cheap one at that (compared with a programme of real technical advance), to give their mechanical components a new suit of clothes. Virgil Exner, with the full support of Tex Colbert, did what he was noted for. He covered the Dodge and Plymouth models with acres of chromium plating, garish colours in duo-tone and tri-tone combinations, and used the greatest styling gimmick of all time, discovering the FIN. Within ten years he had equipped every Chrysler model with a set of rear fins that

Exner's controversial styling of the Stutz Blackhawk's body conceals a humble Pontiac underneath.

The early 1930s design of the Stutz's radiator contrasts with the car's modern bodywork.

The Zimmer's interior is actually a retrimmed version of the Ford Mustang's.

were so extreme that they could almost have served as models for the Space Shuttle!

An early modern Stutz Blackhawk was in Monte Carlo on the occasion of the 1974 Monaco Grand Prix. It appeared out of the car park behind the pits, turning heads as it rolled towards the exit road leading back to the Hotel de Paris. 'Outlandish', was the general comment from all who saw it, and even without a detailed inspection it did not impress in regard to beauty of line and proportion. The gold paintwork, strange sculptured body panels, outside exhaust system that served no functional purpose, the headlight treatment, and the gold-plated interior jarred the senses of anyone who appreciates beautiful cars. Monte Carlo at the time was of course full of superb Italian and German cars. The original Stutz cars when made in Indianapolis were handsome rather than beautiful and were by no means ugly or ungraceful, unlike the 'modern' Stutz, which is surprising bearing in mind that the Pontiac components are shipped out to Italy to Carrozzeria Padana of Modena to have the body and trim finished. There has not been a really ugly Italian road car in the last fifty years, and so it is a great disappointment to learn that the modern Stutz Blackhawk is the work of Italian craftsmen.

The Zimmer Golden Spirit automobile can be described as an extreme clone of the Stutz Blackhawk. The very name gives more than a hint of its true worth. Golden . . . promising luxury and high class value. Spirit . . . a direct effort at associating the car with the Rolls-Royce model of the same name. Would it were the case, but the Zimmer is no more than an attempt at delivering a classic-looking car to customers with little real taste in such matters, but with large bank accounts, and pretensions to owning a high class car.

The Zimmer is produced in Pompano Beach, Florida, and is heavily based on the Ford Mustang. The centre section of the Ford is retained, as are all the mechanicals. New bodywork is

The Zimmer combines up-to-date
practicality with the appearance of a
1930s classic car.

added front and rear, the interior is retrimmed, and several items of 'styling' are added to the overall package.

It is a fact that when cars of this type are laid out on the drawing board three factors are usually included, wire wheels, outside-the-bonnet exhaust with pipes of the flexible type, and separate wings at the front. In these respects the Zimmer does not disappoint; it has all of them. In the case of the exhausts they leave the bonnet side panels some four inches forwards of the actual engine location, and bear no relationship to the functional exhaust system! The wire wheels and the separate front wings are genuine, but the wheels look too small in diameter, being out of scale and out of character with the body styling as a result. The new bodywork is made in that ubiquitous material glass fibre reinforced plastic, very well molded, and of a good heavyweight quality. The sprayed-on paintwork has no more than a mass-produced quality. A Zimmer seen recently that had been in constant use for several years was holding up in the appearance department, the paint a little dulled by the intense Californian sunlight, but the plastic moldings were beginning to show signs of distortion. It is likely that before long the car will become shabby. As a poseur-mobile the Zimmer would rate a 10!

The Gatsby Griffin, like the previous two automobiles is a fake, but it does have two good things going for it, price and good looks. It is constructed in San Jose, northern California at the Gatsby Coachworks, and styled by Sky Clausen. Sky makes no secret of the fact that he designed the car, and makes it for profit only. He has no pretensions to making a classic car, simply one that in some ways resembles a classic of the 1930s.

Sky uses a stretched Ford LTD chassis on which to mount his shapely bodywork, and the car can be powered by any Ford V8 engine up to a 491cu.inch capacity. Californian traffic and speed-restricted conditions mean that the car is pleasant enough to drive. The brakes and ride could be judged as fair to good, but the steering and roadholding are no more than adequate. The suspension feels 'loose', the usual standard Ford poor shock absorber control being the main cause for this sensation, and the steering suffers from the usual over-servoed American power system, lacking in road feel and feedback. For such a large car, the view over the bonnet from the driving seat is impressive for the distance to the front of the car, and the prominent front wings allow the Griffin to be placed on the road with some accuracy. Engine response is sluggish, no doubt partly due to the strangulation effect of the Californian emission equipment with which the poor engine is saddled. These problems are further amplified by the very smooth but slow automatic gearbox performance.

The Clenet, now out of production, was again cast in the mold of the previous cars. Based on a current American production car, using plastic body panels to give it a 1930s look it was really very well made, quite expensive, and only produced in small quantities and has achieved almost star rating among collectors because used examples are in some demand in the USA,

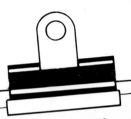

SKY CLAUSEN

Sky Clausen dreamed as so many engineers and mechanics do, of building and selling his own car. His many years in racing and classic car restoration, convinced him that he could produce the car he wanted. He set up his workshop in the northern Californian town of San José and was soon able to show the world his first product, the Gatsby Cabriolet, a car based on a Ford LTD chassis and running gear. It can be bought with either a glass fibre or a steel body. His second vehicle is the Griffin, less restrained in style and better looking on it's Ford LTD under-pinnings.

Sky has been forced to concentrate on re-bodying current production chassis, instead of designing complete cars from scratch. As he explained, 'One step at a time, is my motto. I'm not going to make the mistake so many others have made in this business, of running before they can walk. I intend to establish my business, get it on a firm commercial basis, then I'll get down to making my own, all mine, car!' Time only will tell if Sky can realize his ambitions.

A touch of Italian class—the Nardi steering wheel graces the Griffin's rather cramped interior.

Good looks and a reasonable price have made the Gatsby Griffin a successful seller.

especially on the West Coast.

The Doval Shadow (again another sly reference to a Rolls-Royce model) is a little different from all the previous cars in that the body, which again goes on a Ford LTD chassis, is made by ex-Rolls-Royce and Aston Martin craftsmen in East Haven, Conn. It is manufactured in light alloy material, and as one would expect from craftsmen of this experience, is beautifully constructed. Like the Clenet and the Griffin, the Doval has rather cramped accommodation in the tiny driving compartment; although the trim and seats are excellently made and finished, it is still a struggle for a person of average American proportions to get in to and out of these cars.

Road performance, again, is just like the others. Obviously these manufacturers devote all their efforts towards the

Most American custom cars have glass fibre bodies, but the Doval Shadow, built by ex-Aston Martin and Rolls-Royce craftsmen, has light alloy panels.

LEFT: On the road, the Doval Shadow, which is based on the Ford LTD, drives like an ordinary American car.

FAR LEFT: Alain Clenet was one of the first American custom car makers to offer a well-made, expensive vehicle that combined the comforts of a modern automobile with the appearance of a rare, classic car.

appearance of their vehicles, and virtually nothing to their dynamic qualities. The Doval, for such a large car, has no provision for carrying luggage, the large rear section to the bodywork being no more than an empty shell, without even a floor! Don Hart who operates the Doval Coachworks did confirm this fact, and added that the tail of his car would possibly get a luggage compartment soon, but few, if any, Doval Shadow customers had passed comment about this!

All of the cars in this chapter are American-financed, and styled to cash in on the nostalgia craze on the assumption that any vehicle that can be made to look like a 1930s car with an outside exhaust system, wire wheels, and separate wings can be sold. The old saying, 'You can fool some of the people, some of the time' appears to work in this area of automotive fakery, because all of these vehicles did sell. However, it would seem that even the rich, undiscriminating public are seeing through these efforts to part them from their money, and Doval and Clenet are not producing cars at the moment.

All these cars fit as standard the expensive, and superb Nardi steering wheel, which must demonstrate that the dominant profit motive behind them was not quite strong enough to prevent just a little real class from getting through to the paying customer.

There is a place for such vehicles in the automobile market, and there always has been, but the buyer, without experience and knowledge, should beware, and not be taken in by surface gloss and skilful advertising.

The Packard

Although the Packard Model L's artillery-style wheels look delicate, their quality of construction gave them ample strength.

'Ask the Man who Owns One', for years this was the advertising slogan used by the Packard Motor Company to sell its cars. By today's standards it is a rather low key headline for a major automobile manufacturer to use, but it says a great deal about Packard and its products. The slogan hints that the Packard car is so good, so reliable, of such high quality that all the potential buyer need do is to ask a Packard owner to confirm what he already knows, that the Packard is the best that money can buy.

Like Rolls-Royce, the Packard company came into being after some years as an electrical equipment manufacturer, placing a very high value on good design, careful construction and great durability. These values remained with the Packard company until almost the very end of its life. James Ward Packard began making cars in 1899, but was bought out by a Detroit businessman, Henry B. Joy, in 1901. The new Packard company introduced a four cylinder 12 litre engine into the model L Packard in 1904. A splendid example of the model L in the Nethercutt Collection is housed in the most spectacular style in the Tower of Beauty in Sylmar, California.

However, it was not until 1912 when Jesse Gurney Vincent joined Packard as chief engineer that the company really began to make its mark as a manufacturer of luxury, high class cars. Jesse Vincent designed the first V12 engine to go into mass-production for use in an American automobile. He called his car the Twin-6; the engine was a V12 side valve unit, with a 60° angle between the cylinder banks of 6.9 litre capacity, and was among the first with alloy pistons as part of Vincent's search for lightness and strength. This power unit gave the Twin-6 the necessary refinement and performance that the luxury class customer demanded.

It was so successful that in its first year 3,606 examples of the Twin-6 were built and sold. In 1917 4,140 Twin-6s reached happy customers. In that year Packard made more V12-engined cars, of the highest quality, than the total production of similar vehicles produced by all of Europe's luxury car makers combined!

When Warren G. Harding became the first President of the United States of America to ride to his inauguration by car, he

LEFT AND CENTRE: The Packard Model L equalled the quality of any European rival and set the standard for a long line of top-class American cars.

Phil Hill owns this Packard Twin 6—the first car to have a mass-produced V12 engine.

used a Packard Twin-6.

In 1923 the Twin-6 was replaced by the single-8 model, when over 35,000 examples of the V12-powered car had been made. The new car served further to establish Packard as the name for a top quality automobile, and the company went from strength to strength.

Phil Hill, the first American to win a Formula One Driver's World Championship, in 1961, is an avowed Packard enthusiast. He has a Twin-6 at home and wished to demonstrate it.

He drove the car out of his garage, checked it for fuel, took up some adjustment on the rear brakes (the only brakes the car has) and made ready to take the car for a run.

He quickly drove down to the Santa Monica Freeway, and thrusting his precious car into the crowded road he proceeded to put the Packard through its paces, giving the machinery no mercy. In his day as a top racer Phil always drove hard with 101 percent effort. Now, taking maximum revolutions in first and second gears, gearchanging with lightning speed he quickly reached a cruising speed on the freeway of 75mph. At this speed, which is well over the national speed limit of 55mph, the big car sat on the road as solid as a rock, the high placed seats giving marvellous visibility in all directions, and in spite of the author's concern about the car having only rear brakes, Phil's driving ability, anticipation, and reflexes ensured that the car invariably slowed smoothly and without panic. All the time Phil kept up a commentary on the car's abilities and after 30 minutes of practical demonstration there was no doubting Packard quality and Phil's competence behind the steering wheel.

Phil said, almost as an aside, that he considers that his Twin-6 would make the perfect vehicle in which to take his family back to New York during the summer. 'It will cruise at a very happy 60-65mph all day, there is enough room for the rest of the family to stretch out in the back without getting in each other's way, and the suspension would make for a very comfortable journey! And he was serious, as he is about all motoring matters.

When in 1923 Packard introduced four-wheel brakes, and four-speed gear boxes, they continued to make that masterpiece of automotive power units the V12, this time yet another Jesse Vincent design, but of 7.3 litre capacity. This engine remained in production, with updating modifications, until 1939.

Two Packards that featured this engine were the Le Baron Towncar, and one of the most covetable cars in the world, the V12 convertible by Dietrich, known as the 'Orello', and, like the model L, to be found in the Nethercutt Collection. For sheer style and glamour these two cars must rank with the best.

This latter car is known as the 'Orello' because although it is a model 1108 Packard its colour is a combination of yellow and orange, specially selected by Jack Nethercutt to match the famous Packard advertisement in Fortune magazine which ran in 1934, the year the 'Orello' was built. The car is a four-door convertible sedan by Dietrich, one of the very best of American coachbuilders. It is a model of quiet good looks and proportions,

yet because of its splendid V12 engine, fast, comfortable, and able to cover long distances at high speed. Maintained in mint condition by the restoration staff at the Nethercutt Collection it is, like all the cars at Sylmar, ready for the road at short notice, requiring no more than fuel and a battery to run. Unlike so many desirable and rare cars these days, the 'Orello' Packard could be put to everyday use now, without any concern from the driver at using such a vehicle in today's traffic conditions. To be able to say that about a fifty-year-old motor-car speaks volumes about the Packard's design and construction. For a convertible the 'Orello' looks just as impressive and handsome with the top up as with it down, a truly magnificent automobile.

If the 'Orello' has glamour it is because of its striking good looks, beautiful finish, performance, and sheer class, the Le Baron Towncar scores in the glamour stakes with its aura of grand style. To anyone who thinks of the typical American car as a flashy, chromium plated, extravagance on wheels, then the first sight of the Packard Le Baron would quickly effect a change of opinion. The Le Baron towncar is quite simply a superb carriage for the grandest occasions. Travelling in the grand manner is the sole reason for its existence. It is a sober, stately vehicle in the best possible taste.

The 7,298cc V12 engine sighs into life at no more than a touch of the starter button, and remains quiet and unobtrusive throughout its working range, giving the heavy car a performance quite out of keeping with its appearance. The steering, brakes, and ride are all perfectly matched to the engine,

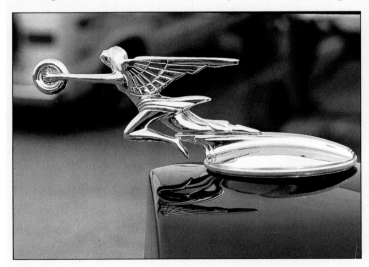

The Packard radiator mascot, just like the car itself, is distinctive, simple and attractive.

THE AMERICAN ROLLS-ROYCE

In just 59 years, the Packard company had slipped from the height of luxury and technical advance to bankruptcy.

But the Rolls tag was well-earned. With its slogan 'Ask the man who owns one', Packard established itself as America's number one luxury car manufacturer. In its hey-day, the Packard company may even have been the best in the world. And during the war, it built the celebrated Rolls-Royce Merlin engine which powered the Spitfire, the Hurricane and the Mosquito.

The Merlin, however, was the company's first flirtation with greatness. By 1959, after its disasterous merger with Studebaker, it was no more. The field was left free for Cadillac and Lincoln.

No European car was better made than the Packard of the mid-1930s as exemplified by the 1935 Le Baron Towncar.

going about their business in an efficient, smooth manner that is so right for the car and the use for which it is intended.

In its day the Packard had many competitors for the luxury car trade: the Rolls-Royce Phantom II; the superb Hispano-Suiza J12; the Isotta-Fraschini, and the excellent Cadillac V16, but none of these cars could really match the Packard's combination of very high quality, bearing in mind that the Packard was a truly 'mass-produced car. In 1937 Packard made more than 109,000 cars, and were building straight-6s, straight-8s as well as the V12 engines, all going into several different body styles. Despite the crippling effects of the depression, Packard appeared to be riding high, avoiding the problems that were afflicting so many of the other American car-makers like the Auburn-Cord-Duesenberg company. But the writing was on the wall by the mid-1940s, even for Packard.

Packard used independent front suspension and low-pressure tyres (above) to give their cars a comfortable ride.

Even today, this 1934 Packard V12 'Orello' (left) is a pleasure to drive, on the open road or in traffic.

During World War Two, Packard had further enhanced their engineering reputation by manufacturing aero-engines, possibly the most famous being the Rolls-Royce Merlin engine that made such a major contribution to British victory in the Battle of Britain. Packard quality was built into it, and this earned warm praise from the pilots and maintenance crews in all the theatres of war where Merlin-powered aircraft flew, and even Rolls-Royce themselves. At the end of the War Packard had been persuaded to sell the body dies for their luxury model, the Senior Series 8-cylinder car, to the Russians in a forlorn gesture of American/ Soviet goodwill, a move that left Packard with no true luxury car for the post-war period. The Russians went on to make their version of the Packard for many years, calling it the ZIS-110 model, but it was only available to members of the Politburo.

Packard returned to making cars after 1945 with the wrong class of automobile, and with a new president, James J. Nance, who wanted desperately to return to luxury car manufacture. Packard was faced by a buoyant General Motors Corporation intent on holding on to their preeminent position in the domestic market, and a hungry Chrysler Corporation equally keen on retaining their reputation for the finest mass production engineering. The Ford Motor Company were in dire straits, beset with internal conflict that nearly destroyed them. Even so, Packard never really regained their position in the market place. Their problems increased further when they purchased the dying Studebaker company in 1954 in a desperate attempt at broadening their market appeal, but as one might have supposed, two dying companies can never really restore each other's fortunes. The shrinking luxury car segment of the market only made life even more difficult for Packard; besides, Cadillac and Lincoln had that piece of the action firmly in their tight grip, so Packard were frozen out of even their special area of operation. Within four years of making the disastrous merger with Studebaker, the famous and prestigious name of Packard had gone for ever from the lists of great American car makers. That year, 1958, was a sad year for lovers of grand luxury cars, and you have only to see examples of the best of the Packard range to fully appreciate what has been lost.

Carefully designed and built, and carrying some of the most beautiful bodies made by such names as Dietrich, Le Baron, Murphy, and Darrin, the Packard effortlessly covered the market for high quality cars. Whether the customer was a head of state, a film star, a socialite, a country doctor or simply someone who fully appreciated fine automobiles, there was a Packard in the range for them. Just take a look at the Packard Super-8 of 1932, which the company entitled the Phaeton. Introduced to a public at the height of the Depression, it demonstrated that Packard was capable and willing to fight on against the odds with quality cars. Offered with a choice of two engines, the straight-8 with 135hp, the new V12 with 160hp, the car delivered stunning good looks with reliability, durability, and performance. The Super-8 could

cruise at 85mph, and the V12 could easily attain a speed of over 110mph. The green Super-8 in the photographs was spotted in Los Angeles this year outside the Museum of Contemporary Art. It is in regular use, yet it looks so good that that it ought to be on display inside the Museum! However, inside the Museum there is a Packard Super-12 Phaeton occupying a stand in the exhibition of classic cars.

The Packard story could be described as one of riches to rags in only 59 years. Thankfully they left behind a dynamic record of many good cars and several really excellent ones, and an aero-engine that was a positive factor in victory in the Second World War; there cannot be many other automobile manufacturers who have as good a claim to fame.

LEFT AND FAR LEFT: No museum piece, this fine Packard Super 8 is used all the year round.

Racers

ABOVE AND RIGHT: The Mercer Raceabout 35C could be called the first American hot-rod. A simple, well-made car, it offered little more than pure performance with little concern for the driver's comfort.

It is generally held by the public that motor-racing is glamorous. To those directly involved in the activity, racing is simply very hard work under difficult conditions, usually hundreds of miles away from the home-base. It is also dangerous and exciting, and at times is frustrating, inconvenient, noisy, dirty, and always very, very expensive. Sir Thomas Lipton once said that racing a yacht in the America's Cup can be accurately compared with standing under a cold shower for hours on end, and tearing up £5 notes at the same time! The same thought must have entered every motoring journalist's head when covering some motor-racing events.

Yet to the occasional spectator any mention of being involved, even on the very edge of the sport, brings a gleam of envy into their eyes. Throw in a hint that the next race to be visited will be the Monaco Grand Prix, or the Italian G.P. at Monza, and their immediate response will be to exclaim, 'You lucky so-and-so!' Although a car race itself is very glamorous, one must not forget that, were it not for the machinery involved, the event would not happen.

The Mercer Raceabout was built in Trenton, New Jersey in the early days of this century. Mercer stopped producing cars as early as 1925, but their great days were those prior to 1915 when the Raceabout was in production. The Raceabout was, in fact, probably the best car that they ever made and certainly the most famous.

By 1910 their fastest car was the Speedster, but in that year Mercer's chief engineer, Finlay Robertson Porter, designed a road-going version of the Type 30-M racing car, and called it the Raceabout. It was an instant success, guaranteed to be safe at over 70mph, which was a remarkable speed for a roadster in those days. It looked the part of a racing car, its mechanicals barely covered by the bodywork—this gave the car a purposeful, uncompromising appearance. The engine, a four cylinder, T-headed Continental unit of 5 litres capacity had a revolution limit of 1700rpm, and produced a meagre 50hp. This large, but low powered engine endowed the Mercer with shattering performance which was helped by a primitive lightweight chassis. The monocle windscreen was just one example of weight-saving by the factory at the expense of comfort. Only the Stutz Bearcat could approach the Raceabout on the roads of America in the four years before the Great War.

After the death of the Roebling family of Brooklyn Bridge fame, and the founders of the Mercer company, Emlem Hare acquired the concern. In the ten years to 1925, after production of the Raceabout ceased, Mercer were still to make a few good cars, but as their cars became more civilized they became more conventional and of less interest to potential buyers. By 1925 the Mercer company had been reduced to just another small-time, underfinanced American car maker, under attack from the giants of the industry. They closed their doors that year never to make another sportscar again. But the Raceabout lives on in people's memories. The author saw an elderly gentleman in a wheelchair explaining the intricacies of the Raceabout next to him in the Briggs Cunningham Museum. His enthusiasm was plain to see, and it was clear that he had had more than a little experience of the car. His eyes shone with delight as he talked his son through the starting procedures, and how the car had to be controlled at speed on the rutted, dirt roads of pre-1914 California.

The mighty Daimler-Benz company of Germany, producers of Mercedes-Benz automobiles, have always used auto-racing for one purpose only, to sell their roadcars. In 1968 a graph in the export department demonstrated the success of this policy: after every period of factory racing activity sales of Mercedes-Benz cars increased. This may well be the reason for their not returning to Grand Prix racing; as their cars are always in demand, they may have no need to go back to the race tracks of the world.

But the situation was far different after World War 1, the German economy was in a very bad way, and industry was desperate to earn foreign currency and prestige. Auto-racing has always provided publicity, and success for one company was seen to reflect glory on to other German industries. It was a marvellous shopwindow for the whole German nation after the battering it had taken during the four years of the Great War, and the internal conflict that was taking place afterwards.

At the Berlin Auto Show of 1921 Mercedes-Benz introduced two new cars, the 6/25/40 and the 10/40/65. It is the former car that we are concerned with here. The designation refers to the fiscal horse-power rating of 6 taxable horse-power, the 25 to the maximum horse-power produced without the supercharger, and the 40 to the power produced with the blower. The engine of this car had a capacity of 1.5 litres. The supercharger was of the Roots-

type, an American invention which used twin rotors in a sealed compartment mounted on the front of the engine, and driven by the crankshaft. This is a more efficient method of supercharging an engine than the centrifugal method as it provides boost from very low engine revolutions. It was brought into operation at the fullest extent of the throttle movement, when a multi-plate clutch operated the supercharger. In other words, when the accelerator was pressed to the floorboards the blower cut in!

The author once experienced this effect during a memorable drive in a Mercedes-Benz 540K across London when aged about 15. A doctor friend of the family owned the 540K and offered a ride one Sunday afternoon late in the summer of 1948. In those days there was very little traffic using London's roads, and we made good time to the Blackwall Tunnel under the river Thames. This old tunnel was (and still is) lined with white tiles, and these have an amplifying effect on sound. Halfway through the tunnel the good doctor floored the accelerator in second gear, and with a scream the blower engaged, the walls of the tunnel reflected the sound, amplifying it to an almost unbearable level, and with a rush we stormed out on the other side. To anyone outside the Blackwall Tunnel on that summer's day it must have sounded as though the Hounds of Hell were coming!

This was the device that Mercedes-Benz would use in all their competition cars, and many of their road cars right up to 1939. It was first used in their 1922 Targa Florio racing car. The cars for the Sicilian race were heavily modified, and carried the first twin overhead camshaft cylinder heads fitted to any Mercedes-Benz car. The engines were fitted into three converted 1914 Grand Prix chassis, given mudguards and windshields to make them look like sportscars, as the Targa Florio is for sportscars, and not G.P. machines! Count Masseti won the race in front of two French Ballots, using one of these supercharged Mercedes.

The 38/250 Mercedes-Benz sportscar of 1928 may be worthily described as one of the greatest sportscars ever built. It combined in the one vehicle high performance, superb good looks and a level of construction for which the Stuttgart factory had always been famous. The 38/250 in the Blackhawk collection looks today as if it had just left the factory, being quite immaculate in all respects. It exudes an aura of power and speed that can be felt almost as a physical thing. The engine, the heart of any car, is a 7,069 cc, six-cylinder, single overhead cam unit providing the driver with 140bhp in unsupercharged form, and 200bhp when using the blower. The supercharger was not to be used for periods of more than 20 seconds—in other words it was an overtaking device, definitely *not* to be used on long fast stretches of autobahn for mile after mile, unless frequent engine rebuilds were to be undertaken!

Even without the aid of the supercharger the Mercedes-Benz SS 38/250 could be cruised at over 110mph for hours on end. The car remained in production until 1933 as the standard sportscar made by the company, although only 111 examples were built in that time.

LEFT AND FAR LEFT: Mercedes-Benz have always used motor racing to develop their cars and to stimulate sales. One of their cars won the 1922 Targa Florio in Sicily by a handsome margin.

Delage Grand Prix cars for the 1926 formula were very few in number, only 7 being constructed in all. The 1.5 litre supercharged straight-8 Delage has been labelled the most beautiful Grand Prix car ever built and it was successful to boot! In one of these lovely cars, Robert Benoist won the 1926 British G.P. at the Brooklands Track.

The Delage engine contained 60 roller and ball bearings, and was recognized as being 'bulletproof'. John Burgess, the Cunningham Museum's director told of when he used to demonstrate some of the collection's cars in the Museum car park (which was very large at the time). He remembers taking out the Delage, and as a very experienced racing driver he was able to show the car off, putting it through its paces in a very thorough manner. It had rained the night before and although the hot southern Californian sun had dried up most of the car park there were still several damp patches under some trees. In crossing one of these wet areas in second gear John was astonished to get wheel spin with the revolution counter flashing round to 9,300rpm! Up to that day previous drives had seen 7,000rpm used as the maximum safe rev. limit. This figure had been calculated when the car had become part of the Cunningham Collection without any details regarding safe engine speeds. 7,000rpm was reckoned to be about right for a car that was over 50 years old. The Delage was rushed into the well-equipped Cunningham workshops, stripped down and checked for valve bounce and any other mechanical derangement. Nothing appeared to be amiss with the engine, and it was reassembled and returned to its place in the hall of the Museum. Later that year John took it to Laguna Seca for the annual Historic Car Races held there every September. He was to put on a driving display on the track of about five quick laps. Before he went out on the track, and still mindful of what had happened in the car park, John was approached by an elderly Frenchman who introduced himself as one of the Delage mechanics from the factory racing days. John

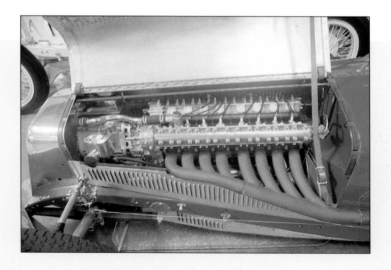

immediately asked him about rev limits for the engine. The reply was that 10,000rpm was regularly used by all the team drivers, and 9,300rpm was perfectly O.K.!! The Delage company really knew what they were doing when they designed and built these marvellous engines at 140, Avenue des Champs Elysées, Paris, back in 1926.

The Talbot Lago could be described as a racing Cinderella. A tough, French racing car of the 1950s, it carried the French colours with some distinction across Europe, competing in the Grand Prix racing programme against the might of Alfa Romeo, Ferrari and Maserati. It used an overhead valve six-cylinder engine mated to a Wilson pre-selector gearbox. What success it achieved, 1st, 2nd and 3rd in the 1937 French G.P. and 1st in the French G.P. of 1947 was largely due to its inherent durability, and its frugal fuel consumption. The car was often able to go through a full race without needing to make a pit stop for fuel. Talbot Lagos are still to be seen in the historic car races now held in many countries of the world.

The 1937 Rolls Bentley can more accurately be described as a two-seater, open Rolls-Royce. It was a much more civilized car that the vehicle made by W. O. Bentley, but lost a great deal of excitement and driver interest as a result. It will never have quite the same appeal as a W. O. Bentley car, or the same financial value. However, it is still a delightful car of the mid-1930s, and the one featured in this chapter has one special claim of interest. It was entered in the 1984 Great American Race, from Los Angeles to Indianapolis. It went on to win this new event on the public highway, and in doing so it secured for its owner a cheque for $100,000!

The Bentley is for sale as this is written, with a price tab of $100,000.

The story of the Arnolt-Bristol is very much more the story of Stanley Harold Arnolt III than that of just an automobile.

'Wacky' Arnolt was born in Chicago in 1907 into a family of bookbinders, not poor, but not wealthy either. The young Arnolt attended the University of Wisconsin and took a degree in mechanical engineering, but when it was time for him to find a

RIGHT AND FAR RIGHT: The Talbot Lago
was a French racing car of the 1950s.
Although its design was already out
of date when the car was new, its
fuel economy and durability brought
it some success.

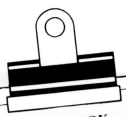

TONY CROOK

Tony Crook, the managing director of the Bristol Company, can be variously described as a gentleman, businessman, racing driver, salesman, and test-driver.

It was as a racing driver that he first came to the notice of the general public, having the distinction of never having been beaten by another driver in a car of equal performance. His greatest success was as a driver of a Frazer Nash sportscar in the race that supported the Monaco Grand Prix. He had a tremendous tussle with the Lancia of Valenzano before taking the lead, and holding it to the line. From 1946 to 1955 he drove Bristol-engined cars in more than 400 races all over Europe.

With the then Mr George White, and two other directors he took over the car making part of the Bristol Aeroplane Company in 1956 when the parent company split it off to become Bristol Cars Ltd. In 1960, with Sir George White, he bought up the company separating it from any further control of Bristol Aeroplane. It is no coincidence that it was in this year that the first V-8 engined Bristol appeared, the 407 model.

His company has full order books, a world-wide reputation for excellence and yet is run in the most friendly, easy manner. Tony apparently knows each and every owner (and car) made and sold over the last thirty years.

job the Depression was well under way in the USA, and jobs for young mechanical engineers were in short supply.

For the next seven years Wacky, like millions of his countrymen got by, but it was a struggle for someone so eager to make his mark in the world. Then in early 1939 the big chance came along—Arnolt was offered the full manufacturing rights to a small marine engine, the Sea-mite. Scraping together the small amount of necessary capital to buy up the complete company, Wacky moved into ownership of the concern that was to make his fortune. The secret was in his timing; within months of his take-over, World War Two had broken out, and for the next six years the USA was to be the free world's shipbuilder. Every one of the thousands of American-built ships needed a whole host of small powered craft such as lifeboats and tenders. Luckily for Arnolt, nearly all of these small boats were powered by a Sea-mite. The Arnolt Sea-mite factories expanded to service the government contracts, and in doing so allowed Wacky to move into other products. Very soon the Arnolt enterprise was a coast to coast conglomerate, and making lots of money.

In 1931, Rolls-Royce took over the bankrupt Bentley company. Bentleys of the early 1930s were refined cars that lacked real performance. This American-owned 3½-litre example competed in the 1984 Great American Race.

At the 1952 Turin Motor Show Wacky appeared in his Stetson hat and Texas cowboy boots looking every inch the European's idea of the typical American millionaire. On the Bertone stand he noticed two very attractive M.G.-based sportscars that Nuccio Bertone had produced in a last minute attempt to stave off the collapse of his company. Bertone was hoping to persuade a major car-maker of his enormous talents as a coachbuilder, and was bowled over when this American giant ordered 200 finished Bertone-M.G.s, a move that saved the Bertone company. When two years later he saw the Bristol 404 sports coupé, it increased his desire to go in to motor-racing, but the 404 as it came from the Bristol company was too heavy to be really competitive, so Arnolt turned to Bertone for the answer. With the help of one of Bristol's best engineers, Jim Watt, Bertone produced the sensational looking Arnolt-Bristol coupé. Nuccio built a steel body on to the Bristol chassis as the lines of the car could be duplicated only in this material, alloy plainly ruling out the possibility of following the Bertone lines. It is interesting to note that the alloy-bodied Bristol 404 as it came from the factory weighed 300lbs more than the steel-bodied Arnolt-Bristol! Not only was the Arnolt-Bristol lighter, but in 1954 it was almost half the price of the Bristol 404; $4645 against the $9946 of the 404!

Using the brakes from the Bristol 403 helped to keep costs down, as did using Italian craftsmen, but even so it is remarkable that Wacky could make and sell his version of the Bristol so much more cheaply than the original model.

In all Arnolt sold 130 out of a total of 142 cars built—the remaining 12 were destroyed in a warehouse fire. The film star Lee Marvin owned one, as did Air Force General Curtis Le May, and the model labelled the 'Bolide' was raced all over the USA with some success. But probably the car, and Wacky's, greatest success came in 1955 when he persuaded the retired French racing driver René Dreyfus to lead a team of Bolides in the Sebring International Sportscar Race in Florida. The team did rather well finishing in 1st, 2nd and 4th positions!

American money, an Italian body and a British chassis and engine were the formula for the Arnolt-Bristol. Its fantastic handling often helped it to beat more powerful cars.

Even by the standards of the day the Arnolt-Bristol was not a really high performance car, not having a great deal of horse power. However, the car was balanced by agility and good roadholding, together with fine braking and steering characteristics. The Arnolt-Bristol team worked on the basic racing principle of, 'To finish First, first one has to Finish'.

As it came from Wacky's showrooms, the Bolide could only boast a top speed of 112mph, and a standing-start quarter mile in 17 seconds, with a 0-60mph time of 10.1 seconds. The model was last raced in 1960, by which time there were many other cars that were cheaper and faster. The beauty of the car, its racing history, and the story of its founder all make it a candidate for a glamorous car.

Stanley Harold Arnolt III died in 1963, and because he made no allowance for anyone to properly succeed him, the Arnolt car died with him.

Briggs Cunningham is the other face of the Wacky Arnolt coin, a wealthy man in his own right, and an established hero in the view of the American public by virtue of his exploits as a successful yachtsman before he turned to racing car production and driving. He manufactured cars for a very short period, only five years. Briggs was quite successful on the race tracks of America and Europe, then at the height of his fame he closed down his Florida factory and returned to California to establish his excellent Automobile Museum at Costa Mesa.

Briggs' racing programme began in 1949 with a modified Cadillac sedan at Le Mans with a Frick-Tappet modified engine. This apparently unsuitable car finished 10th! In the same race that year Briggs entered another Cadillac-engined special which was so big and ugly that the French dubbed it 'Le Monstre'. The alloy body might have been aerodynamically sound, but it really was awful to look at. Even so it finished the punishing race just behind his other car, in 11th place.

For the 1952 Le Mans race Cunningham developed and entered his most successful sports/racing car the C-4R model. This

Briggs Cunningham was a rich amateur racing driver who wanted to win the Le Mans 24-hour race in a car bearing his own name. He almost succeeded in this Cunningham C-4R (right), finishing in 4th place.

was powered by a 300hp Chrysler V8 engine driving through a ZF four-speed gearbox. The whole car, like all the Cunninghams, was most beautifully crafted—the brakes, of the drum variety, were so elegant that a set has been mounted on a wall plaque in the Museum and looks like a piece of modern sculpture. However, beautiful as they undoubtedly were, they suffered from heat fade because they were too large in diameter, and too narrow in width! These two factors meant that the peripheral speed of the drums was so great that the heat build-up could not be dissipated quickly enough. Smaller, wider drums would have handled the problem much more easily, but at the time of the French classic the problem had been neither located nor rectified.

But despite this braking deficiency the C-4R gave Briggs Cunningham his best Le Mans finish—he drove the car into 4th position at the end of the 24 hours. The following year saw a development of the Cunningham sports/racer with the appearance of the C-5R which, driven by Walters and Fitch got even closer to the winner's circle finishing in 3rd position.

At this point it was becoming obvious that with the involvement of the massively financed Mercedes-Benz racing programme, small-scale efforts such as those of the Cunningham team stood virtually no chance in international racing, and Briggs ran his car operation down, finally closing the Palm Beach factory in 1955.

1966 was the year that the Ford sportscar racing effort finally, after immense expenditure of men, materials, and money, achieved success at the one race that really counts, the Le Mans 24 Hours race.

In 1962, the Ford company had made approaches to Enzo Ferrari with a view to buying his company. Enzo was interested, and for a few months teams of lawyers, engineers, and administrators commuted between Dearborn and Maranello. But in the end, and following delay after delay, Ferrari pulled out of the deal. Ford then scouted Europe for a car that could be developed as a Ford racing-car. In England they finally narrowed the list of possibles down to two, Lotus and Lola.

Len Terry explained how the final decision was made between these two companies. Colin Chapman the Lotus boss was confident that his company would secure the very lucrative contact with Ford, and was devastated when it was announced that Eric Broadley and his tiny Lola concern would be the ones to gain the support that Ford were offering. Broadley had shown his idea of what a modern sports/racing coupé should look like at the London Racing Car Show earlier that year—he simply called it the Lola GT, and it was beautiful. Broadley was a more amenable partner than Chapman, his car had the potential to do what Ford wanted and much of the hard work had already been done, so Broadley was the man that Ford selected.

As an aftermath to this decision Lotus rushed into producing their Type 30 sports/racing car, with Colin Chapman swearing to use it to blow the Ford/Lola car off the race tracks of the world. The Type 30, and its successor the Type 40, were probably the worst Lotus competition cars ever built; most drivers hated them as on the track they were obviously very difficult to drive competitively, only the genius of Jim Clark ever succeeding in keeping the Type 30 on the road and over the line at the finish. Eric Broadley signed a two-year contract with Ford, John Wyer was engaged to manage the racing operation, and Carroll Shelby would handle the Ford GT racing team. In June 1963 the Ford Advanced Vehicle Operation was formed to research, build, and develop the ex-Lola GT now called the GT-40, because it stood 40 inches (actually 40½ inches!) high.

The GT-40 engine would be the Fairlane alloy-block Indy 4-cam engine of 4.2 litre capacity developing 350hp. A Colotti 4-speed gearbox was fitted and was to prove a constant source of problems from then on.

The Le Mans 24 Hours race was the target for the Ford effort, as it is the most prestigious race in the sportscar racing world. Ford had ten months to prepare, and after a period of intense activity entered the 1964 season with high hopes.

Of their efforts in this, their first year in this highly competitive class of international motor-racing all that need be said is that

they entered ten races, and failed to finish in any of them!!

Eric Broadley did not renew the offered extension to his contract, and left after the 1964 season.

Ford contracted the Shelby-American organization to take over the preparation and development of the GT-40 programme. Phil Remington and the Englishman, Ken Miles, were given the task of making the car competitive, and with Carroll Shelby they set about this task. One improvement made was to replace the Fairlane Indy engine with a race-proven Cobra 289cu. inch unit. New ZF gearboxes were substituted for the unreliable Colotti that had been the cause of so many breakdowns in 1964. The engine cooling system was improved, aerodynamics sorted out, cast magnesium Halibrand wheels replaced the Borrani wire wheels, and bigger, better brakes were installed.

As a result the new GT-40s won the first two races of 1965 at Daytona and Sebring. But the Ferrari threat was getting stronger all the time, and the pressure from them meant that no more races were won by Ford that year, the failure to win Le Mans being the ultimate bitter blow. They withdrew from the remaining races after Le Mans that year!

During the 1965 season a bigger 427 cu. inch engine had been tried out since it delivered a reliable 500plus horsepower, and this was obviously the way forward in the 1966 season. With this engine the GT-40 became known as the Mark II.

1966 and 1967 saw the Ford racing effort finally gain the coveted win at Le Mans, in 1967 by the greatest margin over the previous race record in history. Gurney and Foyt drove the winning GT-40 Mark IV covering 3249.6 miles in the 24 hours period, at an average speed of 135.48mph. Nobody will ever know the final cost to Ford of winning those two Le Mans races—one can only guess at the number of zeros on the balance sheet.

When Phil Hill was asked which racing cars he most liked driving, his answer was just a little surprising; he listed only two cars, the Ford GT-40, and the Chaparral—the highest accolade any racing car racing car manufacturer could wish for. In the Briggs Cunningham Auto Museum there is a yellow GT-40 on display. It is there on loan from Jim Toensing of Newport Beach, close by the Museum. Jim is a remarkably fine machinist, and he has restored the GT-40 to its original specification, that is with the Fairlane 4-OH Camshaft engine. In view of the problems that Shelby-American had with this engine, even with the fullest backing from the giant Ford company. Jim Toensing might have been suspected of going about his restoration the wrong way. However the Toensing touch was good enough to convert the fractious engine into a docile, well behaved unit that is not only immensely powerful, but can be driven on the public highway without any problems. The whole car is as beautifully turned out as the engine, and looking at it in the Cunningham Museum makes one wish it could be demonstrated by John Burgess around the car park at the side of the Museum building. A very great competition car in splendid condition.

By using its almost unlimited resources, the Ford Motor Company developed the Le Mans-winning GT40. After victories in the 1966 and '67 races, the car became an instant classic.

Specials

The Bucciali was a complex machine that was never marketed with any real conviction; its constructors were already dogged by the effects of the Depression in the early 1930s.

Many of the early car designers had an engineering background in steam locomotive and railroad work, or in heavy electrical equipment construction. However, one make of automobile can claim a musical design history on the part of its designer and constructor. This vehicle is the Bucciali, made by the Bucciali brothers, Angelo and Paul-Albert in Paris between 1922 and 1933.

Their father had been born in Corsica, but had left that island to move to Boulogne-sur-Mer to repair and build church organs. His two sons worked for some time at this profession before leaving Boulogne to go to Paris to make their fortune.

They had already turned their hand to car building, but until they got to Paris their work had not been very successful. In the capital city they established themselves, and began to construct their masterpiece, a car of very radical design. Firstly it featured front wheel drive, at the time a controversial method of driving a vehicle. They used a rather inefficient transmission system that was heavy, expensive, and made driving the car irksome in the extreme. In fact, the author's first sight of a Bucciali was seeing it at the foot of the steep hill that leads up to the garage that houses the pick of the Blackhawk Collection. The large car was sitting there, the side valve straight-8 Continental engine rumbling away as the driver searched for first gear so as to be able to tackle the hill. It took him several minutes before he located the right slot, and with a mighty jolt the selector went home, and the Bucciali was able to ascend the hill.

During the short life of the Bucciali company, the two brothers stayed in business by the skin of their teeth, full of very interesting ideas, but there was never enough money to realize their full potential, and the times were not the right ones for launching radical approaches to automotive problems.

In their TAV-8 and Double Huit series of designs the Buccialis came up with such features as front-wheel drive, electrical operation of the front brakes, servo-assistance for the mechanical rear brakes, and the oddball transmission system that had step-

down gears between engine and road wheels before the clutch, which imposed a four times increased loading on the gearbox which component consequently had to be very much heavier, with bigger and stronger internals than would otherwise have been required. This made driving the Bucciali very difficult, and gave the driver a hard time!

For engines the Buccialis offered the Continental 3.8 litre straight-8 with 120hp, and a remarkable V16 side-valve unit that they only claimed produced between 155 and 170hp; not a great deal of power for a 7.8 litre motor! However, the lack of same was probably an advantage as it had to drive the front wheels of the car and more would have caused extra problems. Apart from a show display chassis there seems to be no record of a Double Huit ever reaching a customer's hands and being driven on the road.

The owner of the TAV-8 shown in the photograph explains that driving a Bucciali was not one of the great motoring delights. In a nutshell, it was very slow, very expensive, difficult to stop and had an awkward gear change, and its fuel consumption was never better than 10-12mpg. However, the stork emblem on the bonnet a reminder of Paul-Albert's service in the French Air Force during World War One in the Squadron Cigogne (Stork)—its sensational looks—set the car apart. With a Saoutchik body, a Bucciali could cost over $50,000 in 1930, a very substantial sum of money.

Just before the Bucciali factory closed down in 1933, the two brothers accompanied Coldwell S. Johnson, an American

Cadillac, in the 1930s, built some of the best quality mass-produced cars ever made. This example was used for many years in India for hunting tigers.

Pierce-Arrow, despite producing this stylish vehicle (left), was one of the many fine American automobile makers that failed to survive the death blow dealt by the Wall Street Crash.

businessman who had interests in the American Peerless Motor company in Detroit, to the USA to visit several American automakers with the idea of selling them some of the Bucciali engineering patents, and hopefully manufacturing rights for their cars also. This last throw attempt to save their company failed doubly, because not only was there no interest in their cars, but several of the Bucciali transmission ideas for military vehicle use were incorporated most successfully into American military vehicles. No royalties were ever paid to the Buccialis. After 1945 Paul-Albert spent all of his money on unsuccessful litigation in European and American courts to claim his financial rewards on these patents. It is sad to have to report that he was equally unsuccessful in the courts as he was as a luxury car maker.

One of the loveliest cars of all time must have been the Cadillac V16, not only a great car, but one that can be said to have represented the very peak of Cadillac quality. Unlike the poor Bucciali, the Cadillac went on to become one of the most successful, and profitable, divisions of the giant General Motors Corporation. The Blackhawk Cadillac V16 that really catches the eye is the one that is simply known as 'The Tiger Car'.

The Maharaja of Indore commissioned Pinin Farina to design a tiger hunting car for him based on the Cadillac V16 chassis. Now this Cadillac model was more suitable for cruising, chauffeur-driven, down 5th Avenue in New York, or Piccadilly in London than being rushed across the hot Indian plains chasing after tigers. Nevertheless a special elevated shooting seat was fitted and six individual gun compartments.

Today the design of a car for this purpose would be more like a stretched Land Rover—very functional and basic, which highlights even more the sheer beauty of the Cadillac 'Tiger Car'. The Cadillac is so elegant that even today it would not be out of place delivering its owner to the grandest of occasions.

The V16 Cadillac really does make sense of the hackneyed phrase, 'They don't make them like they used to'. A Cadillac collector, a man who has a selection of the world's best from the 1940s still runs Cadillacs but has to change the car every six months to avoid mechanical problems! He is of the firm opinion that from the mid-1930s Cadillac quality has steadily declined, and that the V16 models were the greatest cars that the company

During the late 1920s the small
Belgian automobile industry
produced its finest vehicle, the
Minerva, a car built to the highest
standards, and valued by many
fastidious buyers. Sadly it did not
survive the economic depression of
the 1930s.

ever produced.

In 1933 the Pierce-Arrow factory, makers of many of the very best American cars of all time, shocked the crowds at the New York Car Show with their Silver Arrow model.

This car, the brainchild of designer Phil Wright, introduced the all-steel roof, radical styling with concealed sidemounts and running boards, and 12-inch thick doors with recessed handles. The car was a sensation, but the Pierce-Arrow concern was in serious financial difficulties, and only five Silver Arrows were ever built, with only three left in existence. Like the Cunningham (James, rather than Briggs) the Pierce-Arrow was built in Buffalo, New York, but unlike the Cunningham, after closing down their car production the company faded away. Cunningham do not make cars anymore, which is a very great pity, as their automobiles were truly fine machines, but their engineering business is alive and well.

Not much is generally known about the Minerva car because, like so many luxury car makers, they were forced out of the business by the depression of the 1930s. Made in Antwerp, Belgium the Minerva was one of the very finest cars made in the world. It was beautifully designed along conventional lines, exquisitely constructed with the strictest of quality control, and purchased by owners with the highest standards and fattest wallets.

The Minerva in the photographs resides in the Nethercutt Collection in Sylmar, California. It was given the gorgeous coachwork by Floyd Derham, the son of the original Derham bodymaker. Floyd had set himself up in competition with his father, but after making only three bodies he went bankrupt. Before going into total decline he did complete the Minerva contract, and the results indicate what a great craftsman was lost to the luxury automobile world.

The Nethercutt Minerva's beauty can be judged by the fact

GABRIEL VOISIN

Gabriel Voisin (1880-1973) lived to be 93 and he would have been the first to agree that living to the hilt, with passion, is the best recipe for a long and interesting existence! His autobiography, *Men, Women and 10,000 Balloons* fully reveals his extrovert nature in work and play.

Voisin was a dynamo of a man: he worked with skill, dedication, judgement and more than a touch of genius. He was an aviation fanatic and built, tried out and flew kites and balloons.

He turned away from aircraft production, after the First World War, towards car production at his Issy-les-Moulineaux factory to take up the slack as aircraft orders fell away.

His cars reflected his individuality — they all used the sleeve-valve type of engine. In 1936 he even presented a 6-litre straight twelve engine, highly unusual! Lightness of weight was, perhaps because of his experience with aircraft, always a major consideration in his cars and he consistently favoured the use of light alloys.

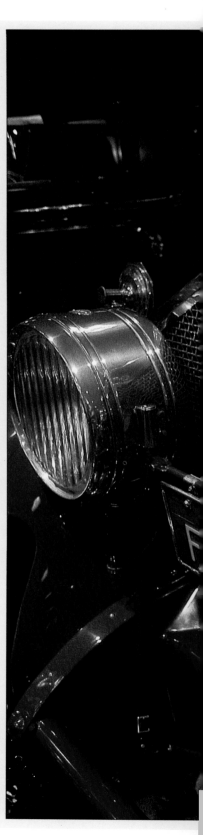

that it scored a perfect 100 points in the 1978 Monterey/Pebble Beach Classic Car Show, and won the Best of Show award.

The 1923 Twin Valve McFarlan Knickerbocker Cabriolet was at one time owned by a great American personality, the film star 'Fatty' Arbuckle.

Made in Connersville, Indiana the model 154 McFarlan was one of the many excellent American automobiles of the period. Its six-cylinder engine produced 129hp. At the time the McFarlan engine was so 'torquey' that it was described as 'big enough for a truck'. Two interesting features on the Arbuckle car should be mentioned; a set of snap fastenings on the outside edge of the roof, (and it was some long time afterwards that it was realized that they served to attach an awning to the side of the car to protect 'Fatty' when he was filming on location). Secondly, the supplementary mudguards fitted in front of the rear guards so as to protect the passenger's clothing from road dirt thrown up on to the car by the wheels on entering or leaving the McFarlan.

'Fatty' Arbuckle is remembered today, if at all, because of his involvement in a rather nasty criminal case. It is now believed that the charge was trumped up against him, but at the time it was

CENTRE: The T. V. McFarlan was selected by the film star 'Fatty' Arbuckle as his location vehicle. It was a quality car, made in small numbers, and is practically forgotten today.

Rudolph Valentino favoured the unusual in his choice of automobiles, hence his purchase of the Voisin Sporting Victoria (far right), a French vehicle made to aircraft standards, and very collectable today.

enough to finish his career in the movie business.

The 1923 Avions Voisin Sporting Victoria was first owned by the acknowledged greatest silent film star of all time, Rudolph Valentino. His films, 'The Sheik', and 'The Four Horsemen of the Apocalypse' were two of the biggest films of their time both in terms of numbers who paid to see them, and box office takings. Valentino died a very young man after a simple appendix operation, from blood poisoning. On news of his death fans all over the world went into mourning, and a few supposedly even committed suicide because of their grief.

Valentino's Voisin model C-5 was made in France by one of the most original aero and automobile engineers, Gabriel Voisin. Voisin has claimed, with some justification, that it was he who first flew in a powered aircraft, and not the Wright brothers at Kittyhawk. Voisin argued that the Wright brothers used a catapult-assisted take-off to get themselves into the air, as their puny engine did not have the required power to perform this

task. Less than a year later, and before the Wrights could find and fit a powerful enough engine, Voisin had flown under powered flight, ie covered the necessary distance etc to meet all the criteria set for defining genuine powered flight, and landed safely. Gabriel Voisin went to his grave convinced that he should be considered as the father of Powered Flight!

The C-5 was one of Voisin's best cars, and the body fitted for Rudolph Valentino a great asset to the rest of the vehicle. Voisin commissioned J. Rothschild and Sons of Paris to build him a suitable carriage for the number one film star, and they did a fine job. The coachwork is both stylish and simple, and reminiscent of the passing horse-drawn age. Like the T. V. McFarlan, the Voisin has supplementary mudguards, but this time for the front wings, so as to afford protection to passengers and bodywork. These can be seen behind the front wheels, and below the mudguards proper. The car is in perfect running order, as. are all the Nethercutt Collection cars, needing only gasoline and a battery to be driven away.

The cars in this chapter are special, either by virtue of their makers or because of their owners. All of them are more than simply vehicles, and were so even when new.

The elegant Voisin that belonged to Rudolph Valentino required very little restoration to bring it up to as-new condition, a tribute to its original builders, and the kind Californian climate.

Sportscars

Carroll Shelby's Cobra, with its 427 cubic inch engine, was essentially a racing car slightly modified for road use, with very little concession made to real comfort and convenience. It is avidly sought after by collectors the world over.

CARROLL SHELBY

In 1962 Carroll Hall Shelby retired early from a career as a top line driver of Formula One and Sports/Racing cars. His greatest success, in terms of international fame, had come in 1959 when he had co-driven the winning Aston Martin at Le Mans.

He persuaded the Ford Motor Company, and A.C. Cars in England to combine a Ford engine and an A.C. chassis to produce one of the greatest sportscars of all time, the Cobra.

Today he is still 'fixing'. He is fit, busy — not too busy to keep closely in touch with the Shelby/American Car Club, and follow motor-racing.

There have been many candidates for the title of the greatest sportscar during the near hundred years of the automobile. Mercedes, Mercer, Alfa Romeo, Bugatti, Bentley, Jaguar, Aston Martin, Shelby Cobra, Stutz, Porsche, Ferrari, Maserati, the list is endless and the choice entirely dependent upon personal taste and national preference. One method many people use to judge the ultimate value for the greatest is to consider the cash value of the car in question on the open market. While not all people will approve of this idea, it does at least have a bearing on the status of the vehicle being considered. A true sportscar in the simplest terms (and again, different people have different views on this subject), should be an open model, very fast, and with good styling. It is not necessary for it to have the best brakes, steering, and roadholding, because many of the accepted great cars in this class did not have these attributes, but they all *were* good looking, fast cars. The Shelby Cobra is a case in point. The Cobra came about following the early retirement, of Carroll Shelby the American racing driver. After his best season, 1959, when he co-drove an Aston Martin to the marque's only Le Mans win, it was discovered that he had a heart condition that made any future driving a hazard, so he hung up his famous striped racing overalls and retired as a driver.

Wanting to stay in the sporting car business he persuaded the Ford Motor Company, and the tiny British sportscar makers A.C., to allow him to put the Ford 260 cubic inch V8 engine into the A.C. Ace chassis, and then made additional chassis modifications so that the new car would handle well and stop. By late 1961 his new sportscar was ready to go into production in the Shelby-American plant in Los Angeles. The story goes that it was in the middle of the night that the name for the car, 'Cobra', came to Carroll, but however it came about, a better name for the Shelby/Ford/A.C. concoction could not be imagined.

75 260-engined cars had been made when Ford introduced the 289 cubic inch engine which Shelby immediately set about using instead of the 260. In this form the Cobra really took off, and 579 of the bigger-engined Cobras were produced in the next three years. In 1965 Shelby substituted the 427 engine in a successful bid to keep the Cobra competitive on the race tracks of the world. Shelby made 348 of these cars in the following two years.

As Carroll Shelby admitted, the Cobra was an old-fashioned sports car, but what a fire-eater it was. Performance was its sole reason for existing, and despite marginal brakes, massive heat transfer into the driving compartment from the engine bay, a distinct lack of torsional strength, and a firm, harsh, ride, the Cobra was king of the roads, and the best value for money of any sportscar in the world. Armed with the 427 engine Shelby won the G.T. world racing championships in 1965 with his Daytona Cobra coupé.

Despite the advantages of the massive horsepower produced by the stock 427 engine, the 289 Cobra is generally better balanced in its handling. There is more than enough power together with quite reasonable fuel economy, and the brakes have an easier time than with the 427!

Today a mint-condition Cobra realizes a vast sum of money on the market, and this fact has encouraged many copyists both in Europe and the USA to attempt to cash in on the popularity of the twenty-year-old sportscar. Only one succeeds in duplicating the original, and that is the highly expensive 'official' Autocraft A.C. Mk. IV, made from the original A.C. patterns, so Shelby's creation still stands supreme. Carroll Shelby's reaction to all the copies being made of his car was, 'I find it strange that anyone should want to copy a car that was already outdated when we developed it. Surely their money would be better spent on producing a modern car?'

This is accepted as an indication of just what a realist he is, and it is not surprising to learn that Carroll Shelby will be helping the Chrysler Corporation develop a series of production-based high performance cars. The early signs are that he has not lost his touch!

A sportscar that failed, but should have made it, is the Triumph

Kas Kastner and Pete Brock had hoped that their interpretation of the Triumph sportscar (the 250-K) would become the new TR-7. But this prototype remains the only example in existence.

The super-charged, six-cylinder engine in the Lyon sportscar is based on a Jaguar unit, but very heavily modified by Russ Lyon to produce reliable high performance.

Entirely hand-made by Russ Lyon and his wife, their car's driving compartment gives a good idea of their artistry and high standards of work.

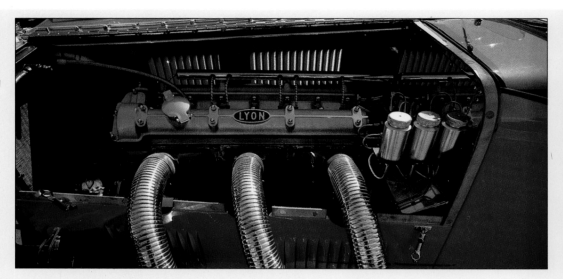

250-K. This car was the result of a collaboration between the Triumph North American racing team manager Kas Kastner, and stylist Pete Brock.

Kastner had made the American Triumph racing team into the most successful and feared, outfit in American racing. He is not only a very fine engineer, organizer and motivator, but also (behind the wheel of a racing car) a frequent US champion. In June 1967 Kas was called to Triumph's Headquarters in Coventry to discuss racing matters for the season. It was his custom always take something new with him which he had under development. On this occasion he was caught napping, and was going to have to arrive in England empty handed. However, for some time he had been examining possibilities for the replacement of the TR-6 model which was selling poorly in the USA. In this connection Kas had discussed design ideas with Brock, who had roughed out some sketches of the car that they felt could replace the TR-6, and boost Triumph sales.

With less than two hours before flight time Kastner called Brock around to his house, and asked him to produce some better layouts of their dream car for him to take to Coventry. Kas just made the flight, and during the short stop-over in New York he showed them to Leon Mandel, then editor of *Car & Driver* magazine. Leon agreed to feature the 250-K, as Kas called the car, on *C & D*s front cover three issues later. This must have been worth a massive amount of publicity, and armed with this additional weapon Kas presented his 250-K to the Triumph top men. He persuaded them to come up with $25,000 of development money to allow the car to be built, but they insisted that it be ready to RACE in the following February's Sebring meeting! What Triumphs were getting for their money was a free magazine front cover and an actual prototype car which would feature in the Sebring races in six months time!! It must have seemed like the bargain of the century to Coventry, because Kas Kastner had never let them down.

The Lyon sportscar is the fruit of 13 years' hard work by Russ Lyon. A vehicle cast in the mold of a 1930s sportscar, it combines many modern design features with vintage looks, and delivers astonishingly high performance, but at an equally high price.

Kastner built the car and race-prepared it in less than six months, a miracle compared to modern automotive development schedules. Unfortunately, with only five laps of a race track completed to sort the whole machine out, the 250-K went to Sebring, and was retired with a broken wheel, but not before it had been pored over by the world's motoring press, with valuable follow-up coverage. Triumph did not put the car into production in an attempt to rebuild their fading image, in the export markets especially, possibly not liking the idea of making an American-designed sportscar, maybe considering that Coventry should be the source of the new vehicle. So the one and only remaining 250-K sportscar lives in the Blackhawk Collection in California. Everyone who has seen it remarks on its superb looks—on looks alone it would have been a winner against the TR-7.

Another American who nurtured a dream of making a sports car that would set the world back on its heels is Russ Lyon. He has been planning his car for the last 13 years and this year sees that ambition realized in his Lyon sportscar.

With qualifications in mechanical and aeronautical engineering behind him, Russ has produced his first prototype Lyon, and has taken several orders for production models. Each Lyon is hand-built over six months by Russ himself, and costs $135,000—the Lyon is something very special.

A Jaguar-derived six-cylinder, supercharged engine powers the Lyon, giving it a very high performance with a top speed of over 130mph and acceleration from 0-60mph in under 5 seconds—fast in any language. The whole car is most beautifully finished with Russ making the patterns, having castings made from them, machining the castings, fitting and adjusting the components. Even the Roots-type supercharger was designed and made this way by Russ. About the only items he did not make himself are some brake parts, tyres, electrics, basic engine, gearbox and differential, and the chromium plating!

The finished article not only looks fabulous, but it goes just as well. It may look like a sportscar from the 1930s, but it goes, brakes, and handles like a modern machine. With a production rate of only two cars per year Russ looks like being a very busy man for the next 8 or 10 years just meeting the current demand for his creation.

In a similar fashion, Chris Lawrence is making his own sportscar, but basing it closely on the famous Maserati 450S sports/racing car from 1956. In his tiny Norfolk workshop Chris is reproducing this marvellous competition car using Maserati engines and transmissions assembled into his own chassis (which closely follows the original car's design). His bodywork is as the 1956 Maserati, and it is difficult to tell between the Lawrence car and a genuine 450S, the results are so good.

The original Maserati 450S was the car that Stirling Moss, and his navigator, Denis Jenkinson, were to use in the 1956 Mille Miglia. They had won the classic race for Mercedes the year before, setting a new course record for the 1000-mile circuit. The

The V-8 engine in the Lawrence Maserati 450S delivers more than enough horsepower to make the car very fast, yet flexible and easy to drive.

The work of one man. It accurately recreates the famous Italian sportscar that promised so much in the late 1950s.

The last Bugatti to leave the Molsheim factory was rebodied by Virgil M. Exner in the early 1950s in a vain attempt to keep the company in business, but it was doomed to failure.

Maserati, with its very high speed potential was to be the machine in which they expected to gain a repeat win. After weeks of testing and practicing race day came and the Moss/Jenkinson car was flagged away from the start in Brescia. Less than ten miles down the road, braking for a medium-speed corner, Moss was horrified to feel the brake pedal snap off under his foot! But a combination of superb driving skill and more than a modicum of luck enabled the car's occupants to climb out unhurt and hastened the 450S's exit from the race.

The Maserati 450S continued to be unfortunate as a race car, although its engine carried on to become the power unit for several production road cars from Modena. A combination of lack of money, and an overstretched racing department meant that the 450S never received the development that it deserved. The final blow came when the World Sports/Racing engine capacity formula was reduced to 3 litres, and the car could no longer qualify to race. Maybe the new Lawrence 450S will give the model a new lease of life.

A car that every enthusiast would fervently wish to see back on the road again has to be the Bugatti. But with the deaths of Ettore (1947), and his son Jean, the company too faded away, not immediately after Ettore's death but three years later. The Bugatti automobile is so tied to the life and style of *le patron* that it really would be difficult to imagine the Molsheim factory without him. When the small Bugatti factory finally closed its doors in early 1951 there were six chassis waiting for customers (and bodies) sitting on the workshop floor. One of them, a type 101-C was purchased by Virgil M. Exner, who had the idea of somehow continuing the production of Bugatti automobiles, but with much more up-to-date styling. He commissioned the Italian designer Bertoni to style a two-seater body, and Ghia to build it.

It was ready for the 1965 Turin Auto Show, and was judged to be a styling success, although today the marriage of the 1930s chassis and road wheels with the 1960s coachwork looks uncomfortable, the skinny wheels appear to lift the car too high off the road giving the whole machine a rather 'strange' look.

On the road, this Bugatti drove like the late 1930s car that it is under the modern skin, with a stiffly-sprung chassis, heavy steering and even heavier brakes. This clashed with the overall styling which promised a more civilized road manner. As a work of automobile art it is excellent, the fit and finish to a very high standard, but as a vehicle it must rate below par for the intentions of those involved in it production. But it is the last complete Bugatti, and as such has a place in automotive history. It is one of the very few cars that should end its days in a collection or museum rather than being driven on the road.

Commissioned to promote the increased use of copper, brass, bronze, and their alloys, the Mercer Cobra rolled out of the bodyworks of Sibona-Basano in Turin in 1964.

Virgil M. Exner accepted the job of producing a unique, one-of-a-kind automobile to travel the world's auto-shows and, hopefully, catch the eye of car makers and persuade them to

make more use of these metals.

In association with Sibona-Basano, Exner designed the
extraordinary body for the car and took as his inspiration the
Mercer Type 35 of 1912. He loved the stark racer-look of that
famous model with its liberal use of highly polished brass fittings.
He used an A.C. chassis and lengthened it to 182 inches, with a
wheelbase of 108 inches. The car has the standard 289 cubic inch
V8 engine, but with special Shelby twin carburettor intake
manifolds.

The copper items on the car were available in eleven shades,
and the brass trim was of cartridge quality. Exner wanted to give
the Mercer Cobra a 'warm metal look', as he felt that it would be
more eye-catching than cold chromium plating. Of special
interest are the disc brakes which feature copper discs, this metal
having a ten times greater thermal conductivity than cast iron, the
usual material used. The valve covers of the V8 engine, the air-
cleaner, oil filler cap and dip stick tube are all in cartridge brass.
The steering wheel is made from a chromium/copper alloy, and
the exhaust shield is of silicon bronze.

Its pearl-white body colour makes the Mercer Cobra most eye-
catching, with its pivoting headlights being another striking
feature. On the auto-show circuit the car interested many people,
but the use of copper and brass as alternatives to chromium
plating has never caught on.

The Mercer Cobra remains a unique one-off motor car, and is a
new addition to the Blackhawk Collection.

Index